Monographs in Computer Science

Editors

David Gries
Fred B. Schneider

Springer
New York
Berlin
Heidelberg
Barcelona
Budapest
Hong Kong
London
Milan
Paris
Santa Clara
Singapore
Tokyo

Monographs in Computer Science

Flemming Nielson

Editor

ML with Concurrency

Design, Analysis, Implementation,
and Application

With 18 Figures

Springer

Flemming Nielson
Computer Science Department
Aarhus University
Ny Munkegade
DK-8000 Aarhus C
Denmark

Series Editors:

David Gries
Department of Computer Science
Cornell University
Upson Hall
Ithaca, NY 14853-7501
USA

Fred B. Schneider
Department of Computer Science
Cornell University
Upson Hall
Ithaca, NY 14853-7501
USA

Library of Congress Cataloging-in-Publication Data
Nielson, Flemming, 1955–
    ML with concurrency: design, analysis, implementation, and
application / Flemming Nielson.
      p. cm. — (Monographs in computer science)
    Includes bibliographical references and index.
    ISBN 0-387-94875-9 (hardcover: alk. paper)
    1. ML (Computer program language) 2. Functional programming
(Computer science) 3. Parallel programming (Computer science)
I. Title. II. Series.
QA76.73.M6N54   1996
005.2—dc20   96-35926

Printed on acid-free paper.

Production managed by Natalie Johnson; manufacturing supervised by Johanna Tschebull.
Camera-ready copy prepared from the author's LaTeX files.
Printed and bound by Maple-Vail Book Manufacturing Group, York, PA.
Printed in the United States of America.

9 8 7 6 5 4 3 2 1

ISBN 0-387-94875-9 Springer-Verlag New York Berlin Heidelberg   SPIN 10524137

Preface

Pure functional languages are easy to reason about but are not in widespread use. By the skillful integration of imperative features, Standard ML has achieved much wider use. However, existing systems often have many components that must execute at the same time, and the integration of concurrency primitives shows promise of being useful for such tasks. Software development then can take place in the secure world of the strong polymorphic typing and modules system of Standard ML.

This book surveys a number of recent approaches to the integration of the functional and concurrent programming paradigms. This is a wide spectrum, and in this book we concentrate on extensions of Standard ML with new primitives for concurrency. This involves the design of multiparadigmatic languages, methods for describing their semantics, techniques for the analysis of fragments of the languages, and finally, approaches to distributed implementation. Closely related, but not covered in this book, are the higher-order process calculi and the parallel implementations of existing functional languages.

Readers of this book are likely to be graduate students of computer science, researchers at industrial laboratories, and professional computer scientists. The book may be useful to programmers in conveying the basic opportunities offered by mixed functional and concurrent programming languages and in providing pointers to existing systems.

Production of this book would not have been possible without the patience of Martin Gilchrist, at Springer-Verlag, and without the assistance of Kirsten Lackner Solberg and René Rydhof Hansen, at Aarhus University.

Aarhus, Denmark   *Flemming Nielson*

Contents

Contributors

Bernard Berthomieu   LAAS-CNRS, 7, avenue du Colonel Roche, 31077 Toulouse, France.

Dominique Bolignano   VIP, Dyade, Le Chesnay, B.P.105 78153 Le Chesnay Cedex, France.

Mourad Debbabi   Computer Science Department, Laval University, Sainte-Foy, Quebec, Quebec G1K 7P4, Canada.

Tsung-Min Kuo   Quickturn Design Systems, Inc., 440 Clyde Ave., Mountain View, CA 94043, USA. (Work performed while at ECRC, Arabellastrasse 17, D-81925 Munich, Germany.)

Lone Leth   ICL, Technology Businesses, Research & Advanced Technology, Lovelace Road, Bracknell, Berkshire RG12 8SN, UK. (Work performed while at ECRC, Arabellastrasse 17, D-81925 Munich, Germany.)

David C.J. Matthews   Department of Computer Science, University of Edinburgh, The King's Buildings, Mayfield Road, Edinburgh EH9 3JZ, Scotland.

Flemming Nielson   Computer Science Department, Aarhus University, Ny Munkegade, DK-8000 Aarhus, Denmark.

Hanne Riis Nielson   Computer Science Department, Aarhus University, Ny Munkegade, DK-8000 Aarhus, Denmark.

Prakash Panangaden   School of Computer Science, McGill University, Montreal, Quebec H3A 2A7, Canada.

John H. Reppy   AT&T Labs Research, Murray Hill, NJ 07974, USA.

Bent Thomsen   ICL, Technology Businesses, Research & Advanced Technology, Lovelace Road, Bracknell, Berkshire RG12 8SN, UK. (Work performed while at ECRC, Arabellastrasse 17, D-81925 Munich, Germany.)

1
Introduction

The programming language *Standard ML* is an eager (or call-by-value) functional language with sufficient imperative aspects so as to overcome some of the major performance penalties of (so-called) pure functional languages. It allows one to write well-structured code where imperative constructs are the exception (when they are needed) rather than the rule (when they might not be). This allows writing code that highlights the overall algorithms and data structures used. It leads to code that is easier to read, easier to maintain, and easier to reuse for other programming tasks.

Originally defined as the metalanguage of the *LCF* theorem prover [62], Standard ML has taken on a life of its own as it has gained in popularity, and its use in industrial applications is increasing. It is now used in undergraduate teaching at a growing number of universities, sometimes even as the first programming language taught, because of the ease with which it allows the instructor to teach and express fundamental concepts like structured programming, data structures, and algorithmic techniques. It is remarkable for a programming language to have such well-developed formal descriptions [112, 111] and for these to have played such an essential role in the development of the language as is the case for Standard ML. Consequently, it appears to the user as a well-engineered language offering few surprises and anomalies.

Use of Standard ML is facilitated by the appearance of several textbooks [181, 142, 133, 178]. High-quality implementations of the language are now available from many sources and for many machine platforms; this includes the industrial-strength SML/NJ implementation (from AT&T Bell Labs., USA), the commercial Poly/ML system (from Abstract Hardware Ltd., Edinburgh, United Kingdom), the commercial ML Works system (from Harlequin Ltd., Cambridge, United Kingdom and also Cambridge, Massachusetts, USA), the French CAML systems, and Moscow ML. An entire newsgroup on the Internet is devoted to the discussion of issues related to Standard ML (see `comp.lang.ml`).

A hallmark of Standard ML is the presence of *polymorphism* by means of the `let`-construct. This offers the ease and reusability of type-free programming while the implementation guarantees the type-security of the programs developed: that program bugs are preferably caught at compile-time (when the programmer is still available) rather than at run-time (when he/she is not). The generality and power of the `let`-polymorphism present in Standard ML means that only occasionally is the type system regarded as a constraining factor in the code that can be written; however, most extensions of the Standard ML type system turn out to be undecidable (and hence not implementable), and so it would seem that the design of Standard ML strikes a good balance between expressiveness and implementability.

Another hallmark of Standard ML is the *modules* system, with parameterized modules called functors. This gives the necessary primitives for programming in the large, so as to make code reusable and to allow separate compilation, and at the same time strong typing is maintained. Recently the modules system has been extended with the automatic inference of "types" (actually so-called signatures) for modules (and functors) and so extends the illusion of type-free programming to the modules level.

Despite all these strong points of Standard ML there are situations where other programming features might be desirable. An obvious candidate is the exploitation of object-oriented (or object-based) features; indeed, this is an active research area. Another obvious candidate, not completely unrelated to this, is the addition of constructs for the exploitation of concurrency and distribution. There are many example applications where this is the case: the more modest aims include systems for windows management on a uniprocessor, and the more ambitious aims include complex systems for fully distributed systems running on heterogeneous processors.

In this book we have selected six chapters that illustrate various approaches to extending an eager functional language like Standard ML with features for communication and/or distribution. The first four chapters discuss the design and implementation of different programming languages that evolved out of this approach; it will be clear from the chapters that the aims have been different, and that this in turn has affected the design of the languages. The final two chapters are concerned with more theoretical developments focusing on semantics and analysis.

Chapter 2, by Prakash Panangaden and John Reppy, discusses the essential concurrency features of *Concurrent ML*. These concurrency features were originally designed to allow the execution of a number of processes on a *single processor*, and an early application programmed in the language is the *eXene* window management system. The more basic primitives allow sending and receiving messages over typed channels, creating channels and new processes, and choosing between as yet unsynchronized communications; more advanced primitives are covered in the chapter. The language is based on the New Jersey implementation of Standard ML and is included in the widely available New Jersey compiler package.

Chapter 3, by David Matthews, describes the concurrency features of *Poly/ML*. The original motivation behind the design of the language was the need to support a window management system, and the basic primitives are rather close to those of Concurrent ML, although there are important differences. The language is based on the Standard ML implementation developed and marketed by Abstract Hardware Ltd. The paper describes a number of implementations of the concurrency features, highlighting the achievements and open problems. The simplest implementation concerns a uniprocessor (as in the case of Concurrent ML); next comes an implementation taking advantage of a shared-memory multiprocessor; then comes an implementation exploiting a *distributed network* of workstations; finally, on-going work on improving some of the shortcomings of this distributed implementation is presented.

Chapter 4, by Bernard Berthomieu and others[1], discusses the programming language *LCS*. This is an asynchronous programming language that integrates the process algebra CCS into Standard ML. This means that concurrency is directly expressed in terms of executing two or more threads in parallel, rather than by having a thread responsible for spawning new processes. The language is given a polymorphic type system based on a novel use of extensible record types, and the properties of substitutions and unification in this scenario are investigated. Next, an operational semantics is defined by means of a three-level evaluation relation. Finally, the implementation model is discussed in some detail.

Chapter 5, by Bent Thomsen, Lone Leth, Tsung-Min Kuo, and others[2], describes the *FACILE* language and run-time system. Based on Standard ML of New Jersey, the language adds communication primitives (along the lines of Concurrent ML and Poly/ML) as well as distribution primitives (as found in Poly/ML, but with a view towards the programming of *fault-tolerant distributed systems* on loosely coupled processors). Example applications include the Calumet teleconferencing system, the Einrichten collaborative design system, and a system for Mobile Service Agents. Furthermore, FACILE has an explicit syntactic category for expressing operations on behaviors in the style of process algebras, i.e., in terms of parallel compositions rather than the spawning of processes, thus incorporating some of the constructs also found in LCS. Additionally, there are facilities for dynamically querying a database for servers matching a given signature; this is important for distributed systems where the presence of servers may evolve over time and where new services should become available to existing applications. The chapter discusses the language design, the implementation, and the applications in some detail.

Chapter 6, by Mourad Debbabi and Dominique Bolignano, considers semantic properties of languages like those exposed above. Usually such languages are given an operational semantics (in the manner of Chapter 7) due to the difficulties involved in giving a sufficiently abstract denotational semantics of the communication constructs. This motivates the development of the present chapter: to present a way to structure denotational semantics by basing it on the judgments of the static semantics; in this way semantics is only defined for well-typed programs, unlike what is often the case in denotational semantics. Furthermore, fewer recursive domain

---

[1]Contributions from Thierry Le Sergent and Camille le Moniés de Sagazan.

[2]Contributions from Pierre-Yves Chevalier, Pierre Cregut, Alessandro Giacalone, Fritz Knabe, Andre Kramer, Sanjiva Prasad, and Jean-Pierre Talpin.

equations result because the semantics (including the semantic domains) have been "specialized" for the program at hand. The static semantics itself is an annotated type-and-effect system along the lines of [160] that records the sets of values that may be communicated over channels in addition to specifying the types. The dynamic semantics is based on the model of acceptance trees.

Chapter 7, by Hanne Riis Nielson and Flemming Nielson, takes a subset of Concurrent ML as the starting point. For this language an annotated type-and-effect discipline is developed; unlike Chapter 6, the behaviors retain a high degree of causality and take the form of process algebra terms in an algebra that corresponds directly to the scenario of Concurrent ML. The annotated type-and-effect system is proved semantically sound using a notion of simulation and a subject reduction result. The chapter ends by investigating decidability issues of the simulation and the syntactic approximation used in the annotated type-and-effect system.

All the languages described in this book share the underlying idea that processes may be dynamically spawned, channels may be dynamically created, and values may be (synchronously) sent over channels and (synchronously) received over channels. They differ in a number of other respects, not least concerning the amount of distribution that may take place.

The reader should be aware, however, that the languages do not always use the same names for the same constructs. An example of this concerns the primitives for sending and receiving values over a channel; to avoid adding to the confusion we shall temporarily write put(ch,val) for sending the value val over the channel ch and get(ch) for receiving a value over the channel ch. One possibility is that the operations perform the actions immediately; we write putI(ch,val) and getI(ch) for this. This allows the thunks[3] fn () => putI(ch,val) and fn () => getI(ch) to be passed along as values that can then be enacted by applying them to (). Another possibility is that the operations are delayed and only performed when explicitly synchronized by the sync primitive; we write putD(ch,val) and getD(ch) for this. This allows the delayed communications putD(ch,val) and getD(ch) to be passed along as values that can be enacted by giving them as argument to sync. These two viewpoints are closely related; for example, sync(putD(ch,val)) may be coded as putI(ch,val), and putD(ch,val) may be coded as fn () => getI(ch). The reader should be aware that the chapters in this book, in accord with the programming languages described, use constructs like send (or transmit) for sending values, but that in some chapters they stand for putI and in others for putD; similar remarks apply to the constructs receive (or accept) used for receiving values. The choices made are clearly explained in each chapter.

---

[3]A thunk simply means a procedure without parameters.

2
The Essence of Concurrent ML

Prakash Panangaden and John Reppy

ABSTRACT Concurrent ML (CML) is a programming language that integrates high-level abstraction mechanisms with concurrency primitives. Like other similar, recent languages, CML embodies the idea that concurrent programming can be done in a modern high-level language like ML. The fundamental new ingredient is the notion of a (polymorphic) *event*. This is a piece of code packaged as a new abstraction. Combinators are provided to build new events from old ones. The key subtlety is the interaction of external choice with abstraction. Ordinary functional abstraction conceals the communication actions on which choices need to be made. The event mechanism allows one to build abstractions that expose the communication. The language CML features mobility, polymorphism, and ordinary lambda-abstraction as well as events. In this article we discuss the basic features and explain how CML can be used to implement new concurrent abstractions.

2.1   Introduction

At the heart of any formalism for programming or reasoning about· concurrent systems is the notion of interaction between autonomous entities. When formalisms for concurrency differ in an essential way, the interaction mechanism is invariably the central point of difference. In concurrent programming, interaction manifests itself through *communication* and *synchronization*. Because of the presence of several processes executing independently, the possible execution scenarios are subject to the complexity of combinatorial explosion, and one needs methods for coping with the resulting complexity.

Abstraction is a key tool for managing complexity. In the development of software, a fundamental advance in programming languages was making procedural abstraction and data abstraction available to the user. This has proved to be enormously useful in practice; one is hard-pressed to imagine a serious language without procedures. The theoretical tool needed to analyze procedural abstraction, namely the λ-calculus, had already been developed by logicians. There followed almost thirty years of fruitful (if not always amicable) interactions between theoreticians and practitioners. One of the high points of this development was the wonderful paper by John Reynolds, called "The essence of Algol," which spelled out the key ideas in Algol [153].

What is the right notion of abstraction for concurrent programming? This is a question that has been asked surprisingly infrequently. Current programming practice largely adheres to the idea that "systems" programming requires working in a low-level language. Such languages provide abstractions of the underlying hardware but very little in the way of support for programmer-defined abstractions. Theoretical research in concurrent programming has been primarily focused on the algebraic properties of process calculi. When abstraction mechanisms are considered at all, they are usually attempts to combine lambda-abstraction with familiar process calculi. But as we shall argue below, this is not always the appropriate mechanism for concurrent programs. On the other hand, concurrent programs are notoriously complex, even when not particularly large; thus the need for an abstraction mechanism is particularly acute.

The languages Concurrent ML (CML) [150] and its precursor PML [149] provide a unique abstraction mechanism for concurrent programming. The key idea is to separate the operation of synchronization from the mechanism for describing synchronization and communication protocols. A new type of first-class values is introduced to represent the descriptions of synchronization and communication, and a small collection of combinators is provided for creating more complex protocols from primitive ones. This mechanism allows application programmers and library providers to design and implement new synchronization and communication abstractions that have the same status as the built-in primitives.

CML is not another process calculus with a new set of combinators; the new feature of the language is the new abstraction mechanism and the way that it is smoothly integrated with the higher-order features and polymorphic type discipline of Standard ML. Indeed, the primitives are fairly conventional: rendezvous-style communication (with value passing) as in CCS or CSP, selective choice between events, concurrent spawning of processes and the standard constructs of a sequential language. Since the language is an extension of Standard ML, the usual notion of higher-order entities is available (and used!). We emphasize, however, that CML is not just "a higher-order functional language with concurrency features." The new abstraction mechanism that is present in CML is specifically designed for concurrent programming and cannot be built out of λ-abstraction.

For the benefit of the theoretically-oriented reader, the most important point to be made about CML is that the language was designed to be used in large-scale concurrent programming. Thus, the key design decisions were not made in order to produce a pleasing algebra, but nevertheless, certain mathematically pleasant properties naturally emerged. From a foundational point of view, the choice of primitives in CML is guided by the desire to build other concurrency abstractions on top of the given primitives. In a forthcoming book on CML, it is shown how a wide variety of concurrency primitives can be expressed in CML [148].

The intended application area of CML is concurrent programming rather than parallel or distributed programming. In other words, the idea is not to get speedup by exposing and exploiting parallelism in the hardware nor to function in a loosely coupled distributed environment, but rather to express programs where the underlying algorithm imposes only a partial order on the actions taking place. One of the most important examples of such software is interactive applications. Indeed, the most significant application of CML has been eXene, which is a multi-threaded X Window System toolkit [57].

2.2   The Fundamental Ideas

Three fundamental ideas are essential to understanding CML. These are:

- abstraction and choice

- scoping and mobility

- polymorphism.

Abstraction is of course the key tool in managing complexity, but what is new in CML is the way choice interacts with abstraction. Scoping turns out to provide a vital idiom — namely a mechanism for keeping communication channels private. However scoping by itself would keep channels so secure that no process would be capable of communicating along a private channel. What is crucial is the ability to send channels along channels thus expanding the scope in a dynamic but controlled fashion. This phenomenon, called *scope extrusion* by Milner [109], was of great interest and novelty to concurrency theorists and has been much studied from the theoretical point of view. It was recognized as an important programming idiom and used in PML and CML from the outset. Polymorphism is one of the outstanding features of ML and it is important that the concurrent extensions were smoothly integrated into the polymorphic type system.

2.2.1   *Abstraction, Choice, and Synchronization*

The basic design philosophy in CML is to provide abstraction mechanisms that allow a programmer to organize complex programs in a structured way while allowing the expression of concurrency, synchronization, and choice. In this section we motivate and discuss the abstraction mechanism of CML. In order to do so, we introduce a possible interface for synchronous communication in CML and discuss the interaction between choice and abstraction.

One of the first design decisions that must be resolved is how processes communicate. In CML, communication is effected by two-way synchronization, or rendezvous, as in CSP. Communication through shared variables, though useful when one does have to do low-level implementation, makes it very hard cleanly to separate processes and thus vitiates any attempt at abstraction. Message passing, on the other hand, clearly expresses communication as an interaction between processes while keeping the two processes separated.

One still has to choose between asynchronous communication, as in dataflow for example, and synchronous communication. In CML, synchronous communication was chosen because it gives a better handle on the information flow between processes. More precisely, when one uses synchronous communication the two processes involved achieve common knowledge of the information exchanged. This makes reasoning about a number of protocols much easier. In asynchronous communication, processes achieve concurrent common knowledge when a message is sent [131]. This is substantially weaker than common knowledge, and while still useful for many purposes it is often not enough. One can use acknowledgment messages to achieve a stronger form of knowledge exchange, but this loses the performance advantages of asynchronous communication and adds programming overhead. Practical arguments for the use of synchronous communication over asynchronous communication are presented in a forthcoming book [148].

From the point of view of expressiveness, synchronous communication is to be preferred. In a forthcoming paper, we show that one cannot *abstractly* implement $n+1$-way synchronous communication using n-way synchronous communication. Of course, if one wants nonabstract implementations one can use one of many existing committee-coordination protocols [44]. Thus, in CML it is easy to set up asynchronous communication as a buffered process encapsulated in an abstraction. The reverse is in fact impossible: in order to implement synchronous communication with asynchronous communication, one has to have assumptions about what the processes involved in the communication can do, which breaks the abstraction.

We now address the main issue of this section, namely the interplay between abstraction, communication, and choice. The most important single new idea in CML is the *event* mechanism as a new abstraction mechanism appropriate for concurrent programming. A basic question that arises is why one needs a new abstraction mechanism rather than just using ordinary procedural abstraction (i.e., λ-abstraction). The answer is best presented through an example.

Suppose that we have a protocol for requesting a service from a server. Let us say that we have a procedure req1(x) for making the request; the parameter x contains information that is specific to each request. Inside the body is the code describing the communication protocol that needs to be obeyed. For example, the protocol might demand that the client issue a request and await exactly one response before issuing another request. Following this protocol allows one to ensure that the requests and their responses are properly synchronized. Whatever the details might be, the point is that the communication is hidden inside the body of a procedural abstraction. By using the abstraction we ensure that the protocol is followed. Suppose that we have another procedure, req2(x), for making similar requests of another server. We might want to make both requests and choose the one that responded first. If our choice mechanism allows us to select between communication events, we can write code to choose between the two servers, but *we cannot do this using the existing abstractions.* Thus, if we had a choice operator like the + of CCS, we would be making a blind choice between req1 and req2. Such a choice operator would be quite expensive, if not impossible, to implement, and one is not found in practical concurrent programming languages. Thus, there is a fundamental conflict between the traditional λ-calculus notion of abstracting, leaving only the parameters visible, and the need to keep the communication exposed for effective use of choice.

The solution is to have an abstraction mechanism that hides the implementation while preserving the synchronous nature of the abstraction. The approach followed in CML is to introduce a new abstract type of values, called *events*, that represent *potential* communication and synchronization actions. Event values are quiescent; they only perform their communication action when a thread uses them for synchronization. This is entirely analogous to λ-abstraction; a λ-abstraction is a value; computational actions are triggered only when it is applied. There are combinators that allow one to construct more complex events from simpler ones. In particular, one can use these combinators to "wrap up" a complete protocol inside an event, thus creating abstractions that expose the communication while concealing the details of the protocol. The syntactic details are presented in the next section.

2.2.2 Scoping and Mobility

It is very common in concurrent programming to have several pairs of processes participate in the same protocol concurrently (using different channels). It is essential that the communications be kept separate so that there is no confusion about which message is intended for which recipient. One way is for the programmer to keep track of all the relevant names of communication channels and make sure that the proper message is sent along the appropriate channel. This is exactly the sort of complexity that an appropriate linguistic mechanism can help resolve.

An obvious mechanism is scoping. One can imagine that two processes could be declared inside a single let block and that a channel name is declared in the let block. Now if they use this channel to communicate they are guaranteed that no other process will accidentally receive the message. On the other hand suppose that there are three processes that might engage in any pairwise combination and run some protocol. We cannot have three different let scopes for each pair of processes.

In CML, one can send channels along channels; this is called *mobility*. In fact, if a private channel, say c, is sent along a channel, say c', to another process, the scope of c expands to include the process that receives c. Of course c' has to be a name that is known to the receiving channel. This scope expansion (or extrusion) can be used to make separate but overlapping scopes so that our three processes could indeed have three different scopes that allow private channels to be set up for each pair. Of course, lexical scoping just cannot do this; the combination of local scoping and the ability to send channels along channels is essential.

2.2.3 Polymorphism

In sequential programming, there are two important sources of polymorphism. Crudely speaking, these arise from lambda abstraction and from the presence of pointers. Thus, one sees that a lambda term like $\lambda x.x$ has a polymorphic type and that the list constructor cons has a polymorphic type. The polymorphism of the latter expresses the idea that pointer manipulations are independent of the type of data that the pointers are pointing at. In concurrent programming, there is a third kind of entity that naturally leads to polymorphism, namely communication channels. Protocols for sending, receiving, and acknowledging are often not dependent on the type of data being communicated. In CML, channels and events are polymorphic in the same sense that lists are polymorphic. This is in fact not something that had to be contrived, but fits naturally into the programming paradigm.

2.3   Overview of CML

In this section, we give an informal overview of the central CML constructs. Figure 2.1 gives the signature of the most commonly used CML primitives. The first four of these operations are fairly standard:

spawn f creates a new thread to evaluate the function f and returns the ID of the newly created thread.

channel () creates a new channel.

recv ch receives a message from the channel ch. This operation blocks the calling thread until there is another thread sending a message on ch.

send (ch, msg) sends the message msg on the channel ch. This operation blocks the calling thread until there is another thread accepting a message from ch.

The remaining functions support the mechanism of events. We use the phrase "synchronize on an event" to indicate that activity has been initiated

```
type thread_id
type 'a chan
type 'a event

val spawn : (unit -> unit) -> thread_id

val channel : unit -> 'a chan
val recv    : 'a chan -> 'a
val send    : ('a chan * 'a) -> unit

val recvEvt : 'a chan -> 'a event
val sendEvt : ('a chan * 'a) -> unit event

val guard   : (unit -> 'a event) -> 'a event
val wrap    : ('a event * ('a -> 'b)) -> 'b event
val choose  : 'a event list -> 'a event

val sync    : 'a event -> 'a
val select  : 'a event list -> 'a
```

FIGURE 2.1. The common CML operations

and that the events are being executed. One should think of this as being analogous to saying "apply the λ-abstraction."

recvEvt ch constructs an event value that represents the operation of receiving a message from the channel ch. When this event is synchronized on, it receives a message from the channel and returns it as the result of synchronization.

sendEvt (ch, msg) constructs an event value that represents the operation of sending the message msg on the channel ch. When this event is synchronized on, it sends the message on the channel and returns unit as the synchronization result.

guard f creates an event out of the pre-synchronization action f, which is called a *guard function*. When this value is synchronized on, the guard function is evaluated and its result is used in the synchronization.

wrap (ev, f) wraps the event value ev with the post-synchronization action f, which is called a *wrapper function*. When this event is synchronized on, the function f is applied to the synchronization result of ev.

choose [$ev_1, \ldots, ev_n$] forms the nondeterministic choice of the event values $ev_1, \ldots, ev_n$. When this event is synchronized on, one of the events ev_i will be selected, and its result will be the synchronization result.

sync *ev* forces synchronization of the event value *ev*, returning the synchronization result.

We illustrate these constructs with a very simple example. The interested reader can consult the second author's thesis [151] or forthcoming book [148] for more extensive examples. Suppose one has two servers, each with a different protocol that must be used. A client wishes to issue requests to both servers and interact with whichever server accepts the request first. We can write this as an event constructed using choose and wrap, without having to expose the details of the protocols, as follows:

```
choose [
    wrap (sendEvt(req1, serverCh1), protocol1),
    wrap (sendEvt(req2, serverCh2), protocol2)
]
```

If upon synchronization, the first server accepts the request first, the code that gets executed is protocol1(). One can use guard if one wants to send out two requests and choose the server that honors the request first, rather than the one that accepts the request first.

```
choose[
    guard (fn () => (send(req1, serverCh1); recvEvt(replyCh1))),
    guard (fn () => (send(req2, serverCh2); recvEvt(replyCh2)))
]
```

When one synchronizes on this event, the choice is made on the reception of the replies from the server.

The "let" construct of SML provides CML with local scoping. The process calculus notion of *restriction* is captured by this. For example, if one wants to have a private channel for two processes to communicate along, one can use a let to achieve this. On the other hand, the mobility of CML allows "scope extrusion" to occur. The type system allows one to declare a channel of type, say, integer-channel channel and to send integer channels along it. Thus, one has mobility in the sense of the π-calculus, except, of course, that channels are typed. With this possibility it is clear that scope extrusion is possible.

2.4   The Semantics of Mini-CML

In this section, we formalize the semantics of the operations described above. We define a small language, called "Mini-CML," which is Clément et al.'s Mini-ML [45] extended with concurrency primitives. This language includes the core idea of treating synchronization operations as values but omits some of the CML combinators.[1]

---

[1]Our language might better be called "Mini-PML," since it covers the PML subset of CML primitives.

For a full treatment of the semantics of CML, see either [151] or [148].

2.4.1 Syntax

The expressions of our language have the following syntax:

$$
\begin{array}{llr}
e & ::= & x \qquad\qquad\qquad\qquad\qquad\qquad variables \\
& | & b \qquad\qquad\qquad\qquad\qquad\qquad constants \\
& | & \kappa \qquad\qquad\qquad\qquad\qquad channel\ names \\
& | & (e_1,\ e_2) \qquad\qquad\qquad\qquad pairs \\
& | & \texttt{fn}\ x\ =>e \qquad\qquad function\ abstraction \\
& | & (e_1\ e_2) \qquad\qquad function\ application \\
& | & \texttt{let}\ x=e_1\ \texttt{in}\ e_2 \qquad\qquad let\ binding \\
& | & \texttt{chan}\ x\ \texttt{in}\ e \qquad\qquad channel\ binding \\
& | & \texttt{spawn}\ e \qquad\qquad\qquad process\ creation \\
& | & \texttt{sync}\ e \qquad\qquad\qquad synchronization \\
& | & e? \qquad\qquad\qquad\qquad receive\ event \\
& | & e_1!e_2 \qquad\qquad\qquad\qquad send\ event \\
& | & e_1 \Rightarrow e_2 \qquad\qquad\qquad\qquad wrap\ event \\
& | & (e_1 \oplus e_2) \qquad\qquad\qquad event\ choice \\
& | & \Lambda \qquad\qquad\qquad\qquad\qquad never\ event \\
& | & \mathbf{A} \qquad\qquad\qquad\qquad\qquad always\ event
\end{array}
$$

It is useful to distinguish two subsets of expressions: *values* and *event values*. These are defined as the least subsets of expressions satisfying the following rules:

$$
\begin{array}{lll}
v & ::= & x \\
& | & b \\
& | & \kappa \\
& | & (v_1,\ v_2) \\
& | & \texttt{fn}\ x\ =>e \\
& | & ev \\
ev & ::= & \kappa? \\
& | & \kappa!v \\
& | & ev \Rightarrow v \\
& | & (ev_1 \oplus ev_2) \\
& | & \Lambda \\
& | & \mathbf{A}
\end{array}
$$

While channel names (κ) are included in the syntax of Mini-CML, they are not part of the surface syntax. Rather, they are introduced during the course of evaluation.

2.4.2 Typing Rules

Mini-CML has a standard polymorphic type system; the only twist is that we use Wright's *value restriction* to handle the combination of let polymorphism and imperative features [184]. This simplifies the type system, since we avoid having two classes of type variables. The semantics of CML under the full SML type system have been described in [151].

Our notation in this section is standard (e.g., see [177] or [182]). Let $\iota \in \mathrm{TyCon} = \{\mathtt{int}, \mathtt{bool}, \ldots\}$ designate the set of *type constants*, and $\alpha, \beta \in \mathrm{TyVar}$ the set of *type variables*. Then, the set of types, $\tau \in \mathrm{Ty}$, is defined by

$$
\begin{array}{rlll}
\tau & ::= & \iota & \text{type constants} \\
& | & \alpha & \text{type variables} \\
& | & (\tau_1 \rightarrow \tau_2) & \text{function types} \\
& | & (\tau_1 \times \tau_2) & \text{pair types} \\
& | & \tau\ \mathtt{chan} & \text{channel types} \\
& | & \tau\ \mathtt{event} & \text{event types}
\end{array}
$$

and the set of type schemes, $\sigma \in \mathrm{TyScheme}$, are defined by

$$
\begin{array}{rll}
\sigma & ::= & \tau \\
& | & \forall \alpha_1 \cdots \alpha_n.\tau.
\end{array}
$$

We write $\mathrm{FTV}(\sigma)$ for the free type variables of σ.

Type environments assign type schemes to variables in terms:

$$
\mathrm{TE} \quad \in \quad \mathrm{TyEnv} = \mathrm{Var} \xrightarrow{\text{fin}} \mathrm{TyScheme}.
$$

We use $\mathrm{FTV}(\mathrm{TE})$ to denote the set of free type variables in an environment. We write $\mathrm{TE} \pm \{x \mapsto \sigma\}$ for the extension of TE by a binding of x to σ. To associate types with the constants, we assume the existence of a function

$$
\mathrm{TypeOf} : \mathrm{Const} \rightarrow \mathrm{TyScheme}.
$$

We need two more definitions before presenting the typing rules.

Definition 2.4.1. A type τ' is an *instance* of a type scheme $\sigma = \forall \alpha_1 \cdots \alpha_n.\tau$ (written $\sigma \succ \tau'$) if there exists a finite substitution, S, with $\mathrm{dom}(S) = \{\alpha_1, \ldots, \alpha_n\}$ and $S\tau = \tau'$. If $\sigma \succ \tau'$, then we say that σ is a *generalization* of τ'. We say that $\sigma \succ \sigma'$ if whenever $\sigma' \succ \tau$, then $\sigma \succ \tau$.

Definition 2.4.2. The *closure* of a type τ with respect to a type environment TE is defined as $\mathrm{Clos}_{\mathrm{TE}}(\tau) = \forall \alpha_1 \cdots \alpha_n.\tau$, where

$$
\{\alpha_1, \ldots, \alpha_n\} = \mathrm{FTV}(\tau) \setminus \mathrm{FTV}(\mathrm{TE}).
$$

The typing rules for Mini-CML are divided into two groups. The first set of rules, given in Figure 2.2, are the standard rules for ML-like languages. We follow the approach proposed by Wright [184] and only introduce polymorphic types for *values*. This is captured in the two rules for `let`: the first applies in the nonexpansive case (i.e., when the bound expression is

$$\frac{\text{TypeOf}(b) \succ \tau}{\text{TE} \vdash b : \tau}$$

$$\frac{x \in \text{dom}(\text{TE}) \quad \text{TE}(x) \succ \tau}{\text{TE} \vdash x : \tau}$$

$$\frac{\text{TE} \vdash e_1 : (\tau' \to \tau) \quad \text{TE} \vdash e_2 : \tau'}{\text{TE} \vdash (e_1\ e_2) : \tau}$$

$$\frac{\text{TE} \pm \{x \mapsto \tau\} \vdash e : \tau'}{\text{TE} \vdash \mathtt{fn}\ x \Rightarrow e : (\tau \to \tau')}$$

$$\frac{\text{TE} \vdash e_1 : \tau_1 \quad \text{TE} \vdash e_2 : \tau_2}{\text{TE} \vdash (e_1, e_2) : (\tau_1 \times \tau_2)}$$

$$\frac{\text{TE} \vdash v : \tau' \quad \text{TE} \pm \{x \mapsto \text{CLOS}_{\text{TE}}(\tau')\} \vdash e : \tau}{\text{TE} \vdash \mathtt{let}\ x = v\ \mathtt{in}\ e : \tau}$$

$$\frac{\text{TE} \vdash e_1 : \tau' \quad \text{TE} \pm \{x \mapsto \tau'\} \vdash e : \tau}{\text{TE} \vdash \mathtt{let}\ x = e_1\ \mathtt{in}\ e_2 : \tau}$$

FIGURE 2.2. Core type inference rules for Mini-CML

$$\frac{\text{TE} \pm \{x \mapsto \tau\ \mathtt{chan}\} \vdash e : \tau}{\text{TE} \vdash \mathtt{chan}\ x\ \mathtt{in}\ e : \tau}$$

$$\frac{\text{TE} \vdash e : (\mathtt{unit} \to \tau)}{\text{TE} \vdash \mathtt{spawn}\ e : \mathtt{unit}}$$

$$\frac{\text{TE} \vdash e : \tau\ \mathtt{event}}{\text{TE} \vdash \mathtt{sync}\ e : \tau}$$

$$\frac{}{\text{TE} \vdash \Lambda : \tau\ \mathtt{event}}$$

$$\frac{}{\text{TE} \vdash \mathbf{A} : \mathtt{unit}\ \mathtt{event}}$$

$$\frac{\text{TE} \vdash \kappa : \tau\ \mathtt{chan} \quad \text{TE} \vdash v : \tau}{\text{TE} \vdash \kappa!v : \mathtt{unit}\ \mathtt{event}}$$

$$\frac{\text{TE} \vdash \kappa : \tau\ \mathtt{chan}}{\text{TE} \vdash \kappa? : \tau\ \mathtt{event}}$$

$$\frac{\text{TE} \vdash ev : \tau'\ \mathtt{event} \quad \text{TE} \vdash e : (\tau' \to \tau)}{\text{TE} \vdash ev \Rightarrow e : \tau\ \mathtt{event}}$$

$$\frac{\text{TE} \vdash ev_1 : \tau\ \mathtt{event} \quad \text{TE} \vdash ev_2 : \tau\ \mathtt{event}}{\text{TE} \vdash (ev_1 \oplus ev_2) : \tau\ \mathtt{event}}$$

FIGURE 2.3. Type inference rules for concurrency features

a value), and the second applies when the expression is expansive. This avoids the soundness problems that can be caused by the combination of imperative features and polymorphism [177]. The second set of rules, given in Figure 2.3, cover the typing of the concurrency constructs. It is worth noting that the syntactic form of a term uniquely determines which typing rule applies.

2.4.3 Dynamic Semantics

Following some necessary definitions, we present the dynamic semantics of Mini-CML top-down, starting with concurrent evaluation.

Preliminaries

We use the following sets of objects in our dynamic semantics:

$$
\begin{array}{rcll}
e & \in & \text{Exp} & \textit{expressions,} \\
v & \in & \text{Val} \subset \text{Exp} & \textit{values,} \\
ev & \in & \text{Event} \subset \text{Val} & \textit{event values,} \\
\kappa & \in & \text{Ch} \subset \text{Val} & \textit{channel names,} \\
\pi & \in & \text{Proc} & \textit{process names.}
\end{array}
$$

We also need finite sets of channels:

$$
\mathcal{K} \overset{\subset}{\underset{\text{fin}}{}} \text{Ch}
$$

and sets of processes:

$$
\mathcal{P} = \text{Proc} \overset{\text{fin}}{\longrightarrow} \text{Exp}.
$$

We treat a set of processes as both a finite map from process names to expressions and as a set of pairs. Note that each process in a set has a unique name. We write $\langle \pi, e \rangle$ for an element of a process set and $\mathcal{P}, \langle \pi, e \rangle$ for the set $\mathcal{P} \cup \{\langle \pi, e \rangle\}$ (with the implicit side condition that $\pi \notin \mathcal{P}$). A *configuration*, written $\mathcal{K}; \mathcal{P}$, is a pair of a channel set and a process set. A *well-formed* configuration is one in which the free channels in $\mathcal{P}$ are contained in $\mathcal{K}$ and the terms in $\mathcal{P}$ are all closed. We assume that all configurations are well-formed in the discussion below.

Our semantics consists of the following three relations:

$$
\mathcal{K}; \mathcal{P} \Rightarrow \mathcal{K}'; \mathcal{P}' \qquad \textit{Concurrent evaluation,}
$$

$$
(ev_1, \ldots, ev_k) \rightsquigarrow_k (e_1, \ldots, e_k) \qquad \textit{Event matching,}
$$

$$
\mathcal{K}; e \hookrightarrow \mathcal{K}'; e' \qquad \textit{Sequential evaluation.}
$$

Each of these is defined in detail in the sequel. While it would be possible to collapse these into two relations (concurrent evaluation and event matching), we prefer this organization because it separates logically distinct concepts.

Our semantics is given as a transition system, and we use Felleisen's notion of an evaluation context to define the concurrent and sequential evaluation relations [55]. An *evaluation context* is a single-hole context where the hole marks the next redex (or is at the top if the term is irreducible). The evaluation of Mini-CML is call-by-value and left-to-right, which leads to the following grammar for the evaluation contexts:

$$E \quad ::= \quad [\,] \mid (E\ e) \mid (v\ E) \mid (E, e) \mid (v, E)$$
$$\mid \quad \mathtt{let}\ x = E\ \mathtt{in}\ e \mid \mathtt{spawn}\ E \mid \mathtt{sync}\ E.$$

Concurrent evaluation

The concurrent evaluation relation describes the evolution of process configurations. The most basic evaluation step is that in which one of the processes does a sequential evaluation step:

$$\frac{\mathcal{K}; e \hookrightarrow \mathcal{K}'; e'}{\mathcal{K}; \mathcal{P}, \langle \pi, e \rangle \Rightarrow \mathcal{K}'; \mathcal{P}, \langle \pi, e' \rangle}$$

This evaluation changes the "state" of the process π and may introduce new channel names. As can be seen below, the rules for sequential evaluation guarantee that $\mathcal{K} \subseteq \mathcal{K}'$. Creation of new processes is described by the following rule:

$$\frac{\pi' \notin \mathrm{dom}(\mathcal{P})}{\mathcal{K}; \mathcal{P}, \langle \pi, E[\mathtt{spawn}\ e] \rangle \Rightarrow \mathcal{K}; \mathcal{P}, \langle \pi, E[()] \rangle, \langle \pi', e \rangle}$$

Here a new process (π') is created to evaluate the expression e. Lastly, process synchronization is described by

$$\frac{(ev_1, \ldots, ev_k) \leadsto_k (e_1, \ldots, e_k)}{\mathcal{K}; \mathcal{P}, \langle \pi_1, E_1[\mathtt{sync}\ ev_1] \rangle, \langle \pi_k, E_k[\mathtt{sync}\ ev_k] \rangle \Rightarrow \mathcal{K}; \mathcal{P}, \langle \pi_1, E_1[e_1] \rangle, \langle \pi_k, E_k[e_k] \rangle}.$$

This rule is an abstraction of synchronization involving one (or more) processes. The details of the synchronization are defined by the k-way event-matching relation.

Event matching

The *event-matching* relation is used to describe synchronization involving one (or more) processes. By separating this notion from the concurrent evaluation relation, we avoid tying concurrent evaluation to a specific notion of rendezvous.

The actual rules used to specify the event-matching relation depend on the rendezvous primitives provided by the language. In Mini-CML, we have synchronization involving pairs of communicating processes (2-way rendezvous), and synchronization involving a single process and the `always` event. In both cases, the involved processes synchronize using the `sync` operation. For 2-way rendezvous, we have the following definition of matching:

$$\overline{(\kappa!v, \kappa?) \rightsquigarrow_2 ((), v)}$$

For synchronization on an *always* event (we might call this 1-way rendezvous), we have the following:

$$\overline{\mathbf{A} \rightsquigarrow_1 ()}$$

With the semantics for the base events defined, we can extend the definition of k-way matching to include the event combinators. We have two rules for choice:

$$\frac{(ev_1, \ldots, ev_i, \ldots, ev_k) \rightsquigarrow_k (e_1, \ldots, e_i, \ldots, e_k)}{(ev_1, \ldots, (ev_i \oplus ev'), \ldots, ev_k) \rightsquigarrow_k (e_1, \ldots, e_i, \ldots, e_k)}$$

$$\frac{(ev_1, \ldots, ev_i, \ldots, ev_k) \rightsquigarrow_k (e_1, \ldots, e_i, \ldots, e_k)}{(ev_1, \ldots, (ev' \oplus ev_i), \ldots, ev_k) \rightsquigarrow_k (e_1, \ldots, e_i, \ldots, e_k)}$$

and a rule for wrapping:

$$\frac{(ev_1, \ldots, ev_i, \ldots, ev_k) \rightsquigarrow_k (e_1, \ldots, e_i, \ldots, e_k)}{(ev_1, \ldots, ev_i \Rightarrow f, \ldots, ev_k) \rightsquigarrow_k (e_1, \ldots, (f\ e_i), \ldots, e_k)}$$

Sequential evaluation

Our sequential evaluation relation is defined in terms of evaluation contexts and specifies a standard call-by-value semantics. The first rule defines the meaning of the primitive function constants (e.g., `+`) in terms of the auxiliary function δ:

$$\mathcal{K}; E[(b\ v)] \hookrightarrow \mathcal{K}; E[\delta(b, v)].$$

To ensure sensible typing of these constants, we impose a typability restriction on the definitions of δ and TypeOf.[2] If TypeOf(b) $\succ$ ($\tau' \rightarrow \tau$) and TE $\vdash v : \tau'$, then $\delta(b, v)$ is defined and TE $\vdash \delta(b, v) : \tau$. The next two rules are the standard β-reductions for λ and `let`:

$$\mathcal{K}; E[((\mathtt{fn}\ x\ \mathtt{=>}\ e)\ v)] \hookrightarrow \mathcal{K}; E[e[x \mapsto v]],$$

$$\mathcal{K}; E[\mathtt{let}\ x = v\ \mathtt{in}\ e] \hookrightarrow \mathcal{K}; E[e[x \mapsto v]].$$

---

[2]Note that this restriction does not account for partial functions, such as integer division, but the semantics can be extended to support exceptions.

The last rule deals with the creation of new channels:

$$\mathcal{K}; E[\text{chan } x \text{ in } e] \hookrightarrow \mathcal{K} \cup \{\kappa\}; E[e[x \mapsto \kappa]], \qquad (\kappa \notin \mathcal{K}).$$

It should be clear that these rules preserve the well-formedness of configurations.

2.5   Events and Their Algebra

Events are the basic entities on which the concurrent programming paradigm embodied by CML is founded. Events are organized into (polymorphic) types introduced by a new type constructor and possessing an algebraic structure.

In this section, we describe this structure and show that it possesses some categorical structure reminiscent of the λ-calculus. It also turns out to obey many, but not all, of the equations required to form a monad [113]. The discussion of the present section is informal in the sense that we talk about equational "laws" of CML without spelling out what equality means in the sense of providing a denotational semantics.

Given any datatype T, we define a new datatype $\mathcal{E}(T)$. If T is the type variable α we have a type of polymorphic events $\mathcal{E}(\alpha)$. Recall that events are abstractions analogous to λ-abstractions. Just as with λ-abstraction, there are constructs for introducing events and constructs for eliminating them, i.e., for using them to construct values that are not in the event type. In addition to event types, one has *channel* types. Both events and channels are *first-class* entities, and one can send, for example, an α event along an α-event channel or an α channel along an α-channel channel. The ability to send channels along channels makes CML *mobile* in the sense popularized by the π-calculus [110].

The event combinators satisfy some important equations. The most basic are

```
fun recv ch = sync (recvEvt ch)
fun send (ch, msg) = sync (sendEvt (ch, msg)).
```

The interaction of sync with wrap and guard is given by

```
sync(guard f) = sync(f())
sync(wrap(e,f)) = f(sync e).
```

The equation for **wrap** shows how one can package a complex protocol in the function f that is invoked *on the result of the communication* when synchronization occurs.

It may seem strange to introduce the notion of event as a potential action and then to use sync to trigger the actual communication actions. Why not just introduce recv and send directly and forget about events? The point is that the algebra is defined on the events; the algebra of processes is trivial by comparison. We have event combinators that allow one to construct complex events, and then one can use sync to produce a value.

We have enough structure to make some category-theoretic observations. A thorough investigation of the categorical structure as well as denotational semantics for a closely related language has been developed by Alan Jeffrey [79]. For the most part we ignore the choose combinator. We consider the collection of types to be a category **Type** where the objects are the types and the morphisms are functions between the types. We need not concern ourselves for this discussion with a precise description of exactly which functions we are talking about; we can, for example, take the functions to be the functions definable in CML. The event type constructor, $\mathcal{E}(.)$, is an endofunctor on the category **Type**. Its action on morphisms is given by wrap as follows: If $f : \alpha \to \beta$ is a function then $\mathcal{E}(f)$ is the function

$$\lambda e : \mathcal{E}(\alpha).\texttt{wrap}(e, f) : \mathcal{E}(\alpha) \to \mathcal{E}(\beta).$$

Given this setup, sync and always are natural transformations from $\mathcal{E}(.)$ to the identity functor and from the identity to $\mathcal{E}(.)$ respectively. The naturality diagrams for sync and always are shown in Figure 2.4. The fact

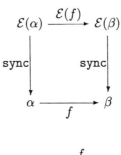

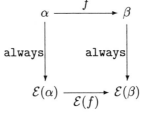

FIGURE 2.4. Naturality diagrams

that the naturality diagrams commute simply amounts to the equations

$$\texttt{sync} \circ f = \texttt{sync} \circ \mathcal{E}(f),$$

which is the basic equation relating sync and wrap, and

$$\texttt{always} \circ f = \mathcal{E}(f) \circ \texttt{always}.$$

To see the first equality, let e be an event of type $\mathcal{E}(\alpha)$; then the equation just says that $\texttt{sync}(\texttt{wrap}(e, f)) = f(\texttt{sync}(e))$. The function $\texttt{sync}$ is a retraction, i.e., it is a left inverse for some function, in this case for $\texttt{always}$. If we did not have the communication primitives between threads then we would have that $\texttt{sync}$ and $\texttt{always}$ are inverses of each other and we would have an isomorphism between $\mathcal{E}(.)$ and the identity functor.

It is worth seeing what the effect of $\texttt{choose}$ is. In the absence of communication, $\texttt{choose}$ faithfully mimics the behavior of finite sets. To see this we ignore the communication primitives and look at what happens if we just have events introduced by $\texttt{always}$, $\texttt{choose}$, and $\texttt{wrap}$. In the present context we work with sets of values rather than of individual values. We use the notation $\mathcal{P}(X)$ to represent the set of finite subsets of a given set X. We redefine $\texttt{sync}$ to be of type

$$\texttt{sync} : \alpha - event \to \mathcal{P}(\alpha);$$

it gives the set of possible results produced by the synchronization. Now we define $\texttt{always+} : \mathcal{P}(\alpha) \to \alpha - event$ by

$$\texttt{always+}\,(\{e_1, \ldots, e_k\}) = \texttt{choose}([\texttt{always}(e_1), \ldots, \texttt{always}(e_k)]),$$

with $\texttt{always+}(\emptyset) = never$. Note that $\texttt{always+}$ is part of the semantics and not part of the syntax on CML. We write $\mathcal{P}(f)$ for the pointwise extension of a function from X to Y to $\mathcal{P}(X)$ to $\mathcal{P}(Y)$. It is now obvious that $\texttt{always+}$ and $\texttt{sync}$ are inverses and that they are still natural transformations. Thus we have an isomorphism of functors between $\mathcal{E}(.)$ and $\mathcal{P}(.)$, the covariant powerset functor.

Finally, we discuss to what extent one can view the CML synchronization events as forming a monad. It turns out that they are quite close to being a monad. It is worth seeing what exactly breaks down. We recall that a monad is an endofunctor T on a category $\mathcal{C}$ with two natural transformations $\eta : I \to T$ and $\mu : T^2 \to T$. These natural transformations are required to obey the following commutative diagrams shown in Figure 2.5.

In the case of events, we want to view $\mathcal{E}(.)$ as a monad. An obvious candidate for η is $\texttt{always}$. In looking for μ one might be tempted to use $\texttt{sync}$, but one can check that the equations for a monad are not satisfied. However, one can use $\mu_A = \lambda e : \mathcal{E}(\mathcal{E}(A)).\ \texttt{wrap}(e, \texttt{sync})$. In verifying the naturality of η, one needs to check that $\texttt{wrap}(\texttt{always}(v), f) = \texttt{always}(f(v))$, which is clearly true from the definition of $\texttt{always}$. To verify the naturality of μ we need to have $\texttt{wrap}(\texttt{wrap}(e, \texttt{sync}), f) = \texttt{wrap}(\texttt{wrap}(e, \lambda e'.\texttt{wrap}(e', f)), \texttt{sync})$. Informally, one can see that these are equal by applying $\texttt{sync}$ to both events and getting $f(\texttt{sync}(\texttt{sync}(e)))$ in both cases. Of course, one really needs to show that they behave the same in all contexts.

In order to verify that the diagrams commute we need to show that

$$\texttt{wrap}(\texttt{wrap}(e, \mu), \texttt{sync}) = \texttt{wrap}(\texttt{wrap}(e, \texttt{sync}), \texttt{sync})$$

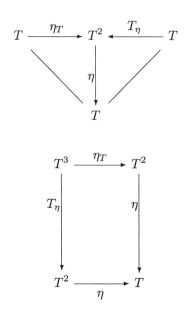

FIGURE 2.5. Commutative diagrams for a monad

holds. Again, one can check that applying sync to either side gives $\mathtt{sync}^3(e)$. Finally, we need to check the triangle diagrams. One of them is just

$$\mathtt{wrap}(\mathtt{always}(e), \mathtt{sync}) = e$$

and the other is

$$\mathtt{wrap}(\mathtt{wrap}(e, \mathtt{always}), \mathtt{sync}) = e.$$

Here we can demonstrate that these equalities do *not* hold if we are observing deadlock. Let never be an event that never synchronizes—an attempt to synchronize on it leads to deadlock. We can see that

$$\mathtt{sync}(\mathtt{choose}(\mathtt{always}(0), never))$$

will always return 0, because choose will select a non-deadlocking alternative. On the other hand, we can synchronize with $\mathtt{wrap}(\mathtt{always}(never), \mathtt{sync})$; after one step it leads to deadlock. Thus, if we had

$$\mathtt{sync}(\mathtt{choose}(\mathtt{always}(0), \mathtt{wrap}(\mathtt{always}(never), \mathtt{sync}))),$$

the choose could select the second alternative and wind up in a deadlock.

A rigorous denotational semantics of CML is under development by Alan Jeffrey using (variants of) ideas from Moggi's computational monads program. Jeffrey has shown that if one develops a trace semantics, in which deadlock information is not recorded, then one will indeed have a monad [80].

2.6   Expressiveness

The treatment of synchronization and communication in CML provides a uniform framework for many kinds of synchronous operations. These may be provided as primitives or implemented as user-defined abstractions, with the only difference being the efficiency of the implementation. It turns out, however, that this is not quite true, since some operations must be primitive, since they cannot be implemented as abstractions using weaker primitives. In this section we discuss informally some of the expressiveness considerations that guided the choice of CML primitives.

The expressive power of concurrency constructs has been studied by several researchers. One of the consequences of this research is the realization that certain constructs are *nonmonotone* [130]. Roughly speaking, this means that there is negative information being conveyed. Thus, for example, **fair merge** in dataflow languages is nonmonotone and is equivalent to having *timeouts* or *signal handlers* or *polling*. These last three constructs are present in the full CML language and are all important for a variety of "systems programming" applications. These may be removed or modified in future versions of CML, but some version of at least one of these constructs has to be provided since they cannot be implemented at all by the usual (monotonic) constructs.

A very important practical construct is the `guard` construct discussed in our overview section. This can in fact be defined as a derived construct, but we would have to introduce a second event-type constructor, which would muddy the type system. For this reason `guard` is provided as a primitive in CML but is not defined in the semantics of mini-CML.

One of the significant design choices arises with the synchronization construct. In the language CML, 2-way rendezvous is the primitive provided. In the discussion of the semantics of mini-CML we have formulated rendezvous as a general k-way synchronization leaving the k as a parameter; thus we leave open the possibility that future implementations of CML may provide 3-way rendezvous as a primitive.[3] One can prove that one cannot *abstractly* implement a $k + 1$-way rendezvous using a k-way rendezvous. In order to understand what this result signifies we need to elaborate on the concept of an abstract implementation.

Consider how one would implement asynchronous communication between a producer and a consumer using a two-way rendezvous. One would write a buffer process that would engage in synchronous communication with the producer and with the consumer. The buffer process could be packaged, and as far as the producer or the consumer is concerned, the details of how the buffer works can be hidden. Imagine now that asyn-

---

[3]There are practical reasons for using three-way rendezvous, for example, in debuggers, but we have not found a natural example of four-way rendezvous.

chronous communication is supported directly, and one wishes to support rendezvous. One can no longer write a "synchronizer" with the details of the protocol hidden away. The standard implementations of rendezvous all require that the participants follow protocols that have to be built into each instance of the communication. In short, the protocol cannot be implemented abstractly. A rigorous proof that an abstract implementation is impossible can be given using concepts from epistemic logic. This kind of expressiveness result gives support to the decision to provide synchronous communication as the primitive, rather than asynchronous communication.

2.7 Implementing Concurrency Abstractions in CML

One of the main design goals of CML was to be able to implement other concurrency primitives *as abstractions*. Of course there are expressiveness limitations that make it impossible to achieve this in full generality. Nevertheless, there are several examples that illustrate what can be done. In this section we discuss two simple examples. A much more extensive discussion with elaborate examples will appear in the forthcoming expository text on CML.

2.7.1 Buffered Channels

The first example shows how one can implement asynchronous communication as an abstraction on top of CML. Of course it is well known that one can do this; the point of this example is to illustrate some CML programming techniques as well as to emphasize the abstract nature of the implementation. *Buffered channels* provide a mechanism for asynchronous communication between threads. Buffering of communication is useful in a number of situations. One important example is when a cyclic communication pattern is required, which would result in deadlock if programmed using synchronous communication. Buffered communication is the fundamental form of communication in the dataflow framework and is one of the most well-studied forms of asynchronous communication. The implementation below shows that we can implement buffers as an abstraction, i.e., one can use buffered communication without being aware of how it is implemented in CML.

A buffered channel consists of a queue of messages; when a thread sends a message on a buffered channel, it is added to the queue without blocking the sender. If a thread attempts to read a message from an empty buffered channel, then it blocks until some other thread sends a message. The signature of this abstraction is given in Figure 2.6. Since the bufferSend operation is nonblocking, it is provided as a unit-valued function. Receiving a message from a buffered channel is a potentially blocking operation, so we provide an event-value constructor (`bufferRecvEvt`) for it.

The queue of messages is maintained by a *buffer thread*. Communication to the buffer thread is via a pair of channels, one for `bufferSend` operations and one for `bufferRecvEvt` operations. The implementation is given in Figure 2.7. The function `bufferChannel` creates the channels that represent the buffer channel and spawns the buffer thread. The channel `inCh` is used to send messages to the buffer thread, while the channel `outCh` is used to receive messages from the buffer. As usual, the buffer thread is a tail-recursive function, with its state maintained in its arguments. The state is the message queue. When the queue is empty, the buffer thread can only offer to accept messages from `inCh`, which means that any attempt to read a message from the buffer will block. When there is at least one message in the queue, then the buffer thread offers both to accept an additional message, which gets added to the rear of the queue, and to send the queue's first message on the `outCh`. The operations `bufferSend` and `bufferRecvEvt` perform the corresponding CML operation on the appropriate channel in the buffer channel's representation. Note that although the `bufferSend` is implemented using the blocking `send` operation, it cannot be delayed indefinitely. This is because the buffer thread is always willing to accept a communication on the `inCh`.

2.7.2 Swap Channels

In this section, we present a simple example of a communication abstraction called a *swap channel*. This is a new type of channel that allows two processes to swap values when they rendezvous; one might call this *symmetric rendezvous*, since there is no distinction between sender or receiver. The interface consists of an abstract type

`type 'a swap_chan,`

and functions for creating channels and "*swap*" events:

`val swapChannel : unit -> 'a swap_chan,`
`val swapEvt     : ('a swap_chan * 'a) -> 'a event.`

When two processes communicate on a swap channel, each sends a value and each receives a value. Implementing this correctly requires some care.

Our implementation is based on the asymmetric message-passing operations; so to insure the symmetry of the operation, each thread in a swap must offer both to send a message and to accept a message on the same channel. We can use the `choose` combinator for this purpose. Once one thread completes a send (which means that the other has completed an accept), we need to complete the swap, which means sending a value in the other direction. A first solution might be to use another channel for completing the swap, but unfortunately, this results in a race condition

```
signature BUFFER_CHAN =
  sig
    type 'a buffer_chan

    val bufferChannel : unit -> 'a buffer_chan

    val bufferSend    : ('a buffer_chan * 'a) -> unit
    val bufferRecvEvt : 'a buffer_chan -> 'a event

  end; (* BUFFER_CHAN *)
```

FIGURE 2.6. The buffered channels interface

```
structure BufferChan : BUFFER_CHAN =
  struct

    datatype 'a buffer_chan = BC of {
        inCh : 'a chan,
        outCh : 'a chan
      }

    structure Q = Fifo

    fun bufferChannel () = let
          val inCh = channel() and outCh = channel()
          fun loop q = if (Q.isEmpty q)
                then loop(Q.enqueue(q, accept inCh))
                else select [
                    wrap (recvEvt inCh,
                      fn y => loop(Q.enqueue(q, y))),
                    wrap (sendEvt(outCh, Q.head q),
                      fn () => loop(#1(Q.dequeue q)))
                  ]
          in
            spawn (fn () => loop(Q.empty));
            BC{inCh=inCh, outCh=outCh}
          end

    fun bufferSend (BC{inCh, ...}, x) = send (inCh, x)

    fun bufferRecvEvt (BC{outCh, ...}) = recvEvt outCh

  end; (* BufferChan *)
```

FIGURE 2.7. The implementation of buffered channels

when two separate pairs of threads attempt swap operations on the same swap channel at the same time. For example, Figure 2.8 shows what might happen if threads P_1, P_2, Q_1, and Q_2 all attempt a swap operation on the same swap channel at roughly the same time (where the swap channel is represented by the channels ch and ch'). In this scenario, P_1 and P_2 are

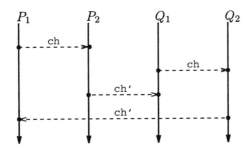

FIGURE 2.8. A swap mismatch

initially paired, as are Q_1 and Q_2. But there is a race in the second phase of the swaps, and P_1 ends up being paired with Q_2, and P_2 ends up with Q_1 (because Q_1 beats P_1 to reading a value from ch', and P_2 beats Q_2 to sending a value on ch').

To avoid this problem, we need to allocate a fresh channel for completing the second phase of the swap operation each time the swap operation is executed. Figure 2.9 gives the implementation of the swap channel abstraction. The representation of a swap channel is a single channel that

```
datatype 'a swap_chan = SC of ('a * 'a chan) chan

fun swapChannel () = SC(channel ())

fun swapEvt (SC ch, msgOut) = guard (fn () => let
      val inCh = channel ()
      in
        choose [
            wrap (recvEvt ch,
                fn (msgIn, outCh) => (send(outCh, msgOut); msgIn)),
            wrap (sendEvt (ch, (msgOut, inCh)),
                fn () => recv inCh)
        ]
      end)
```

FIGURE 2.9. The swap channel implementation

carries both the value communicated in the first phase, and a channel for communicating the other value in the second phase. Note that the ability to send channels along channels is crucial here. Furthermore, local scoping and mobility combine to make a channel available to only the two processes that should use them. The channel for the second phase must be allocated before the synchronization on the first message, which is the kind of situation for which guard was designed. The guard function first allocates the channel for the second phase, and then constructs the swap event using the choose combinator. Because of the symmetry of the operation, each side of the swap must allocate a channel, even though only one of them will be used. Fortunately, allocating a channel is very cheap, and the garbage collector takes care of reclaiming it after we are done.

The swap channel example illustrates several important CML programming techniques. The dynamically allocated inCh channel serves as a kind of transaction ID, and lexical scoping is used to control its visibility. By sending the response on the local channel, the respondent is guaranteed that the message is going to the proper process. The other side of this is that the partner in the symmetric exchange must have access to the private channel. This is done by sending the channel to the process along with the data; in short, *scope extrusion* is used in a crucial way. This is a paradigmatic example: local scope is used to guarantee that a channel is private, and scope extrusion is used to make the channel available to another process to use.

It is also an example where nondeterministic choice is used inside an abstraction, which is why we have both choose and sync, instead of just the select operator. And lastly, this example illustrates the use of the guard combinator.

2.8   Conclusions and Related Work

The earliest attempt known to the authors to add concurrency to ML is Holmström's PFL language [77]. Around the same time, Cardelli developed the concurrent language Amber [43]. The dynamic thread creation, synchronous message passing, and generalized selective communication of Amber provided the inspiration for the second author's design of PML [149]. CML evolved out of a reimplementation of the PML primitives on top of the SML/NJ system. CML improves PML in two important ways, which we have not discussed in this paper: it provides garbage collection of deadlocked threads, and it extends the event mechanism with a combinator for *negative acknowledgments*.

The concurrent languages FACILE [58] and LCS [25] support communication and synchronization in a way that also allows abstraction. These languages make *behaviors* (a concept taken from the process calculus world) into first-class values. In many respects, these behaviors are like CML's event values; they can encode basic communication, choice, and actions, and can be used to define abstractions.

From the theoretical point of view, there has been substantial activity on mobility and related phenomena, essentially starting with the π-calculus of Milner, Parrow, and Walker [110]. One can view CML channels and the send and recv operations as providing an implementation of a typed version of the π-calculus, but there are key differences. In the π-calculus, one can send *free* channel names along channels. In CML, one cannot quite do this; a channel first has to be created in some scope and then sent. Note, however, that unlike Sangiorgi's πI-calculus [156], which requires that every time a name is sent it be a fresh private name, one can send a channel to multiple other processes. Thus, CML might be viewed as lying somewhere between the π-calculus and the πI-calculus, in terms of mobility.

Recently, Pierce and Turner have proposed a language based on the π-calculus, called PICT [137]. Unlike CML, PICT is not built around a sequential language, but rather is purely concurrent, with sequential features, such as function abstraction and application, encoded using processes and communication. One controversial decision in the design of PICT is that it does not have choice as a primitive. When applications need the non-determinism normally provided by choice, they use application-specific protocols, such as a merge process [137].

Another recent concurrent functional language that does not provide choice is Concurrent Haskell [135], which uses synchronous shared memory as its basis communication and synchronization primitive.[4] As in the case of PICT, the designers of Concurrent Haskell rely on application-specific protocols to implement choice-like patterns of synchronization.

We believe that leaving choice out of a message-passing language is misguided. While choice does have its implementation costs, it is an important mechanism for program composition. Relying on application-specific communication protocols to emulate choice results in nonmodular communication patterns, which can be a serious problem for large-scale software construction.

In contrast, the design of CML is primarily motivated by a desire to provide support for modular construction of concurrent applications. First-class event values provide a compositional abstraction mechanism for managing synchronization and communication.

---

[4]Synchronous shared memory can be viewed as a buffered channel of length one.

3
Concurrency in Poly/ML

David Matthews

ABSTRACT The language Poly/ML is an implementation of Standard
ML. Concurrency primitives were added to Poly/ML in response to a specific requirement: the need to support a windowing system, and not with
the aim of investigating concurrency as such. After a description of the
primitives and the rationale behind them, the major portion of the chapter
is a description of the implementations and the way they evolved. It follows the historical development of the implementations, starting with the
original uniprocessor version and following on with systems on the Firefly
shared-memory multiprocessor and the more recent work on a distributed
network of workstations.

3.1 Introduction

Poly/ML [99] is an implementation of Standard ML [112], which is currently commercially supplied and supported by Abstract Hardware Ltd.
It implements the Standard ML language as closely as possible but also
includes a number of extra features.

The Poly/ML implementation itself is beyond the scope of this paper, but
several features of it are relevant to the provision of concurrency. As well
as the concurrency primitives described in this paper, and an X-windows
package built using them, there is a persistent store system. The persistent
store gives the ML program access to large amounts of data that are brought
into store as required.

Efficient management of store is important for good performance, and
the design of the garbage collector can have a critical effect. All ML objects,
including stacks and executable code segments, are held in the heap. The
normal Unix stack is used only by the run-time system, which is written
in C. This contains the garbage collector, persistent store handler, and the
interface to the operating system. In all there are about nine thousand lines
of C code in the system.

3.1.1 Concurrency

The Standard ML language includes all the features required for sequential programming, but one area that was not addressed in the language

definition was the provision of any mechanism for concurrency.

Concurrency is needed for two quite different purposes. On the one hand there are some applications for which the nondeterminacy implicit in concurrency is an integral part. A window system must be able to respond to a user pointing anywhere on the screen and clicking the mouse button, and one of the easiest ways of programming this is to have separate processes manage events associated with each window. On the other hand there has been the increasing use of multiprocessors to speed up applications, but to use this a mechanism must be provided to enable programs to be split into parts that can be run in parallel.

The initial work on concurrency in Poly/ML focussed on the first of these requirements. The Dialog interface to the Lambda theorem prover, for example, has been implemented using the Poly/ML concurrency primitives. This is a graphical front-end that must be able to respond to user actions while the theorem prover is still computing. Without concurrency it would be necessary for the theorem prover to check periodically to see whether the user had typed or clicked. With concurrency the theorem prover can be written without having to be concerned with events, which are only of relevance to the front-end, and yet they can all run as part of the same ML session.

The second reason for having concurrency, the speedup to be achieved with multiprocessors, has been the subject of more recent attention. Although the semantics of such a system may be the same as for the uniprocessor case, the implementation issues are very different. In particular, if the requirement is to achieve a useful speedup compared with a single processor, it is essential that the implementation be efficient; otherwise the advantages of multiple processors will not compensate for inefficiencies in the implementation.

3.2   The Poly/ML Concurrency Primitives

The reason for providing concurrency in Poly/ML in the first place was purely pragmatic: the need to support a windowing system. The primitives chosen were therefore not the result of a large amount of research, but the result of a few design criteria.

3.2.1   Design Criteria

Poly/ML is first and foremost an implementation of Standard/ML. The most important criterion was that the presence of concurrency in the language should not affect other programs that do not happen to need concurrency. In this respect Poly/ML differs from languages such as FACILE [59] and LCS [25], which are concurrent languages. This immediately rules out the addition of new syntax, since existing programs that might have already used the reserved words as identifiers would no longer compile. The obvious solution was to provide the primitives as a set of functions inside a structure (ML module).

Clearly these primitive functions have to be specially built into the system, but other than that they have no special status. This would allow other concurrency modules to be defined, based on these primitives, that would have the same status as the primitives. This suggests that the primitives should be fairly low-level, since higher-level concurrency operations can be written in terms of them.

The question of semantics was considered as a factor, but only to the extent of an expectation of what would be relatively simple to define. Providing a semantics for a language without concurrency is a major piece of work. Adding the nondeterminacy inherent in concurrency makes the task extremely difficult. Nevertheless, a semantics has been produced [18] for a simple language using a variant of the primitives present in Poly/ML.

Efficiency of the implementation was also a factor but was not an overriding concern. In the intended application, a windowing environment, it was not expected that there would be a large number of processes or that the cost of interprocess communication would be a major factor. More recently, with the use of concurrency on multiprocessors to achieve speedup, the question of efficiency has received much more attention.

The primitive functions and their types are shown in Figure 3.1.

```
val fork: (unit -> unit) -> unit
val choice: (unit -> unit) * (unit -> unit) -> unit
val console: (unit -> unit) -> unit -> unit
type 'a channel
val channel: unit -> '_a channel
val send: 'a * 'a channel -> unit
val receive: 'a channel -> 'a
```

FIGURE 3.1. The Poly/ML concurrency crimitives

Two additional functions, *find_server* and *rfork*, have been added in the distributed implementations and are described in Section 3.5.

3.2.2 Process Communication

The communications system chosen was essentially that of CSP [74]. A process sends a value on a channel to another process that receives it. Both processes are blocked until the value is passed, which happens atomically. The processes are then allowed to proceed. A nonblocking version of *send* could be implemented using the blocking primitives provided, by associating a buffer with a channel. In a distributed system there might well be efficiency gains if this was built in.

When a reference or a channel is passed through a channel it is shared between the sender and the receiver. This allows, for example, a server process to receive a request from a client that includes a channel on which to reply. This definition is easy to implement on a single processor but has serious implications when attempting to implement it on a distributed memory system, as it requires that accesses to the object must be made coherent.

3.2.3   Process Creation

Parallel processes are created using the *fork* function, which takes as its argument a function and runs it as a separate process. When the function returns or raises an uncaught exception the process dies.

There is a related function, *choice*, which provides mutual exclusion between a pair of processes. Of the two processes it creates, only one is allowed to do a communication. The other is allowed to run until it attempts a communication, in which case it dies.

The definition of *choice* is perhaps an unusual aspect of the Poly/ML primitives and comes from the decision to have all the primitives as functions. The basic aim of a *choice* operation is to allow for a process to communicate on one of a number of channels, but on only one. There is no inherent parallelism. Using additional syntax it is easy to provide a guarded choice construction, such as in ADA [41], which ensures that each choice is associated with a send or receive. Another option, which does not require additional syntax, is to have a choice function that associates with each send or receive both the channel and a continuation that will execute if that communication succeeds. This is the solution adopted in PFL [76] and CML [149], and it has a lot to recommend it.

This solution was not used in Poly/ML because it implies a continuation-based view of all the concurrency operations. It was felt that this would require a rather unnatural style of programming of simple operations and that it would be better to have a *choice* operator that was somewhat unusual rather than to distort the *send* and *receive* operations. It must be stressed that this is very much a personal view. Issues of programmability are very important in programming language design, but are, at least at the moment, subjective decisions. It is still open to the programmer to define the primitives of PFL or CML in terms of the Poly/ML primitives, and this has in fact been done.

This left only the possibility of having a *choice* that would take as arguments arbitrary functions. There is no way when *choice* is called that it can check that the first operation that each branch performs is a communication, and therefore it is necessary to run both the branches and to provide interlocks between them. Either branch may contain other calls to *choice* or to *fork*, and so a definition had to be made that allowed for this.

The definition that was finally decided on was that *choice* creates two new processes that initially run in parallel with each other and with the parent. Each of the branches may call any function, including *fork* and *choice*, and do not interact until they attempt to call *send* or *receive*. At that point they interlock so that only one of them is allowed to communicate. More strictly, only processes that are children of one of the branches will be allowed to communicate. This inheritance of the interlock means, among other things, that multi-way choices can be defined in terms of the two-way choice.

The definition of *choice* in Poly/ML has a number of interesting properties:

1. Fork can be regarded as a derived form of choice, and could be defined as follows:

   ```
   fun fork f = choice(f, fn()=>()).
   ```

   This suggests that a single basic primitive, a multi-way choice, could be provided, with the current two-way *choice* and *fork* as derived forms.

2. It is possible for two different choices to send and receive on the same channel:

   ```
   choice(fn()=>send(a, "hello"), fn()=>print(receive a));
   ```

   Since the two branches of the choice are both processes, it is necessary for the implementation to recognise this as a special case and not allow the processes to communicate. They can, of course, communicate with another *send* or *receive* on that channel.

3. If all the observable actions of a process are communications, then the choice operator is very similar to the generalized choice of CCS. A process may, however, have an effect on other processes or the outside world by assigning to a reference or by writing to a file. It would be possible, though expensive, to consider these as communications that committed the choice.

3.2.4 *Interrupts from the Console*

The Definition of Standard ML says that it should be possible to raise an *Interrupt* exception "by external intervention," although the exact details are left unspecified. It seems to be generally accepted that this implies that it is possible to type some key sequence at the console that will raise the *Interrupt* exception in a function that is in an infinite loop. While this is reasonably clear when there are no processes, the addition of multiple processes leads to the question of where the exception should be raised.

Various solutions are possible, the most attractive being those that treat console interrupts as messages on a special channel, but they have problems if an overriding concern is to ensure compatibility with the Definition of Standard ML.

In Poly/ML, most processes do not receive a console interrupt. Only those processes designated "console processes" receive the interrupt. Console processes are created with the *console* function, which is very similar to *fork*. *Console* creates a new process for a function and returns as its result a function that can be used to raise an Interrupt exception in it. In addition, the process is added to the set of processes that will receive an Interrupt if a console interrupt is generated.

The Interrupt exception is also raised if a deadlock is detected. If the scheduler has no processes to run and no processes are waiting for external input or output, it raises the Interrupt exception in all the console processes. This is particularly useful for interactive programming since it is often easy to deadlock the top-level read-eval-print loop when developing programs using process communication. The top-level is a "console process," and so it will receive the interrupt. For the Interrupt exception to work in this way, it is necessary to be able to interrupt not just running console processes but also those that are currently blocked waiting for communication on a channel.

3.3   The Uniprocessor Implementation

The first implementation of the primitives was on a Sun3 to support multiple threaded windows. On a uniprocessor there is no advantage in speed of using concurrency, although for illustration a few example programs were written. The concurrency primitives in ML were mapped directly onto calls into the run-time system, written in C.

3.3.1   Process Creation

Each process runs on a separate stack, with each stack an individual heap object. In keeping with the idea of processes being lightweight, the stacks are initially small, but when a process overflows the end of a stack all the stack values are copied into a new larger stack segment. Other schemes, such as allocating individual stack frames on the heap, were considered, but they put too high an overhead on the garbage collector. Whenever a process makes a call into the run-time system, whether concerned directly with the process mechanism or not, all the registers are saved in the stack segment. The ML processes can be interrupted, resulting in traps into the run-time system, but the run-time system itself cannot be interrupted.

As well as a stack segment, each process has a process base that points to the stack segment and is used for synchronization. The process bases for runnable processes are linked together in a chain, and time slicing involves simply moving a pointer round the chain to select the next process to run. A periodic interrupt is used to provide the time-slicing. There is no priority scheduling, although it would be possible to use some algorithm based on, say, whether a process had used all of its time-slice or whether it had become blocked for a communication on a channel or for external input or output.

Fork creates a new stack segment and process base for the function. The stack is initialized to start executing the function and to call a kill-process function in the run-time system when it returns. The kill-process function is also called by an exception handler if an uncaught exception is raised in the process. A newly created process base is added on to the run queue and so will be run when its turn comes.

The *choice* function is implemented using similar code to *fork* for each of two processes, but a state variable is shared between the two processes created. This state variable provides the interlock between the processes.

3.3.2   Communication

A channel is a two-word updatable object, and the *channel* function merely allocates store for it. Each word is used as the head of a list of processes blocked on the channel waiting to do a send or a receive. Normally only one of the lists will be nonempty, but it is possible for processes to be waiting both to receive and to send on a channel if they are alternative choices. When a process attempts to send or receive on a channel that cannot immediately satisfy the request, its process base is removed from the run queue and linked onto the appropriate chain. Blocked processes use no resources other than the store required for their process bases and stacks, and this store will be garbage collected if the channel is not reachable from a runnable process and so can never be woken up.

Transferring the value is the easiest part of the communication. Since both processes are running within the same memory, only one word needs to be copied, and this is held in the sender's process base until the communication is complete.

Choice

Communication in the presence of the choice function is more complicated and is worth describing in detail. As an example consider the following piece of program:

```
choice (fn()=>(choice (a, b); c), d).
```

Representing the processes executing functions a, b, c, and d by A, B, C, and D, this can be written as

```
((A+B) | C) + D,
```

where + represents alternative choices and | represents parallel execution. Although there is no explicit call to fork in this example, the definition of *choice* in Poly/ML implies that the two processes A and B are run in parallel with C.

Figure 3.2 shows the way the state variables are set up and the way the process bases for the various processes are linked together. Each state variable is a pair consisting of a value, initially either "choice" or "par," and a pointer to another state variable, which may be nil.

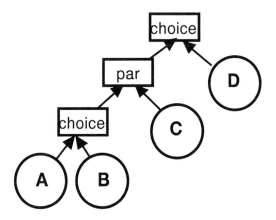

FIGURE 3.2. ((A+B) | C) + D

The state variables are only examined when a process attempts to communicate. Consider the simplest case, when D attempts to communicate with an external process that is not part of a choice. The state variable chain pointed at by D is checked to see whether any of the variables have yet been taken. Since they have not, the communication succeeds and the "choice" pointed to by D is converted to "taken." D itself is detached from the state variable since it can now continue and make other communications (Figure 3.3).

Suppose now that one of the other processes, A, B, or C, wishes to communicate. A search up the chain shows that one of the entries has been taken. The process cannot communicate and is killed.

Consider an alternative possibility, where it is process A that communicates first. As before, the state variable pointed at directly by A is converted to "taken," and the link from A to the state variable is removed. In addition, the rest of the chain is followed, converting "choice" to "taken" and removing the links. The "par" entry remains as "par." The result is a different chain (Figure 3.4).

After this communication, processes B and D cannot communicate, but process C can, since it points to a "par" variable that is not linked to anything else.

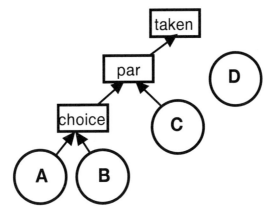

FIGURE 3.3. Choosing D in ((A+B) | C) + D

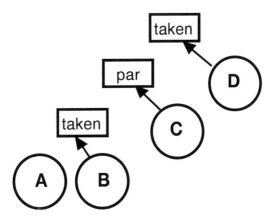

FIGURE 3.4. Choosing A in ((A+B) | C) + D

So far we have considered only communications between these processes and external processes, but there is the possibility of internal communication. Suppose process A attempts to communicate with process D. Since none of the "choices" has yet been taken, it would appear that a communication is possible. However, A and D are the result of alternative choices, and so a communication between them is not allowed, although either could communicate externally. This case is discovered by searching for the first common ancestor of the two processes. In the case of A and D this is the top "choice" box, so these processes cannot communicate, and if no third process is available to communicate, both processes will be blocked.

If the first common ancestor is a "par," communication is allowed. This occurs in the case of A and C.

3.3.3 Input/Output

External input and output, such as to files or to the console, are not dealt with in the same way as communications on channels. The main concern is to ensure that a *read* or *write* does not block, since that would cause the Unix process to be suspended and so prevent any of the ML processes from running. A process that attempts to do an operation that will block is left on the run queue, but set up so that it retries the operation when its time slice comes round again. The alternative, of setting the stream to generate an interrupt, had unfortunate side-effects, and this scheme works satisfactorily provided the time-slices are not so long that the external events are unacceptably delayed or so short that the processor spends too much time polling devices that are not ready.

3.4 A Shared Memory Multiprocessor Implementation

The process primitives and the uniprocessor implementation were designed to support the window system so that there would be a satisfactory interaction with the user. Some examples of other programs were written to experiment with a process-based style of programming and also to see how well the implementation dealt with large numbers of processes, but the overhead of process creation meant that all these examples ran considerably slower than the equivalent programs without processes. On a multiprocessor it is possible to use the process mechanism to split a computation so that it will run faster, but the requirements on a process scheme designed for efficient execution on a multiprocessor might well be different from those required for the window system. The aim of the Firefly implementation was to investigate the consequences of using a multiprocessor.

The Firefly multiprocessor [163] was an experimental system developed at DEC-SRC. Each Firefly consisted of four Microvax processors together with an I/O processor connected to a shared memory. The hardware ensured that the processor caches were consistent. The Fireflies ran a kernel called Topaz that provided lightweight processes called "threads" and multiplexed these onto the available processors. Getting true parallelism in ML was a matter of using these threads to run ML processes. Provided that threads were not used, the Firefly could be run exactly like a uniprocessor Vax with Topaz providing Unix emulation.

Poly/ML had originally been written for the Vax processor, and so porting the sequential part of the system was simple, requiring only a few hours work. The major problem was converting the run-time system to run in a parallel environment since it was not reentrant. In the end the solution adopted was to treat the whole run-time system as a monitor and use a single semaphore for the whole run-time system. A more careful design with monitors on smaller sections of code would almost certainly have improved performance but required considerably more drastic changes.

The run-time system could be entered either by an explicit call, for example to read a character from a file, or by means of a trap. Traps occurred as a result of using an object in the persistent store, resulting in an illegal address trap, or as a result of a trap instruction being executed, indicating that a heap or stack segment was exhausted.

3.4.1   Threads and Processes

The initial design used one thread for each ML process, but although threads were intended to be lightweight, the overhead of thread creation and manipulation were still considerable. Instead, the design was changed to use only four worker threads, i.e., one per processor, each forked at the start and merely stopped if there is nothing for it to do. Each thread took a process off the run-queue and ran it until either the process blocked or its time-slice was exhausted. This is in many ways a simple extension of the uniprocessor implementation. It was obviously necessary to reduce the number of worker threads if there were not enough processes to run, though this was complicated if processes needing to do external input or output were left on the run queue, as in the uniprocessor implementation.

As well as the worker threads there were two threads concerned with trap handling. One dealt with synchronous traps such as heap segments becoming exhausted or persistent store faults; the other dealt with asynchronous traps such as console interrupts and time slicing. These were needed because although Topaz emulated the basic Unix system, once multiple threads were used there were problems with signals.

3.4.2   Garbage Collection

Garbage collection was implemented as a synchronous scheme in which all the processes were stopped, the whole store was garbage collected, and the processes were then allowed to continue. It is probable that asynchronous garbage collection would have considerably improved the performance of the system, but it would have required a drastic redesign of the garbage collector. In any case there has been a considerable amount of work in this area, including work on the Fireflies themselves [53].

Each worker thread had its own segment of heap in which to allocate store. This allowed the threads to run independently and avoided the need for frequent calls to a central heap allocator. When a thread exhausted its segment, it trapped into the run-time system and was allocated a new segment. Only when the allocator was unable to satisfy the request did the store have to be garbage collected.

Garbage collection required all the worker threads to stop so that there was no activity that would affect the store. When a process trapped into the run-time system it had to acquire the run-time monitor lock, and this was used as a way of stopping activity. Each worker thread was persuaded to make a run-time system call as soon as it was in a safe state, and then it became blocked on the run-time system semaphore, since the semaphore was already held by the thread performing the garbage collection. As soon as all the threads had become blocked, the store could be garbage collected. When garbage collection was complete the thread allocated itself the store it needed and returned from the run-time system, releasing the semaphore. This then allowed one of the other threads to do its run-time system call, which then gradually released the other threads.

3.5   The Development of a Distributed Implementation

Although the underlying implementation of processes on the Fireflies was substantially different from the uniprocessor version, the semantics was the same. It is important that any distributed implementation should have the same semantics so that users can move their programs from a uniprocessor to a distributed multiprocessor without seeing any difference in behavior, except one hopes, a substantial speedup.

The Fireflies had one serious disadvantage, namely, that the individual processors were very slow, and so there was little incentive for further work on them when a four-processor Firefly could be outperformed by a single uniprocessor. To continue to develop multiprocessor applications it was necessary to look for a distributed implementation.

One approach would be to design for a network of transputers, but there are a large number of personal workstations in the Laboratory that are left idle out of office hours, and it seemed sensible to design a system that would make use of them.

3.5.1   Additional Primitives

Although the eventual aim is to have only one set of primitives for all concurrency architectures, during the development of the distributed system two additional primitives, *rfork* and *find_server*, were added.

The model used is of a client machine and a number of servers that only provide processing power. The user initially runs the Poly/ML system with the top-level read-eval-print loop on the client machine. Elsewhere on the network are server machines that are waiting to receive connections from a client. The servers provide only computing power and do not retain any state between sessions.

Establishing connections between the client machine and the servers is done by the *find_server* function. It returns *true* if it has established a connection with a new machine and *false* it if has not. It can be called repeatedly to get several servers into the pool of servers on which the client can run processes. Once a server is connected to a client it remains allocated to that client until the client quits. Servers themselves cannot call *find_server*; it can only be called by the client.

Eventually there will probably be a mechanism for migrating processes, but at the moment a process stays on the machine on which it is created. The *fork* function creates processes that run on the same machine as the caller, and there is an *rfork* function, which behaves in the same way as *fork* but creates a process on another machine. Processes created by *choice* always run on the same machine as the caller. From the point of view of the behavior of the system, there is no difference between processes created locally with *fork* or remotely with *rfork*. The reason for making the distinction is that it is very useful to have some control over process placement when trying to evaluate the performance of the system. Communication between processes is with *send* and *receive*, which behave in the same way whether the processes and the channel on which they are communicating are on the same or different machines.

The types of *rfork* and *find_server* are shown in Figure 3.5.

```
val rfork: (unit -> unit) -> unit
val find_server: unit -> bool
```

FIGURE 3.5. The additional distributed primitives

3.5.2 Implementation of a Distributed System

The distributed system[100] is essentially an extension of the uniprocessor system, with a scheduler on each machine running its own processes but with a mechanism that allows the schedulers on different machines to cooperate.

The implementation can be divided into two main areas. The interscheduler communications system provides the mechanism for creating processes on remote machines and communicating on remote channels. In addition to this there is a distributed memory system that is responsible for handling large data structures and for ensuring that objects that are shared between different machines are consistent. Both the interscheduler communications system and the distributed memory system use the same underlying message stream.

The implementation was remarkably easy, by extending the persistent storage system of Poly/ML [98]. Most of the mechanisms needed to implement the distributed memory space were already present and needed little adaptation. Most of the difficulties were found in the communications systems, involving deadlocks and even a bug in the operating system.

Communication Protocols

The distributed system is implemented on Unix-based machines connected by an Ethernet. The Internet protocols available are a datagram protocol (UDP) and a stream protocol (TCP). UDP provides a mechanism for sending blocks of a limited size to a specific port number on a specific machine or to broadcast. It does not establish a connection. It is possible for a UDP message to fail to arrive, so it is the responsibility of higher-level protocols to ensure reliability. TCP provides connections between streams on two machines. It takes care of flow control and reliability at the cost of adding extra overhead to the communication system. For this system UDP broadcast messages are used during the initial connection protocol, but TCP connections are set up to carry the communications between the schedulers on different machines. The Unix signal mechanism is used to interrupt the executing ML code when a message arrives and alert the scheduler.

Initial Connection and Broadcast

Before any distributed programs can be run, it is necessary for the client machine to make contact with one or more servers. This is performed by the *find_server* function. There may be many servers on the network with different architectures. In the normal client/server model, where there are either a limited number of servers or where every machine provides the service, a name service is used to look up the service address and a connection can be opened directly. In this system we do not know where the servers are or which machines might be providing the service, so we have to use a broadcast. The client broadcasts a message containing an address to establish the reverse connection. Servers that are not connected to any client and that are of the same architecture as the client[1] respond by trying to open a connection. At most one will succeed, and the others will be rejected. The successful server is now able to run processes for the client, while the rejected servers can respond to other connection requests from that client or from others. If the client receives no response within a few

---

[1]The system only allows machines with the same instruction set to cooperate. This simplifies the handling of segments of code that can be passed between machines as ordinary objects. It would be possible to support a heterogeneous system by having a universal machine code form that is translated into a particular machine code on the fly.

seconds it assumes that there are no unconnected servers. Once a server has established a connection to a client, it remains allocated until the client terminates.

When connection is first made to a server, it is allocated a unique number by the client. This number is used to identify addresses of objects created on it, making a single global address space for objects on all the servers connected to a particular client. The first number in the sequence is always the one used by the client, which has special responsibilities.

The Network Memory System

The function of the distributed memory system is to provide the effect of a single memory for all the communicating machines. This is needed because the semantics of *fork* and *send* requires that if a value that represents a complex data structure is sent from one process to another, the data structure is shared between the two processes whether they are on the same machine or different machines. On a single machine this is simple: communication involves passing a single word, which may be the address of a data structure, and so the data structure becomes shared between the processes.

In a distributed system without a single memory things become more complicated. Since there is no shared memory the obvious way of communicating is for the data structure to be copied from the memory on one machine to the memory on another. The data structures are no longer shared, and this can be apparent to the programmer in two ways. If part of one of the copies is modified without ensuring that every other copy is similarly modified, then the copies could be distinguished, and the structures would not be truly shared. They could also be distinguished if it were possible for the programmer to test whether two objects that were supposed to be the same had the same machine address.

Fortunately, in ML this is not such a problem as with other languages. The difference between a copied data structure and a truly shared one is only apparent with **mutable** objects such as references, arrays, and channels, and these represent a small proportion of the total number of objects in typical ML programs. The type system prevents other, **immutable**, data from being modified. In addition, there is no way for the programmer to test for the equality of addresses of immutable objects.

It is therefore possible for an ML data structure consisting entirely of immutable data to be simply copied from one machine to another, whatever the size of the data structure. Although such a scheme is used in FACILE and described by Bailey and Newey [14], it has the disadvantage of requiring the whole of the data structure to be transmitted. Even if the recipient only uses part of the structure, it still has to handle and store the whole structure. It also provides no support for mutable objects. It does, however, have advantages in a truly distributed system where fault-tolerance is an issue, since if a communication succeeds, a machine will have the whole data structure.

The scheme used here limits the amount of data transmitted to a single block at a time, allowing the receiving machine to request more if needed. When the address of an immutable object is to be sent to another machine, the object itself is copied into a special area of memory, the "database area." A *remote address* is constructed for the object, encoding the machine number, making it a global address, and this address is sent to the other machine. This machine can pass it on to other machines.

Remote addresses, like addresses in the persistent storage system, are not valid machine addresses and cause a trap if they are used. The trap handler examines the address and passes it to the distributed memory handler to fetch the block containing the object itself. The distributed memory handler calls back to the machine encoded in the address and forwards the address to it. The response is the block containing the object. Eventually control returns to the trap handler, which replaces the faulting address by the local storage address of the object and retries the faulting instruction.

Typical ML objects are very small, frequently just three words (two words of data such as a list cell with an extra header word used by the garbage collector). Handling large numbers of very small objects is inefficient, and so objects are packed into blocks. The blocks are handled by the system as single entities with maps indicating whether a block has been read and if so where in memory it is located. The maps ensure that when a block has been read, subsequent traps for remote addresses in that block can be handled without needing to copy the block over again.

To avoid wasting the address space, objects are added into a block as addresses for them are needed, until the block is full or the block is requested by another machine. If there is space in the block when it is requested, it is filled by a breadth-first scan of objects already in the block. There is considerable scope for experimentation with different algorithms for packing objects into blocks to optimize communication.

Mutable Objects

This scheme for immutable objects can be extended to mutable objects, but it requires care to ensure that updates are handled correctly. Two mechanisms were tried that proved to be appropriate in different circumstances depending on the way that the references were used. Note that operations on mutable objects do not imply any locking. It is the responsibility of the user-level code to ensure that operations are correctly synchronized by making appropriate use of *send* and *receive*.

References in ML tend to be used in two ways. They are used as counters where they are updated nearly as often as they are read. This use tends to be local to a single process. Alternatively, they are used as flags and are changed very rarely but read frequently and possibly by many processes.

The original mechanism used kept a reference in one place and required other machines to make calls both to make assignments to the reference and to read its current value (dereferencing). While appropriate for the first mode of use, it was unsatisfactory where the reference was updated infrequently, and an alternative scheme is now in use.

As with immutable objects, mutables are copied into the database area and given remote addresses as required. Mutable objects are kept in separate blocks from immutable objects but are copied across when another machine requests them. The address mapping system ensures that there is only one copy of any particular reference on each machine so that equality of addresses is preserved. To ensure that all copies of a reference are consistent, assignments have to involve communications.

The implementation makes use of a spare bit in the header word of mutable objects. All objects have a header word used by the garbage collector that indicates the length of the object and also some bits that indicate whether, for example, the object contains words that could be pointers or bytes that must not be interpreted. This spare bit is used to mark mutable objects that have either been copied to another machine or have been read from somewhere else. In either case, when an assignment is made to an object the bit is tested, and if it is set, the scheduler is called. If the bit is clear, a simple assignment can be made, and the overhead is merely the testing of the bit.

Managing the update of mutable objects is the responsibility of the owner of the reference, that is, the machine on which the reference was originally created. In this way if two machines try to update the same reference at the same time, all copies will have the same value, although which value is indeterminate. The updating machine sends an "ASSIGN" request to the owner, which then sends "UPDATE" requests to all the machines that have copies of the object. To avoid having to record for each object which machines actually have copies of an object it actually sends the "UPDATE" to all machines to which it has connections, and the message is ignored by machines that do not have a copy.

Channels, Process Bases, and Stacks

Although channels, process bases (the data structures that hold information about processes), and stacks are all mutable objects, they are handled differently from references and arrays. They are never moved from the machine on which they are created. Channels are marked by a bit in the header word that indicates that the object is "immovable." Since stacks are only pointed at from a process base and process bases are only pointed to from a channel, this ensures that all of them are "immovable."

It is, however, necessary to construct remote addresses for process bases and channels, but instead of copying them into the database area and then passing that address as the remote address, a "token" is created and its address used. Tokens for process bases can be reused because once a process has completed a successful communication, the token for it is no longer needed. If it needs to communicate later, a new token is obtained.

The Communications Buffer

The standard distributed memory scheme works very well where the address of a particular object is likely to be sent several times or to several different machines. Once a distributed memory address has been created for the object, it can be reused as often as necessary. It is less satisfactory for objects that are created purely for the purpose of being sent to another machine.

The *send* and *rfork* functions both communicate a single word, and any more complex data structure, such as a tuple or a list, would seem to need the creation of an entry in the database area. To avoid some of these overheads, a communications buffer is used to hold some small immutable objects. If the value to be sent is the pointer to a local immutable object that is small enough to fit in the buffer, the object is copied into the buffer. The object is then scanned for other local immutable objects, which are added to the buffer until the data structure has been completely copied or the buffer is full. The full mechanism described above is only needed for mutable objects or for immutable objects that will not fit in the buffer. When the buffer is received, it is copied into the local address area of the machine. This means that if the same data structure is sent several times there will be multiple copies on the receiving machine, but because they are in the local area they can be garbage collected by the normal garbage collector.

Garbage Collection

Once an object has been copied into the database area it can no longer be garbage collected by the local garbage collector. This is partly a consequence of the way the persistent store is handled. Objects read from the persistent store are not garbage collected, so that if they have been read once they remain in memory. This is not a serious problem with the persistent store since objects are only moved from local memory to the persistent store when *commit* is called, which is usually only once or twice during a session. There is a separate garbage collector program that can be run over the persistent database periodically to remove objects that are no longer reachable and to compact the database.

The requirements for the distributed memory system are somewhat different. Objects are added to the database area frequently, possibly every time a machine communicates with another, and it is possible for the space to fill up. There is also the problem that blocks containing mutable objects have to be checked by the garbage collector for local objects to see whether they have been updated with the address of a data structure in the local area, and so the cost of each garbage collection will rise as the number of mutable blocks increases. The lack of a garbage collector for the distributed memory was the most serious deficiency of this system.

The Interscheduler Communication System

Once a connection has been established between a client and a server, a scheduler is started on the server that can receive requests to run processes. This is done using the client calling the *rfork* function. This function takes the address of a closure (i.e., a function together with any nonlocal variables) and sends it to another machine to be run. The choice of server is made simply by cycling around the available servers, and there is no attempt at load balancing at the moment. The ML code to be run is pointed at by the closure and will be copied across under the control of the distributed memory system, as with any other object.

The scheduler is also responsible, as in the uniprocessor system, for communications between processes with *send* and *receive*. The added complication in the distributed system is that either of the processes involved in the communication, and the channel itself, may be on different machines. This could require three different schedulers to cooperate in the communication.

As with the uniprocessor system, channels are two-word objects, with one word used as the head of a list of processes wishing to receive and the other the processes wishing to send. Unlike other mutable objects, a channel is never copied from the machine on which it was created. The responsibility for managing all communications on a channel lies with the scheduler for the machine where the channel is situated.

When a process wishes to send or receive a message, the scheduler for that process examines the address of the channel. If it is a remote address, it sends a message to the scheduler for the channel. The message requesting the communication contains an address of the requesting process, which implicitly encodes the machine making the request, together with the value to be sent if this is a send request. The eventual response is a message to continue the process, together with the value for a receive request. Dummy processes are used by a scheduler to represent processes on other machines while they are attempting to communicate.

Communication between processes on different machines may be relatively simple, but it can be much more complicated if either of the processes is a "choice." The *choice* function creates processes that are interlocked, such that only one is allowed to do a communication. The difficulty lies in the fact that the two alternatives may be trying to communicate on channels on different machines and so may be effectively managed by different schedulers. The schedulers have to coordinate their activity so that they do not both allow the alternatives to communicate. In the uniprocessor system there is just one scheduler; so this problem does not arise. The full protocol is needed when two processes, both of them choices, are trying to communicate. Simpler versions are used when either of the processes is "committed," such as a process created by a call to *fork*.

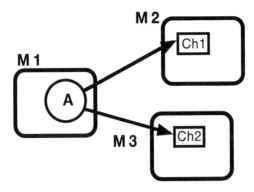

FIGURE 3.6. A ready to choose Ch1 and Ch2

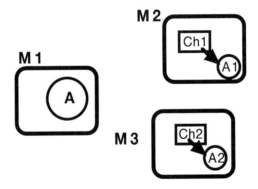

FIGURE 3.7. Ch1 and Ch2 ready to choose A

Figure 3.6 shows a process A on machine M1 that executes a choice of communicating on channel Ch1 on machine M2 or channel Ch2 on machine M3. "Request" messages are sent from the scheduler on M1 to the schedulers on M2 and M3.[2]

Figure 3.7 shows the dummy processes A1 and A2 created by the schedulers, linked to the channel waiting for another process to communicate. The dummy processes are marked as being "choices" and so requiring the

---

[2]In reality process A is a pair of processes linked by state variables. For simplicity it is represented here by a single process.

full protocol. The data structure that interlocks the "choices" remains on machine A.

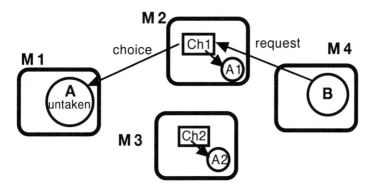

FIGURE 3.8. B selects Ch1

In Figure 3.8 process B, which is not a "choice," wishes to communicate with A1 on channel Ch1. Its scheduler sends a "request" to M2, which finds a potential matching process in A. Before responding, the scheduler on M2 must check with the scheduler on M1 that the choice has not been taken. It sends a "choice" message, which causes the "untaken" choice to be converted to "pending" and the return of an "OK."

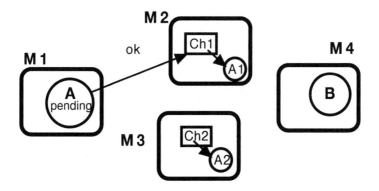

FIGURE 3.9. Ch2 becomes blocked

The result of this is shown in Figure 3.9. As the other process (B) is not a choice, both the processes can be committed by sending "commit" messages (Figure 3.10), and the choice on A is converted to "taken." The communication is complete.

The dummy process on machine M3 has not been affected by this trans-

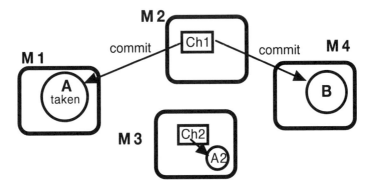

FIGURE 3.10. Ch1 commits to B

action although it cannot now run. It is only removed if another process attempts to communicate on channel Ch2.

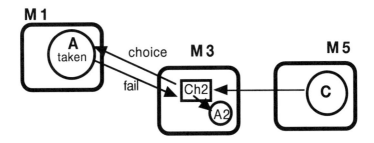

FIGURE 3.11. C selects Ch2

In Figure 3.11 process C attempts a communication, and the scheduler on M3 checks on the state of choice. The choice has now been taken, and so the response is a failure. The dummy process A2 is discarded, and process C is blocked, unless there is another process also waiting to communicate.

It would appear that it should be possible to convert a choice directly from "untaken" to "taken" without going through the intermediate step of the "pending" state. That is true in this example if process B is not also a choice. However, there is the possibility of deadlock in the following circumstances: Suppose that process B is also a "choice" and also wishes to communicate on both Ch1 and Ch2. The scheduler on M4 communicates with the scheduler on M2 and M3 to create dummy processes (Figure 3.12).

The schedulers on M2 and M3 are independent and may communicate with M1 or M4 in any order. Figure 3.13 shows the initial communications.

There are two ways the responses could work. If both messages from

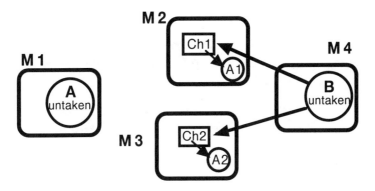

FIGURE 3.12. B ready to choose Ch1 and Ch2

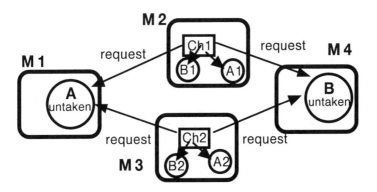

FIGURE 3.13. Resolving the choices

one machine, M2 say, are received by M1 and M4 before the corresponding messages from M3, then the choices at A and B are converted to "pending" and "OK" is returned to M2. M3 received a "wait" message (Figure 3.14).

As M2 has now received "OK" from both sides, it can go on to commit as before. The "wait" messages cause M3 to retry some time later. It will then receive "fail" messages and remove the dummy processes A2 and B2 from its list.

The alternative possibility is that M1 receives the message from M2 at the same time as M4 receives the message from M3. This is a possible deadlock.

Figure 3.15 is identical to Figure 3.14 except that the responses from M4 to M2 and M3 have been reversed. Neither M2 nor M3 can proceed. To avoid deadlock they have to release the "pending" states so that there is another chance to achieve a successful communication.

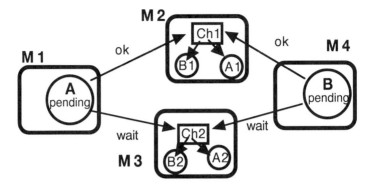

FIGURE 3.14. Ch1 commits to B

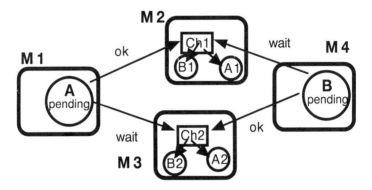

FIGURE 3.15. Possible deadlock

The reset messages restore the original state (Figure 3.16). The protocol starts again from the beginning, and eventually it will arrive at a successful communication. There is a slight danger of "live-lock," where the system forever tries to communicate but has to keep backing off. There are algorithms [39] that avoid this and guarantee termination in a finite number of messages. It seems extremely unlikely that this will be a problem in practice because the random delays in the communications system will tend to favor an eventual termination.

As with the uniprocessor case, it is necessary to check for the case where two alternative choices both communicate on the same channel, one trying to send while the other is trying to receive. This case is checked for when "request" messages are sent out. In addition to sending the address of the process whose status is to be checked, the address of the potential partner is passed as well. Since alternative choices are all on the same

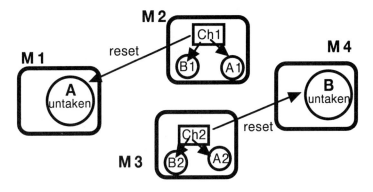

FIGURE 3.16. Resetting the communication

machine, the scheduler on that machine can check that they are distinct. If they are alternatives of the same choice an "alt" response is returned. The effect is then to skip that potential partner and try another. If this case is not treated specially it would result in the "live-lock" condition described above.

Other Issues

If there is more than one server in the system it is possible for the client to pass the address of an object on one server to another server. If that second server needs the object it will have to open a connection to the first. It does this by routing the request through the client. Since the client has connections to all the servers it is able to pass a request for a connection to the appropriate server.

The servers are run as unprivileged Unix processes. Attempts to read from the *std_in* stream give an end-of-file result and writes to the *std_out* stream are sent to the client and interleaved with its *std_out*. Attempts to open any other streams fail. This allows the servers to run independently. A better solution, which would ensure that a process on a remote machine the distributed system behaved the same as a process in the uniprocessor system, would be to have the client operate the streams on behalf of the server.

3.6   Implementation on LEMMA

The major problem with the original distributed system was the lack of a global garbage collector. In addition, there was the difficulty that channels cannot migrate: the machine on which they were first created will always be involved in a communication on a channel, even if all the processes communicating on it are on another machine. The result of this was the decision to build a completely new system based on a distributed memory: LEMMA [102, 101].

3.6.1 LEMMA

LEMMA provides much of the functionality needed to implement Poly/ML, among other things it provides

- a shared virtual memory in which objects are automatically transferred between machines as they are required,

- global garbage collection as well as local garbage collection,

- strict coherency for references with an atomic exchange operation,

- communication between schedulers on different machines;

- it does not assume any particular approach to parallelism and can easily be configured to support different languages in the ML tradition.

This last point shows the origins of LEMMA from collaborative work between me, who had been working on Poly/ML, and Thierry Le Sergent, who had worked on global garbage collection and process migration with particular relevance to LCS.

There is not the space here to describe LEMMA in detail, but it is useful to indicate the differences between it and the network memory system of the previous implementation of Poly/ML.

Most importantly, LEMMA uses only one form of address, avoiding the complications of conversion between local and network addresses. In effect, it uses the virtual memory facilities of the underlying operating system to do this conversion.

Secondly, it provides global garbage collection as a fundamental part of the system, but with local garbage collection on top of this. This allows a machine that is computing heavily and generating a large amount of garbage to carry out a local collection without affecting any of the other machines. A global collection, of course, requires all the machines to synchronize.

Thirdly, LEMMA provides a much improved handling of mutable objects. Coherency is achieved using an invalidation protocol [94], which means that the cost of writing to an object depends only on the number of machines that have read the object since it was last written, rather than, as with the previous protocol, the number since it was created.

3.6.2   Implementation of Poly/ML on LEMMA

Using LEMMA to provide the distributed memory greatly simplified the implementation of the Poly/ML concurrency primitives. LEMMA provides a shared memory with, for mutable data, a write operation that returns the previous value of the word being written. This operation is interlocked so that it can be used to implement a test-and-set operation. LEMMA does not provide any process management, leaving all decisions on processes and language-level communication to the run-time system that uses it. It provides a mechanism for sending data between machines that Poly/ML uses to run a function created on one machine on another.

The Poly/ML process primitives are implemented partly in ML and partly in the C run-time system. The implementation is in many ways similar to that used by Morriset and Tolmach [114] on a shared-memory multiprocessor. That is not really surprising since LEMMA in effect turns the distributed system into a single shared-memory machine. The main difference is that the cost of communications between machines is significantly higher in a distributed system. For that reason Poly/ML uses a separate process scheduler on each machine, each with its own run queue, rather than a single run queue as used by Morriset and Tolmach.

The schedulers are part of the run-time system and deal with time-slicing processes in the run queue. The communications system, written in ML, can call the scheduler to add a process to the run queue or to suspend the current process. Using the LEMMA communications mechanism, it is possible to send a pointer to a process base to another machine and have it add that process to its run queue. This is used to implement the *rfork* primitive and also to run a process after a communication. At present processes always run on the machine on which they were forked, but this mechanism could equally be used to provide process migration.

The *send* and *receive* functions are written using the test-and-set operation rather than by communication between schedulers as in the previous implementation. A channel is not owned by any particular machine, so there is always the possibility that processes on two different machines might attempt to communicate on the same channel at the same time. Indeed, since communication is implemented separately from the scheduler it is possible for the time slice of a process to expire while it is in the middle of the communications code and for another process on the same machine to attempt to communicate on the channel. The issues of deadlock and livelock that arose with the previous distributed implementation are equally relevant here.

The previous implementation used messages between schedulers to implement communication involving processes that have been created by the *choice* function. In the implementation on LEMMA this has been replaced by reading and writing state variables: in effect a return to the uniprocessor implementation. Of course, LEMMA has to implement the reading and writing of references by different machines by sending messages. As with the previous distributed implementation, it is necessary for the state variables to go through an intermediate "pending" state. This is to avoid the deadlock that could arise if state variables were converted directly from "choice" to "taken."

3.6.3 Experience with LEMMA

The full set of Poly/ML primitives has been implemented on LEMMA. It is hoped to start implementing LCS on LEMMA soon. Some work has been done on building applications on top of this implementation of Poly/ML. In particular, there has been some work on implementing a distributed simulation system that showed that a useful speedup could be obtained if the granularity of the parallelism given by the application is not too fine [12].

4
CCS Programming in an ML Framework: An Account of LCS

Bernard Berthomieu

with contributions by
Thierry Le Sergent and Camille le Moniès de Sagazan

ABSTRACT LCS is an experimental highlevel asynchronous parallel programming language primarily aimed at exploring design, implementation, and use of programming languages based upon the behavioral paradigms introduced by CSP and CCS.

The language extends Standard ML with behavior expressions based upon a higher-order extension of the CCS formalism. The extended CCS constructions express concurrency and communication; the SML constructions are used to specify messages, derived behavior combinators, and programs (behaviors). Processes communicate by rendezvous over named communication ports. The language is layered, with behaviors as the highest-level units of computation. New commands are added to the SML user interface to start processes to run in background or in the foreground, in parallel with all already running processes.

The polymorphic typing discipline of SML is extended with the so-called behavior types, assigned to behavior expressions, to enforce consistency of communications between processes. Behavior types bear strong relationships with Wand's row types and Rémy's extensible record types, though they differ in their logical interpretation. Behaviors are assigned a type information that attach a polymorphic type to every possible communication label. Except for the introduction of behavior types, type reconstruction for LCS programs is as in SML.

The operational semantics of the language is given in terms of an observation relation (or labeled transition system), from which various equivalence notions for programs can be defined. As a step towards implementation, this observation relation is refined into a readily implementable reduction relation. The implementation model handles all features of LCS, including preemption; it could be used to implement a large class of process languages. Concrete sequential, parallel, and distributed implementations of the language can be derived from this implementation model.

4.1   Introduction

4.1.1   From Process Calculi to Process Languages

Over the last decade, there has been considerable research interest in process calculi (CCS [107, 108], CSP [74], the π-calculus [110], and a number of related formalisms). Process calculi bring for concurrent programming what the functional paradigm brought to sequential programming, above all strong foundations for their semantics, an explanation of how to compare concurrent programs, and a method for building complex concurrent systems from meaningful smaller pieces.

The central role in process calculi is played by communications: processes describe interaction capabilities with other processes, complex systems (themselves constituting processes) are built as some combinations of interacting processes. The operational semantics of a process is typically given as an observation relation characterizing in some sense its interaction capabilities and from which various equivalence notions can be defined for programs. The approach has been undoubtedly fruitful in the areas of specification and analysis of concurrent systems.

Concurrently, a number of works were aimed at designing, implementing, and experimenting with programming notations based on these paradigms, and hopefully benefiting from their theoretical advances in terms of formal programming techniques. LCS is one of these programming languages; it implements a higher-order extension of Robin Milner's Calculus of Communicating Systems (CCS) with process passing and parametric channels, embedded into Standard ML [112]. Related languages include those described in this monograph, all extending ML with concurrency and communication in various ways, and also some programming or specification notations targeted at specific application areas such as the LOTOS language for specification of open systems interconnection [78].

4.1.2   The LCS Project

LCS processes are described in an SML framework, but concurrent programming capabilities are provided through a specific sublanguage of behavior expressions. Behavior expressions describe processes; they evaluate to behavior values, which are in turn used to spawn processes through specific process creation commands. Processes interact by rendezvous communication over named communication ports. The language is layered, with processes as the highest units of computation.

This contrasts with a number of other parallel programming languages, including Poly/ML [100] and CML [150], discussed in this monograph, in which parallel programming facilities are provided through a set of primitives with a functional interface. Though concurrency and communications are provided through functions, the semantics of these languages depart

significantly from the usual functional semantics due to the complex apparatus needed for incorporating nondeterminism and nonterminating computations into this paradigm. These features are more naturally accommodated in a behavioral framework.

The sub-language of behavior expressions of LCS is based on Robin Milner's Calculus of Communicating Systems [107, 108], which is widely accepted as a convenient formalism for concurrency and communication. As
a bare abstract formalism, CCS lacks several ingredients for constituting
a convenient programming language (e.g., it does not specify messages; it
is untyped; etc.) and also suffers from some known deficiencies in terms of
expressiveness. In particular, CCS does not allow behavior passing or label
passing, which are convenient in implementing mobility and delegation, and
its set of behavior combinators may lack the flexibility required for comfortably programming real applications. LCS proposes solutions to these
problems that as far as possible preserve the underlying theory of CCS
and follow the SML design principles as well. In particular, a nontrivial
extension of the static polymorphic discipline of SML enforces consistency
of communications.

The language and its implementations evolved through several versions
[21, 23] including the one described here, and several implementations have
been investigated. The sequentially running version [23], in which concurrency is limited to a structuring concept, has been used several years as a
workbench for language design, compilation techniques, and experiments.
Implementations on concurrent targets (networks of machines and parallel
machines), allowing one also to take advantage of concurrency as an operational discipline, are forthcoming. An architecture of a virtual machine
suitable for parallel and distributed implementations of LCS on distributed
targets has been designed, and several of its important components have
been developed, including memory management with distributed garbage
collection [88, 102, 101] and distributed scheduling techniques [89].

4.1.3 Overview of the Chapter

This chapter presents in a unified setting the essentials of the LCS project,
previously found in part in separate documents [23, 25, 24, 22]. It is assumed
that the reader has some knowledge of the essential features of both the
language ML and the CCS calculus.

Section 4.2 introduces the language, explains its structure, and discusses
its design decisions. The extended CCS behavior constructions express concurrency and communication, while the SML constructions are used to
specify both messages and derived behaviors. The behavior expressions
typically fall into one of two classes: those concerned with communication
links (creation and naming) and those concerned with composition of behaviors.

Section 4.3 presents the type discipline of LCS. The static and polymorphic typing discipline of SML is extended to enforce consistency of interprocess communication. To the usual SML types are added so-called behavior types, assigned to the behavior expressions. Behavior types bear strong relationships to Wand's row types or Rémy's extensible record types, though they differ in their logical interpretation. Behaviors are assigned type informations that attach a polymorphic type to every possible communication label. Except for the introduction of behavior types, type reconstruction for LCS programs is as in SML.

The operational semantics of the language is given in Section 4.4 in terms of an observation relation (or labeled transition system), from which various equivalence notions for programs can be defined. As a step towards implementation, this observation relation is refined in Section 4.5 into a readily implementable reduction relation. The implementation model handles all features of LCS, including preemption, and could be used to implement a large class of process languages. Concrete sequential, parallel, or distributed implementations of the language can be derived from this implementation model.

The concluding section summarizes the experience, compares it with related projects, and suggests future work.

4.2   Features of LCS

4.2.1   Functions, Behaviors, and Processes

An important decision when designing a high-level concurrent programming language is that of the respective role of functions and processes; the whole shape of the language results in large part from the choice made. With respect to the role of processes, LCS stands between the group of languages Poly/ML [100], CML [150], FACILE [59], in which concurrency and communication are side-effects of functions, and PICT [136], which exemplifies the opposite, "functions as processes," approach. LCS is basically a process language; the highest units of computation are the processes, but abstraction and application are primitives and may be used to build behaviors (process scripts).

Syntactically, LCS extends Standard ML with constructs for building behaviors. The essentials of its syntax are given in Figure 4.1. The set of SML types is also enriched with specific types assigned to behavior expressions; the typing aspects will be discussed in Section 4.3. In addition, LCS provides commands to create processes to run in the foreground or in the background, in parallel with all other running processes.

Behaviors describe interaction capabilities; they are built from primitive behavior expressions and available functional constructions taken from SML (recursion, conditional, abstraction, application, etc.). The primitive constructions include all those of CCS. stop is the behavior that has no

exp	::=	<SML expression> | *beh*	
beh	::=	`stop`	null behavior
	|	`{do` *exp*`=>}`*exp*	commitment
	|	*port*`?{`*pat*`}=>`*exp*	input
	|	*port*`!{`*exp*`}=>`*exp*	output
	|	`signal` *exp* `{with` *exp*`}`	event raising
	|	*exp* `(/|//|/\\|//\\)` *exp*	parallel
	|	*exp* `(\/|\\/|\//|\\//)` *exp*	choice
	|	*exp* `catch` *erules*	event handling
	|	*exp* "`{`"/*lab*$_1$,...,/*lab*$_n$"`}`"	restriction
	|	*exp* "`{`"*lab*$_1'$/*lab*$_1$,...,*lab*$_n'$/*lab*$_n$"`}`"	relabeling
	|	*exp* "`{`"*port*$_1'$/*port*$_1$,...,*port*$_n'$/*port*$_n$"`}`"	aliasing
erules	::=	*erule* `{`||*erules*`}`	event handlers
erule	::=	*exp* `{with` `_}=>`*exp*$'$	event handler
	|	*exp* `with` *match*	message match
port	::=	*lab*`{#`*exp*`}`	comm. ports
match	::=	*pat*`=>`*exp* `{`|*match*`}`	SML matches
pat	::=	<SML pattern>	SML patterns

FIGURE 4.1. LCS expressions

communication capabilities; behaviors are built from `stop`, possibly recursively, by action prefixing (written `=>`), compositions, and port scoping primitives (restriction, relabeling and aliasing).

A communication port is a label (in the syntactic class of identifiers), possibly paired by `#` with an expression. Actions include that of proposing a value on a communication port (output `!` or event raising `signal`), that of accepting a value on a port (input `?` or event handler specifications), and that of performing a preemptive move (do actions). The latter are similar to the silent τ-action of CCS, except that they may encapsulate an expression, evaluated for its side-effects.

LCS is higher order in that one can freely pass behavior values (not processes) as messages, as in the CHOCS calculus [164], or declare functions taking behaviors as arguments and/or returning behaviors as results.

Behaviors must be distinguished from processes. Evaluation of a behavior expression at top level, or locally within some expression, does not produce a process, but rather a closure similar to a function value. Creating a process from a behavior value by one of the process creation commands causes recursive evaluation of the body of the behavior value. The operational semantics of LCS processes is discussed in detail in Sections 4.4 and 4.5.

4.2.2 Naming

Another important design decision is the naming discipline for communication links. CML, Poly/ML, and FACILE, as well as PICT, have first-class channels created by a generative primitive similar to the ref construction of ML for creating assignable values. This approach eases implementation of communications since channels are handled like other values; it also allows the implementation of delegation in a fairly natural way. However, the treatment requires the passing to a process (by parameters or messages) of the full set of channels it needs for interacting with other processes, and channels suffer some polymorphism restrictions (like references in ML).

In contrast with this approach, LCS closely follows the CCS approach for naming. The communication links of a process are here of a structural nature: a process has communication labels a, b, c, etc. just as a record has fields labeled a, b, c, etc. To get around a limitation of basic CCS that does not allow communication labels to be passed between behaviors, LCS uses parametric labels [13]. This permits the retention of most of the underlying theory of CCS while allowing the expression of some forms of delegation and mobility; LCS offers the computation of communication ports, in some sense, instead of offering the passing of labels or channels between behaviors.

LCS communication ports have two components: a *label* and an *extension*, e.g., the port p#(425,true) has label p and extension (425,true). All ports have an extension (the default extension is the value (), of type unit). Dynamically, communication ports identify rendezvous points; three constructions allow the control of their scope:

- The restriction of p in b (written b{/p}) has the effect of delimiting the scope of ports labeled p occurring within b to the process b itself (just as the lambda-abstraction in $\lambda p.b$ delimits the scope of the inner p to the expression b).

- The relabeling b{p/q} restricts label p in b and makes ports labeled q within b appear to the enclosing context as having label p. The restrictive effects of LCS relabelings make them slightly different from those of CCS. Like restrictions, relabelings apply to all ports with the labels involved, whatever their extensions.

- Finally, aliasing allows the renaming of individual ports, rather than collections of ports identified by their labels, e.g., b {p#1/q, p#2/r#true} renames simultaneously port q#() into p#1 and port r#true into p#2. Simultaneously, all ports labeled p are restricted in b.

Relabeling and aliasing are useful for connecting a process defined in isolation with a system of processes obeying a different naming scheme. A typical example of the use of restriction and relabeling is the pipe combinator (^), defined by

```
infix ^;
fun a ^ b = (a {tmp/out} /\ b {tmp/inp}) {/tmp};
```

Assuming a process a producing its results on port out and another process b taking inputs on port inp, the combinator (^) connects the output of a with the input of b. The connection is made using the local auxiliary label tmp.

Labels may be hidden or renamed, but may not be computed or passed as messages or parameters. On the other hand, extensions may be computed or passed, but may not appear in restrictions. This treatment preserves the possibility of static typechecking since the port extensions in use within some process are typically unknown at compile time.

Operationally, one may think of a process as running in a communication environment attaching a channel to each possible communication port. The name scoping primitives dynamically update this association, rebinding existing channels to different ports (relabeling, aliasing), or binding new channels with local scope to some ports (restriction). This interpretation will be developed in Section 4.5.

4.2.3 Compositions

There are three basic forms of behavior compositions: parallel (one of /\, /\\, //\, //\\), choice (one of \/, \//, \\/, \\//), and catch; the first two forms are inherited from CCS, the third is new:

- Processes composed in parallel may communicate values. The single communication and synchronization primitive is synchronous rendezvous over ports: input and output are simultaneous without buffering of the value transmitted.

- Choice compositions permit selection at run-time: the first process in a choice composition that performs an action makes the alternative process(es) in the composition terminate.

- The last kind of composition (catch) is a particular parallel composition with the additional effect of terminating the behavior on the left side of catch as soon as a communication has occurred between members of the composition. The signal and catch constructions implement a process-level exception mechanism that will be shortly described in more detail.

The four variants of parallel and choice compositions differ in how they handle memory locations; the issue will be discussed in a later section. Compositions of any form may be arbitrarily embedded; as in Poly/ML, there are no guardedness constraints on members of any form of composition.

4.2.4 Derived Combinators

New process combinators, such as the previous pipe (^) combinator, are defined as functions taking behaviors and/or other values as parameters and producing behaviors as results. Richer behavior structures are obtained from the basic ones and the available functional facilities, including recursion. Only abstractions and behavior expressions may be recursively defined, however. Some other examples of useful derived combinators are shown below. The NET combinator iterates a binary process combinator Op over a list of behaviors obtained from a parameterized behavior (NET Op a [l1, ...,ln] = (a l1) Op ... Op (a ln). The PAR and PIPE combinators are specializations of NET for parallel and piping compositions:

```
fun NET Op a [] = stop
  | NET Op a [e] = a e
  | NET Op a (h::t) = Op (a h, NET Op a t);
val PAR  = NET (op /\);
val PIPE = NET (op ^);
```

As a simple illustration of naming, piping, and recursion facilities, the behavior shown below offers all prime numbers on a port labeled out by the Eratosthenes sieve method. Behavior primes is built from behavior succs that offers on out all integers greater than or equal to its parameter, behavior filter, which echoes on out the integer it reads on inp, except those that are multiples of its parameter, the previous piping combinator ^ and the recursive sieve behavior. On output of a prime, behavior sieve evolves to itself preceded by a filter that absorbs all multiples of that prime. Note the encapsulated structure of primes, taking advantage of the facilities of SML for local declarations.

```
val primes =
let fun succs n = out! n=> succs (n+1)
    fun filter p = inp? x=> if x mod p = 0 then filter p
                                           else out! x=> filter p
    val rec sieve = inp? x=> out! x=> (filter x ^ sieve)
in succs 2 ^ sieve
end;
```

4.2.5 Exceptions and Events

Events, together with the event raising (signal) and trapping (catch) expressions, implement an exception mechanism at process level. The exceptions we are interested in raising and trapping here are not those found at functional level (such as arithmetic exceptions), but rather those related to communications such as the inability of some process to provide an offer on some communication port. Such exceptions would typically be handled by a reconfiguration of all or part of the current system of processes. Operationally, LCS events are analogous to UNIX signals, though they obey a different scope discipline.

Events are built from event constructors declared through specific event declarations. They may be parameterized (like exceptions) and may carry messages. The message type associated with an event constructor in an event declaration is the type of messages passed to the handlers when events built with that constructor are trapped. Events must be comparable for equality, so their parameter, if any, must admit equality in the SML sense.

Operationally, events implement a particular kind of communication port. Raising an event by signal offers the message associated with the event (or the trivial message (), by default) on a communication port identified by the event itself. Handling an event by catch amounts to a communication between the process that offers the event and its handler. In addition to passing a message, this communication has the effect of terminating all processes on the left side of catch. The operational effect of event trapping is thus that of replacing a system of processes (that on the left side of catch) by another (that specified by the event handler).

Event constructors follow the same static scoping rules as other constructors, but the communication ports they define have particular dynamic scope rules. An event can only be caught by a handler (necessarily introduced by a catch construction) if issued from the behavior on the left side of catch, and its scope stops at the innermost handler found for it. In short, events propagate like exceptions in SML, except that signaling an event has no effect when no surrounding handler may catch it.

The exceptions themselves are propagated as in SML, except that propagation stops at compositions. An uncaught exception x raised within a process makes that process signal event EXN x, in which EXN is a predefined event constructor.

Besides their use as an exception mechanism, events are also useful as a clean-up mechanism to abort, on completion on some work, all the possibly awaiting processes that have been created as part of this work. The next example shows for instance how the previous prime behavior can be used to create another behavior that offers on port out the nth prime number. Behavior nthp spawns primes, skips all primes up to the nth, and then raises a BYE event carrying that nth prime as message. The handler for event BYE offers its message on out; handling the event has the effect of aborting all processes resulting from execution of primes:

```
fun nthp n =
let event BYE with int
    fun skip n = out? x=> if n>1 then skip (n-1)
                               else signal BYE with x
in (primes /\ skip n) {/out}
   catch BYE with p => out! p=> stop
end;
```

4.2.6 Higher-Order Process Passing and Link Passing

Some examples of functions building behaviors have been shown earlier. We are discussing here some potential usages of other higher-order features such as process passing and parameterized labels.

Process passing and link passing are helpful in distributed applications; they allow convenient implementation of mobility and delegation. As a simple example, assume we want to delegate to a remote process the task of reading some value on a given port, processing it, and then returning some result on another given port.

This cannot be directly implemented in LCS since label passing is not provided, but it can be approximated using parameterized ports. Instead of passing labels, an LCS process would pass port extensions applied to implicit labels. That solution can be sketched as follows, in which behavior remote is that of the process executing remotely (function P, left undefined, implements processing). Delegation is implemented by passing indices i and j to the remote process:

```
fun remote =
    rqst?(i,j)=> inp#i?x=> out#j!P x=> done! => remote;
fun application =
    (remote /\  ... rqst!(I,J) => ... => done? => ...) {/rqst};
```

Alternatively, delegation could be done by passing to the remote process the behavior it should execute. That solution is more flexible in that the remote process does not have to keep locally a copy of all potentially remotely requested behaviors. However, the remote process must be equipped with the capability of loading a behavior on some port (say load). This second solution is sketched below. For reasons due to the type discipline, explained in Section 4.3, behavior passing typically requires encapsulation of the behavior passed; type _a Rem below is the type of behaviors loading their behavior on port load.

```
datatype _a Rem = A of {load:_a Rem}_a;
fun remote = load? A b => (b /\ remote);
fun application =
    (remote /\
        ... load!A(inp?x=> out!P x=> done! => stop)=> done? => ...)
    {/load};
```

4.2.7 References, Light and Strong Compositions

As in SML, evaluations take place in the context of a store. LCS reference values are handled as in SML, except that memory locations have restricted scope. LCS provides both light processes (sharing a joint store) and strong processes (operating on private stores).

Each process is dynamically associated with a store; side-effects in evaluation of the process are restricted in scope to the store associated with it. When started, a process inherits the store of the top-level process or a copy of it depending on the process creation command used. Then, the store of a process is determined by the composition combinators from which it results. *Light* compositions (/\ and \/) create processes that both inherit the current store and share it. In the case of *left strong* compositions (//\ and \\/), the process on the left-hand side inherits an independent copy of the current store, while the process on the right-hand side inherits the current store. The other composition operators can be derived from those (see their semantics in Section 4.4). The catch composition acts as a light composition; strong catch compositions can easily be simulated with the existing operators, if required.

Note that with the presence of shared storage, message passing is no more the sole interprocess communication mechanism. No additional means of synchronization are provided, however, and processes cooperating by shared references must still rely on rendezvous for synchronization; semaphores and other usual synchronization devices for shared memory communication can be easily simulated.

Strong compositions are heavily related to distributed programming. A system of two strong processes running on the same LCS machine should not be distinguishable from two processes running on two interconnected LCS machines sharing their communication environment. An important issue for implementation is whether or not passing references between processes not operating on the same store should be allowed. Forbidding it, as was recommended in [25], allows an efficient implementation of strong compositions (store copying can be done incrementally, when stores are written), but the restriction is difficult to enforce statically. The alternative we currently favor is to accept a more important cost for the infrequent strong compositions and message passing between strongly composed processes, and drop the restriction. Passing references between processes operating on different stores is hardly necessary in practice (except when these references encapsulate the internal state of some function or behavior passed between the processes), but it seems more troublesome to forbid it than to give a reasonable operational meaning to it. The issue will be further discussed in Section 4.4.5.

4.2.8   Timers and Other Imperative Features

Other imperative features supported by LCS include timers, stream input and output, and windows. Timing facilities are provided through a sleep primitive function that returns after the expiration of an amount of time equal to its parameter. The implementation of streams input/output is adapted from that of SML, and windows are triples of streams (input, output, and control) associated with a physical window on the terminal.

Timers were introduced for pragmatic reasons, but they do not make LCS a synchronous language; the operational semantics of LCS does not allow relating the starting time of a delay to that of a process. The feature is sufficient in practice for most "non-time-critical" purposes, however. As a simple illustration of the use of timers, function `timeout` below shows how to set up a time bound on an output offer from a process: If process a does not pass any result on port `out` before delay d expires, then it is aborted and process b is started.

```
fun timeout a b d =
let event UP
in (a {tmp/out} /\
    (tmp?x=> out!x=> stop \/ signal (sleep d; UP)))
   catch UP => b
end;
```

4.2.9   User Interface

In addition to the top-level commands provided by SML user interfaces (declarations), LCS user interfaces offer process management commands. These include essentially

- The `start` and `lstart` commands, taking a behavior expression as parameter. They create processes to run in the background and return immediately. The latter creates a process that shares its store with the toplevel process; the former assigns to the process created a private copy of the toplevel store.

- The `call` and `lcall` commands, coupled with the `return` behavior, to create processes running in the foreground and operating on private or shared storage, respectively. Running processes in the foreground is mostly useful when the user processes take input from the same window that the top level does. Evaluation of behavior `return` (semantically equivalent to `stop`) makes the corresponding call command return (evaluation of the called process resumes in the background).

- Finally, a `kill` command allows the user to abort all the processes started, and a `reboot` command permits one to restart the LCS runtime on any user-provided behavior; this last command is used for bootstrapping new versions of the user interfaces and building standalone applications.

4.3   Typing Behavior Expressions

4.3.1   Types for Behaviors

Typechecking must enforce type-safe communications between processes. That problem is shared with CML, FACILE, or Poly/ML, but is solved here in a significantly different way.

In the languages mentioned, communication channels are values typed like locations in a store, and processes are checked in an environment assigning types to channels and other expressions. This "channels as locations" analogy would give a poor typing system for LCS, rejecting many useful programs. LCS channels have no denotations, but are indirectly referred to through port values; the channels used by a process are provided by the context in which the process runs. A better analogy here would be to see processes as records of channels, the communication labels acting as record labels, and to assign to each process the set of types expected on the communication labels it uses, deduced from its local usage of these labels.

Unfortunately, computing statically the set of labels used by a process is not always possible; the exact set of ports through which a process interacts is not necessarily known at compile-time (sub-behaviors may be received by message, or as parameters). This can be solved by making the type of a process assign a type information to all possible communication labels, and not only to those actually used in interactions by the process. To pursue our analogy with records, behaviors should be assigned extensible record types, in which the set of fields is parameterized, rather than fixed field record types: The type of a behavior expression in LCS makes precise for each existing communication label the type of the values that may be passed on ports using that label. In addition, LCS behavior types associate with each label the type of its extension.

For example, the type {q:bool#int,r:unit#('a*bool)}_b, abbreviated {q.bool:int,r:'a*bool}_b, is the most general type for behaviors that may send or receive integers through ports labeled q indexed by booleans and pairs of type 'a*bool through ports labeled r with default unit extensions. The types of the other ports are unconstrained; they are represented by the extension variable _b.

Behavior types are conveniently formalized as a particular subset of the so-called *Tagged Types* discussed in [24] and further elaborated in [86]. Tagged types bear strong relationships with Wand's row types [179] and Rémy's record types [143], though their logical interpretations differ (the differences will be made precise later in the section). They were developed independently, and we believe their interpretation leads to an intuitive and simple technical treatment. For these reasons, the essentials of the theory of tagged types are summarized in the next section; the reader is referred to [24, 86] for a deeper technical treatment and developments. A type system for LCS, using these types, is subsequently introduced.

4.3.2 An Overview of Tagged Types

The language of types

Given a countable set of labels $\Sigma = \{p, q, \ldots\}$, *types* τ, of which the *tagged types* ρ are a subset, and *type schemes* σ obey the following grammar:

$$
\begin{array}{lll}
\tau & ::= & \alpha, \beta, \gamma, \ldots \qquad & \text{plain type variables} \\
& | & a, b, c, \ldots & \text{plain constant types} \\
& | & \tau \to \tau & \text{function type} \\
& | & \rho & \text{tagged types} \\
\rho & ::= & \Delta^\sigma, \Theta^{\sigma'}, \ldots & \text{tagged type variables, } \sigma, \sigma' \text{ closed} \\
& | & \nabla^\mu, \nabla^{\mu'}, \ldots & \text{tagged type constants, } \mu, \mu' \text{ monotypes} \\
& | & \{p : \tau\}\rho & \text{field prefixing, for each } p \in \Sigma \\
\sigma & ::= & \tau \mid \forall(\alpha|\Delta^{\sigma'}).\sigma & \text{type schemes}
\end{array}
$$

As usual, *monotypes* (μ, μ', etc) are types in which no variable occurs (of any sort). In Δ^σ, the scheme σ is called the *kind* of the tagged variable; infinitely many tagged variables are assumed available for each kind. Each monotype defines one and only one tagged constant. For simplicity, we demand that the kinds of tagged variables do not themselves include tagged types, though the treatment developed in the sequel may be extended to such higher-order kinds.

Tagged types have a number of *fields* prefixing a tagged variable or tagged constant (called the *extension*); each field associates a type with a label. The type $\{p_1 : \tau_1\}...\{p_k : \tau_k\}\rho$ is also written $\{p_1 : \tau_1, ..., p_k : \tau_k\}\rho$ when the labels p_i are pairwise distinct.

Substitutions

Intuitively, tagged variables may be read as mappings, assigning a type to every possible label in the set Σ. E.g., the type $\tau = \{p : \alpha, q : \beta \to int\}\Delta^{\forall \alpha.\alpha}$ explicitly assigns type α to label p and type $\beta \to int$ to label q, and implicitly assigns distinct type variables to all other labels. Tagged types are extensible in the sense that a tagged variable may be substituted by any tagged type, possibly resulting in more fields being made explicit. E.g., $\{p : \alpha, q : \beta \to int, r : int\}\Theta^{\forall \beta.\beta \to \beta}$ is an instance of τ, obtained by substituting the type $\{r : int\}\Theta^{\forall \beta.\beta \to \beta}$ for variable $\Delta^{\forall \alpha.\alpha}$.

The kinds associated with tagged variables allow the parameterization of the types they implicitly assign to labels. E.g., $\Delta^{\forall \alpha.\alpha}$ assigns distinct type variables to labels, while $\Theta^{\forall \beta.\beta \to \beta}$ associates distinct copies of type $\beta \to \beta$ with the labels.

The substitution rules must prevent a tagged variable, say of kind σ, from being substituted with a tagged type that assigns to some label a type more general than σ. They are restricted to the *legal* substitutions defined as follows: a plain variable may be substituted by any type; a tagged variable Δ^σ, σ being the closure $\bar{\tau}$ of some type τ, may only be substituted by tagged types such that the types in all their fields are instances of τ (in particular, substituting $\Delta^{\sigma'}$ for Θ^σ requires that σ' be a closed generic instance of σ).

In the sequel, $\leq$ denotes the (legal) substitution instance preorder, defined by $(\tau \leq \tau' \Leftrightarrow \exists S.\tau = S\tau')$, and $\equiv$ is the associated equivalence relation $(\tau \equiv \tau' \Leftrightarrow \tau \leq \tau' \wedge \tau' \leq \tau)$.

Equivalent types

The semantics of types typically follows from that of their monotype instances. Rather than developing such a semantics, we concentrate on an extensionally defined equivalence of types, assumed valid in all their models.

Let Π, Π', denote tagged monotypes. Monotype tagged types are read as mappings: ∇^μ is the constant mapping assigning monotype μ to every label; $\{p : \mu\}\Pi$ is the mapping Π with its $(p, \_)$ element replaced by (p, μ). Equality of monotypes $(=_g)$ is defined as follows:

$$a =_g a \qquad \text{(for each plain constant } a\text{)},$$
$$\mu_1 \to \mu_2 =_g \mu_1' \to \mu_2' \quad \text{if } \mu_1 =_g \mu_1' \wedge \mu_2 =_g \mu_2',$$
$$\Pi =_g \Pi' \qquad \text{if } \forall p \in \Sigma. \, \Pi(p) =_g \Pi'(p)$$
$$\text{with} \quad (\{p : \mu\}\Pi)(p) = \mu$$
$$(\{q : \mu\}\Pi)(p) = \Pi(p) \quad (q \neq p)$$
$$\nabla^\mu(p) = \mu.$$

Let us define then the *less or equally general* preorder $(\preceq)$ and the *equally general* equivalence relation $(\cong)$ as follows:

$$\tau \preceq \tau' \quad \Leftrightarrow \quad \forall \mu \leq \tau. \, \exists \mu' \leq \tau'.\mu =_g \mu',$$
$$\tau \cong \tau' \quad \Leftrightarrow \quad \tau \preceq \tau' \wedge \tau' \preceq \tau.$$

We have for instance (assuming all tagged variables have kind $\forall \alpha.\alpha$),

$$
\begin{array}{ll}
& \{p : \alpha\}\{s : \gamma\}\Delta \to \{p : \beta\}\{s : \gamma\}\Delta \quad (1) \\
\cong & \{p : \phi\}\Theta \to \{p : \delta\}\Theta \quad\quad\quad\quad\quad (2) \\
\cong & \{p : \omega\}\Psi \to \Psi \quad\quad\quad\quad\quad\quad\quad (3) \\
\cong & \Omega \to \{p : \nu\}\Omega \quad\quad\quad\quad\quad\quad\quad (4)
\end{array}
$$

Relation $\cong$ is clearly coarser than the equivalence $\equiv$ obtained from the substitution preorder. Two $\equiv$-equivalent types may differ only by a permutation of their variables, while $\cong$-equivalence is preserved by permutations of fields, for instance, as well as by some substitutions not reduced to permutations of variables (e.g., compare (1) and (2) above).

Characterizing equivalence

Structural congruence $\sim$ is the smallest congruence including identity and the pairs obtained from (permutation) $\{p : \tau\}\{q : \tau'\}\rho \sim \{q : \tau'\}\{p : \tau\}\rho$ $(p \neq q)$

(pruning) $\{p : \tau\}\{p : \tau'\}\rho \sim \{p : \tau\}\rho$

(μ-expansions) $\nabla^\mu \sim \{p : \mu\}\nabla^\mu$

Fields bearing different labels may be permuted. The pruning axiom makes sense of types having several fields identically labeled, like, e.g., $\{p : \alpha\}\{q : \beta \to int\}\{p : bool\}\Theta^{\forall \alpha . \alpha}$. Such types can be obtained as the result of substitutions. Fields with their labels equal to that of some other field occurring on their left side are said to be *hidden*; they may be removed. Finally, so called *redundant* fields may be made explicit by expanding a tagged constant.

$\mathcal{V}(\tau)$ denotes the set of variables occurring in the *normal form* of $|\tau|$, obtained by removing its hidden and redundant fields.

Next, we would like to characterize those substitutions, called *expansions*, that preserve the set of monotype instances of a type (modulo $=_g$). The following construction permits one to choose expansions not introducing variables from some protected set.

Given a set of variables W, an *expansion basis* is a set of substitutions such that (1) There is exactly one substitution $[\{p : \tau'\}\Delta^{\bar{\tau}}/\Delta^{\bar{\tau}}]$ for each possible pair $(\Delta^{\bar{\tau}}, p)$, with $\tau' \equiv \tau$ and $\mathcal{V}(\tau') \cap W = \emptyset$; (2) for any two distinct components $[\{p : \tau\}\Delta^\sigma/\Delta^\sigma]$ and $[\{q : \tau'\}\Theta^{\sigma'}/\Theta^{\sigma'}]$ in the set, we have $\mathcal{V}(\tau) \cap \mathcal{V}(\tau') = \emptyset$; and (3) it contains the empty substitution and is closed under composition of substitutions. Ξ^W denotes the union of all expansion bases away from W; elements of Ξ^W are called *expansions away from W*.

Finally, we say that τ is an *expansion* of τ', written $\tau \preceq_\eta \tau'$, when it is structurally congruent with the result of applying an expansion to τ' protecting its variables, i.e.,

$$\tau \preceq_\eta \tau' \Leftrightarrow \exists W . \exists X \in \Xi^W . \mathcal{V}(\tau') \subset W \wedge \tau \sim X\tau'.$$

All expansions of a type are equivalent by $\cong$. Further, a type is less general than another if and only if some expansion of the former is a substitution instance of some expansion of the latter, i.e.,

$$\tau \preceq \tau' \Leftrightarrow \exists \tau_1, \tau_2 . \ \tau \succeq_\eta \tau_1 \leq \tau_2 \preceq_\eta \tau'.$$

Since both the expansion preorder $\preceq_\eta$ and $\leq$ are characterized in terms of substitutions and structural congruence, so are $\preceq$ and $\cong$.

Unification

Unifying two or more types consists in finding a substitution making them equal types. In addition, we want the resulting instantiation to be the most general possible. Ideally, we should consider here an equality that captures both structural congruence and preservation of meanings through expansions. Unfortunately, it is difficult to formulate the latter requirement in an equational framework, because expansions introduce variables.

So instead, we take $\sim$ as the target equality but compare generality of unifiers by preorder $\preceq$, rather than by the usual substitution preorder $\leq$. The unification problem is rephrased as follows:

$\sim$-unification: A substitution U is a $\sim$-*unifier* of (τ_1, τ_2) if and only if we have $U\tau_1 \sim U\tau_2$. In addition, U is a $\sim$-*most general unifier* of (τ_1, τ_2) when for any other $\sim$-unifier V of (τ_1, τ_2), we have $V\tau_1 \preceq U\tau_1$ (or $V\tau_2 \preceq U\tau_2$).

$\sim$-unification can be reduced to two-sorted unification after an expansion of the types to be unified, and transformations by the axioms of $\sim$, that makes all of their tagged variables and constants prefixed by fields for the same sequence of labels [24]. A better algorithm, incrementally handling expansions, reordering of fields, and pruning, is given in the same reference. As an example, applied to the pair

$$(\Delta \to \Theta \to \{p : a\}\Delta, \Delta \to \Theta \to \{p : a\}\Theta),$$

the algorithm returns the unifier: $[\Omega/\Phi] \circ [\{p : \delta\}\Phi/\Delta] \circ [\{p : \theta\}\Omega/\Theta]$, producing the result type $\{p : \delta\}\Omega \to \{p : \theta\}\Omega \to \{p : a\}\Omega$. Note that the naive $\sim$-unifier $[\Omega/\Delta, \Omega/\Theta]$ is not the most general one in our sense (though it is the most general in the usual sense, by $\leq$). This unifier produces type $\Omega \to \Omega \to \{p : a\}\Omega$, $\cong$-equivalent to $\{p : \delta\}\Omega \to \{p : \delta\}\Omega \to \{p : a\}\Omega$, which is clearly less general by $\preceq$ than the result found by the algorithm.

An elegant alternative to this unification technique is explored in depth in [86]. It consists in introducing an auxiliary *dot* operator for types: $\rho.p$ denotes the type assigned to label p by the tagged type ρ. The equation $\Delta = \{p : \Delta.p\}\Delta$, together with a refined notion of variable, capture then the fact that tagged variables assign independent types to all labels, which was said here differently using expansions. There are obviously extra complications in order to handle the dot operator and tagged variables with nontrivial kinds, but the setting obtained is much closer to the usual equational setting. For simplicity, we stick here to a presentation closer to the actual implementation.

Further issues and related work

Several canonical forms can be defined for types considered modulo $\cong$ (or closed type schemes), relying on the fact that $\cong$ equivalence classes admit only a finite number of maximal elements by $\preceq_\eta$ (modulo $\sim$ and $\equiv$). For the previous example, for instance, there are exactly two such maximal elements, including types (3) and (4), respectively. Any total ordering on maximal elements defines a canonical element (several can be defined, based on the structure of type expressions); the greatest lower bound by $\preceq_\eta$ of those maximal elements defines another canonical element (holding type

(2) in our example).

Apart from their kinds, the technical point making tagged types different from Wand's row types is the domain of tagged variables, e.g., in $\{p : \alpha\}\Delta$, we may read variable Δ as a total map, assigning types to all labels in Σ, as we do, or we may read it as a partial map, assigning types to all labels except p. The latter interpretation is that of [179, 180]; it requires syntactic constraints on row types to make all instances of a row variable in a type have the same domain (e.g., $\Theta \rightarrow \{p : int\}\Theta$ would not be a legal row type). In the general case allowing higher-order kinds (not discussed here), tagged types and the generalized record types in [144] have disjoint expressiveness. However, both formalisms are equally convenient for typing record expressions or behavior expressions.

To summarize their benefits, well-formedness of tagged types reduces to a simple grammatical constraint; extensibility is simply explained as substitutions—they may be unified with simple extensions of the usual algorithms, and closed type schemes admit a variety of canonical forms.

4.3.3   Type Reconstruction in LCS

Behavior types

Behaviors are assigned behavior types, which associate a type with every possible communication label. Behavior types are made from behavior variables (written _a, _b, etc), possibly prefixed by a number of fields of the form $\{p\!:\!\tilde{\tau}\#\tau\}$ (concretely written {p.$\tilde{\tau}$:τ}) in which $\tilde{\tau}$ is an equality type and τ an arbitrary type. In the behavior type $\{\texttt{p1}.\tilde{\tau}_1\!:\!\tau_1,\ldots,\texttt{pn}.\tilde{\tau}_n\!:\!\tau_n\}$_a, the $\tilde{\tau}_i$ are the types of the extensions of communication ports and the τ_i are the types of the messages passed. Extension and message types may be omitted when equal to the default unit type; e.g., {p.int,q:'b}_a stands for the behavior type {p.int:unit,q.unit:'b}_a. The most general behavior type scheme is ∀_a._a, The scheme ∀_a.{p:int}_a is the most general for processes passing integers on ports labeled p with unit extensions.

Behavior variables encode tagged variables of kind $\forall\tilde{\alpha}, \alpha.\ \tilde{\alpha}\#\alpha$, in which $\tilde{\alpha}$ is an equality type variable and α is a plain type variable. LCS also provides a constant behavior type, written ".", and defined as $\nabla^{\texttt{void}\#\texttt{void}}$ in which void is an additional type constant. The purpose of constants "." and void is merely to allow binding of monotype behaviors, e.g., for storing them into memory locations.

Typing rules and type reconstruction

The typing rules for behavior expressions are summarized in Figure 4.2; other expressions of the language are typed as in SML.

A simple rule assures well typing of communications: any pair of ports potentially involved in an interaction must have the same message and

$$\frac{}{A \vdash \texttt{stop}: \_a} \qquad \frac{A \vdash e: \_a \quad A \vdash e': \_a}{A \vdash e \ (/\backslash | \ldots | \backslash / | \ldots) \ e': \_a}$$

$$\frac{A \vdash e: \tau \quad A \vdash e': \_a}{A \vdash \texttt{do} \ e \texttt{=>} \ e': \_a}$$

$$\frac{A \vdash e: \tilde{\tau} \quad A + (x \mapsto \tau) \vdash e': \{\texttt{p}.\tilde{\tau}:\tau\}\_a}{A \vdash \texttt{p\#e?x=>}e': \{\texttt{p}.\tilde{\tau}:\tau\}\_a}$$

$$\frac{A \vdash e: \tilde{\tau} \quad A \vdash e': \tau \quad A \vdash e'': \{\texttt{p}.\tilde{\tau}:\tau\}\_a}{A \vdash \texttt{p\#e!}e'\texttt{=>}e'': \{\texttt{p}.\tilde{\tau}:\tau\}\_a}$$

$$\frac{A \vdash e: \{\texttt{p}.\tilde{\tau}':\tau'\}\_a}{A \vdash e \ \{\texttt{/p}\}: \{\texttt{p}.\tilde{\tau}:\tau\}\_a} \qquad \frac{A \vdash e: \{\texttt{p}.\tilde{\tau}':\tau', \ \texttt{q}.\tilde{\tau}:\tau\}\_a}{A \vdash e \ \{\texttt{p/q}\}: \{\texttt{p}.\tilde{\tau}:\tau, \ \texttt{q}.\tilde{\tau}'':\tau''\}\_a}$$

$$\frac{A \vdash e': \tilde{\tau} \quad A \vdash e'': \tilde{\tau}' \quad A \vdash e: \{\texttt{p}.\tilde{\tau}^3:\tau^3, \ \texttt{q}.\tilde{\tau}':\tau''\}\_a}{A \vdash e \ \{\texttt{p\#}e'\texttt{/q\#}e''\}: \{\texttt{p}.\tilde{\tau}:\tau'', \ \texttt{q}.\tilde{\tau}':\tau''\}\_a}$$

$$\frac{A \vdash e: \tau \ \texttt{evt} \quad A \vdash e': \tau}{A \vdash \texttt{signal} \ e \ \texttt{with} \ e': \_a}$$

$$\frac{A \vdash e: \_a \quad A \vdash e_i: \tau_i \ \texttt{evt} \quad A + (x_i \mapsto \tau_i) \vdash h_i: \_a}{A \vdash e \ \texttt{catch} \ e_1 \ \texttt{with} \ x_1 \ \texttt{=>} \ h_1 | | \ldots | | e_n \ \texttt{with} \ x_n \texttt{=>} \ h_n: \_a}$$

FIGURE 4.2. Type inference for behavior expressions

extension types. In addition, port extensions must have equality types, since comparing extensions for equality is needed at run-time to determine actual communication capabilities.

Variables bound in input are typed like lambda-bound variables in the system of [50] or [49]. The rule for relabeling says that label p after relabeling has the type that label q had before relabeling; the rule for aliasing is similar except that p and q may have different extension types and that the type assigned to q cannot be relaxed in the result type since other ports may still use that label with different extensions. The processes involved in compositions must all have the same (behavior) type. It is assumed that the initial typing environment assigns the scheme $\forall \_a. \_a$ to behavior stop. Events receive type τ evt where τ is the type of the message brought by the event.

Recursion is typed as in [50] too, which explains, e.g., that agent A defined by val rec A = (p!1=>A){/p} cannot be assigned the scheme $\forall \_a. \_a$, but only the weaker $\forall \_a. \{\texttt{p:int}\}\_a$, even though that process cannot communicate through p. Another limitation of the system is that some behavior passing expression, like p?x=>x, cannot be assigned types. In our example, the solution type ρ should solve the equation $\rho = \{\texttt{p:unit\#}\rho\}\_a$. This problem is equivalent to that of typing the function f defined by `fun f x = f` in SML, or that of typing channels communicating themselves in Poly/ML or CML. Clearly, the problem cannot be solved without some form of recursive types, either as part of the language of types or provided at the level of declaration of new type operators as feasible in SML or LCS (an example is given in Section 4.2.6).

As in [106], type synthesis is reduced to unification. The type assignment algorithm is similar to that of ML; the differences essentially lie in the unification algorithm.

As an example, the piping combinator (^) defined in Section 4.2.2 would receive as most general type:

```
^ : {out.''a:'b}_c * {inp.''a:'b, tmp.''d:'e}_c -> {tmp.''f:'g}_c.
```

This can also be written in another, more verbose, canonical form:

```
^ : {inp.''a:'b, out.''c:'d, tmp.''e:'f}_g *
    {inp.''c:'d, out.''h:'i, tmp.''j:'k}_g
 -> {inp.''a:'b, out.''h:'i, tmp.''l:'m}_g.
```

It can be seen from this type that in A^B, port `inp` (resp. `out`) has the type that port `inp` has in A (resp. port `out` has in B), as is to be expected from the operational meaning of a piping operator.

The top-level type, start-time check

Behaviors are typed when declared. At that time, their communication ports are not associated with any channel; that mapping is made when processes are created from behavior values.

It is essential that the processes successively started at top level agree on the types of the ports they use to interact. For this, the LCS top level maintains type information that is the type of the parallel composition of all processes currently running. When starting a behavior, its type is unified with the type maintained at top level (like that for a parallel composition), which is updated accordingly. The top-level type is reset to the most general behavior type by the `kill` command discussed in Section 4.2.9.

4.4 Operational Semantics

The operational semantics of LCS is obtained from the semantics of a more abstract but slightly richer core language introduced in Subsection 4.4.1. The first purpose of an operational semantics is to specify the effects of a program; this is done by defining an observational style semantics for LCS behavior expressions extending similar semantics for CCS or other process calculi. Equivalence of programs is briefly discussed. A second purpose of operational semantics is to provide a basis for implementations; this aspect will be discussed in Section 4.5, where we refine our observational operational semantics to yield a readily implementable reduction system.

4.4.1 Core LCS

Core-LCS includes lambda-expressions with a recursion combinator, the usual ML constants and primitives, and behavior expressions. Core behavior expressions are those in Figure 4.1, except for the **signal** and **catch** expressions, which are derived from the available constructs and an additional combinator < (spelled interrupt). Combinator < acts as a parallel composition having in addition an asymmetric preemptive effect: an interaction performed by a process on its right-hand side aborts all processes on its left-hand side.

The translations of functional expressions, pattern matching, and exception handling are standard (as in SML) and not discussed here. The **signal** and **catch** expressions are translated as follows, in which $\lceil \_ \rceil$ is the translation function, the x_i are assumed not to occur freely in any of the h_j or e, and $\zeta, \chi \notin \Sigma$ (labels ζ and χ are not allowed in user programs):

$$\lceil \text{signal } e \text{ with } e' \rceil = \chi \# \lceil e \rceil ! \lceil e' \rceil \text{=>stop,}$$

$$\lceil e \text{ catch } e_1 \text{ with } y_1 \text{=>} h_1 \mid\mid \ldots \mid\mid e_n \text{ with } y_n \text{=>} h_n \rceil =$$
$$(\text{fn } x_1 \text{=>} \ldots \text{fn } x_n \text{=>} \lceil e \rceil \ \{\zeta \# x_1 / \chi \# x_1, \ldots, \zeta \# x_n / \chi \# x_n\}$$
$$< (\zeta \# x_1 ? y_1 \text{=>} \lceil h_1 \rceil \ \backslash/ \ldots \backslash/ \ \zeta \# x_n ? y_n \text{=>} \lceil h_n \rceil))$$
$$\lceil e_1 \rceil \ldots \lceil e_n \rceil \ \{/\zeta\}.$$

Signaling an event e with message m is interpreted as offering message m on a port $\chi \# e$. A series of handlers for different events is interpreted as their disjunction, the handler for event e_i being guarded by an input on a port labeled $\zeta \# e_i$. Because of the aliasing of event ports in the translation it follows that the dynamic scope of an event extends no farther than its innermost enclosing handler.

The operational semantics discussed in the next sections is restricted to the subset of core language expressions resulting from translation of well-typed LCS expressions. This implies, for instance, that port extensions admit equality, and thus canonical forms. For simplicity, we omit conditional expressions, exceptions, strong versions of the composition combinators (they will be discussed in a later section), and consider only simple versions of recursion, restriction, relabeling, and aliasing; the treatments for the full versions of these constructions naturally follow from those of the simple cases.

The semantics developed is that of an expression passed to the **start** command and creating a process to run in parallel with all existing processes. This is the general case, since the top level itself is implemented as a system of processes, with the **start** command acting as a parallel composition spawning a new process on one side and resuming the top level on the other side.

4.4.2   The Observation Relation ($\xrightarrow{\mu}$)

As for CCS, we associate with a program an *observation* relation, characterizing in some sense its interaction capabilities. Observations $\xrightarrow{\mu}$ are labeled by *actions* μ in a set soon to be described. The intuitive meaning of $p \xrightarrow{\mu} q$ is that the system of processes denoted by expression p may perform the action μ and subsequently evolve into system q.

Beside the differences due to the richer set of behavior expressions, LCS observations differ from those of CCS in that the usual preemptive actions (labeled $\xrightarrow{\mu}$ transitions) may be preceded here by nonpreemptive and nonobservable transitions ($\Rightarrow$ transitions). The transitions of the latter kind result from the use of functional expressions, both to describe the messages passed between processes and to build behaviors. Relation $\Rightarrow$, called *behavior-reduction* (or *B-reduction* for short), will be precisely defined in the next section. In addition, LCS expressions are evaluated in the context of a store; the nonobservable $\Rightarrow$ transitions may have side-effects in that store.

The observation relation for Core-LCS is shown in part (c) of Figure 4.3; it relates *threads* (or *processes*, indifferently) associated with a *store*. We will distinguish elementary threads (those at the origin of some actions) from compound threads (or systems of threads) combining one or more simpler threads. A system of threads evolves by performing actions involving one or more subthreads, possibly following a number of B-reductions.

Variables a, a', b, b' denote threads, i.e., expressions typed as behaviors; e, e' denote arbitrary expressions, x, x' are identifiers, and $e\langle v/x \rangle$ is the expression obtained by substituting the value v for the free occurrences of variable x in expression e. Variables v, v' range over a set V of values, soon to be made precise; W is its subset of values admitting equality. Variables π, π' are communication ports, and η, η' denote port values, that is, pairs p#w with $\text{p} \in \Sigma \cup \{\chi, \zeta\}$ and $w \in W$. The symbol $+$ denotes overriding of mappings; $M + (itm_i, val_i)_{i \in I}$ is the mapping M with its $(itm_i, \_)$ pairs (for $i \in I$) replaced by (itm_i, val_i), and $M + (itm, val)$ matches any mapping such that $M(itm) = val$. For conciseness, rules sharing the same premises are often grouped into single rules with a multiple denominator, and the store components are omitted when unchanged by transitions.

An action is either the *silent* action τ or a triple $(\eta \square v)$ in which η is a port value, $\square$ is a polarity (! or ?), and v is a value (the message). Variable μ matches any action, $\overline{\mu}$ is the action with the same port value and message as μ but with opposite polarity.

The rules for observations in Figure 4.3 extend those of CCS. Rules (i1) to (i3) define the three basic actions. A simple thread matching the left-hand side of one of these rules is called a *suspension*. Rule (i4) expresses that an action may follow a sequence of B-reductions. The basic action transitions themselves have no side-effects, but the B-reductions they may follow may have some, which makes compound actions possibly have side-effects.

$$\frac{e_1, s \rightarrow e_1', s'}{e_1\ e_2, s \rightarrow e_1'\ e_2, s'} \quad (r1)$$

$$v\ e_1, s \rightarrow v\ e_1', s'$$

$$(\texttt{fn}\ x.e)\ v \rightarrow e\langle v/x\rangle \quad (r2)$$

$$\texttt{rec}\ x.e \rightarrow e\langle \texttt{rec}\ x.e/x\rangle \quad (r3)$$

$$\texttt{ref}\ v, s \rightarrow l, s{+}(l, v)\ (l \notin \mathcal{D}(s))\ (r4)$$

$$\texttt{deref}\ l, s{+}(l, v) \rightarrow v, s{+}(l, v) \quad (r5)$$

$$l{:=}v, s \rightarrow (), s{+}(l, v) \quad (r6)$$

$$\frac{e, s \rightarrow e', s'}{p\#e, s \rightarrow p\#e', s'} \quad (r7)$$

$$\frac{\pi, s \rightarrow \pi', s'}{\pi!e{=}{>}a, s \rightarrow \pi'!e{=}{>}a, s'} \quad (r8)$$

$$\pi?x{=}{>}a, s \rightarrow \pi'?x{=}{>}a, s'$$

$$\frac{\pi, s \rightarrow \pi', s'}{a\ \{\pi/\pi''\}, s \rightarrow a\ \{\pi'/\pi''\}, s'} \quad (r9)$$

$$a\ \{\eta/\pi\}, s \rightarrow a\ \{\eta/\pi'\}, s'$$

(a) *F-reduction* $\rightarrow$

$$\frac{e, s \rightarrow e', s'}{e, s \Rightarrow e', s'} \quad (e1)$$

$$\eta!e{=}{>}a, s \Rightarrow \eta!e'{=}{>}a, s'$$

$$\texttt{do}\ e{=}{>}a, s \Rightarrow \texttt{do}\ e'{=}{>}a, s'$$

$$\frac{a, s \Rightarrow a', s'}{a\ \{/\texttt{p}\}, s \Rightarrow a'\ \{/\texttt{p}\}, s'} \quad (e2)$$

$$a\ \{\texttt{q}/\texttt{p}\}, s \Rightarrow a'\ \{\texttt{q}/\texttt{p}\}, s'$$

$$a\ \{\eta/\eta'\}, s \Rightarrow a'\ \{\eta/\eta'\}, s'$$

$$\frac{a, s \Rightarrow a', s'}{} \quad (e3)$$

$$a \setminus\!/\ b, s \Rightarrow a' \setminus\!/\ b, s' \qquad b \setminus\!/\ a, s \Rightarrow b \setminus\!/\ a', s'$$

$$a \wedge b, s \Rightarrow a' \wedge b, s' \qquad b \wedge a, s \Rightarrow b \wedge a', s'$$

$$a < b, s \Rightarrow a' < b, s' \qquad b < a, s \Rightarrow b < a', s'$$

(b) *B-reduction* $\Rightarrow$

$$\texttt{do}\ v{=}{>}a \xrightarrow{\tau} a \quad (i1)$$

$$\eta?x{=}{>}a \xrightarrow{\eta?v} a\langle v/x\rangle \quad (i2)$$

$$\eta!v{=}{>}a \xrightarrow{\eta!v} a \quad (i3)$$

$$\frac{a, s \Rightarrow a', s' \qquad a', s' \xrightarrow{\mu} a'', s''}{a, s \xrightarrow{\mu} a'', s''} \quad (i4)$$

$$\frac{a, s \xrightarrow{\mu} a', s'}{a\ \phi, s \xrightarrow{\phi(\mu)} a'\ \phi, s'} \quad (\phi(\mu)\ \text{defined})\ (i5)$$

$$\frac{a, s \xrightarrow{\mu} a', s'}{} \quad (i6)$$

$$a \setminus\!/\ b, s \xrightarrow{\mu} a', s' \qquad b \setminus\!/\ a, s \xrightarrow{\mu} a', s'$$

$$a \wedge b, s \xrightarrow{\mu} a' \wedge b, s' \qquad b \wedge a, s \xrightarrow{\mu} b \wedge a', s'$$

$$a < b, s \xrightarrow{\mu} a' < b, s' \qquad b < a, s \xrightarrow{\mu} a', s'$$

$$\frac{a, s \xrightarrow{\mu} a', s' \qquad b, s' \xrightarrow{\overline{\mu}} b', s''}{} \quad (i7)$$

$$a \wedge b, s \xrightarrow{\tau} a' \wedge b', s'' \qquad b \wedge a, s \xrightarrow{\tau} b' \wedge a', s''$$

$$a < b, s \xrightarrow{\tau} b', s'' \qquad b < a, s \xrightarrow{\tau} a', s''$$

(c) *Observation* $\xrightarrow{\mu}$

FIGURE 4.3. The observation relation $\xrightarrow{\mu}$

Rules (i5) and (i6) express propagation of actions in the different possible contexts of a thread. Restriction, relabeling, and aliasing specify action substitutions, as follows (in which the labels p, q, r are assumed pairwise distinct):

$$\{/p\}\tau = \{q/p\}\tau = \{\eta'/\eta\}\tau = \tau,$$

$$\{/p\}(r\#w\square v) = \{q/p\}(r\#w\square v) = \{q\#w''/p\#w'\}(r\#w\square v) = r\#w\square v,$$

$$\{q/p\}(p\#w\square v) = \{q\#w/p\#w'\}(p\#w'\square v) = q\#w\square v.$$

Finally, the set of rules (i7) express communication between components of a thread. The rules for /\ and \/ are exactly those of the | and + combinators of CCS, respectively. For core expressions resulting from translation of LCS expressions, a communication involving the component on the right-hand side of < necessarily involves the component on its left-hand side. When interpreting the premises of (i7), it must be kept in mind that basic actions occur last in compound actions, and that they have no side-effects.

Operationally, a communication has two simultaneous effects: that of passing a value from a thread to another (rule (i7), together with (i2) and (i3)), and that of pruning the current threads by removing some of their components (rules (i6)).

4.4.3 Behavior Reduction ($\Rightarrow$) and Functional Reduction ($\rightarrow$)

The B-reduction relation is defined in part (b) of Figure 4.3 from a relation $\rightarrow$, abusively called *functional reduction* (or *F-reduction* for short), and defined in transitional form in part (a) of that table. F-reduction is simply the eager version of the beta-reduction relation of the lambda-calculus, extended here to handle behavior expressions. When F-reduction terminates, it produces a value; the set of values V includes the usual constants and primitives, the subset W of equality values (definition omitted), the function values (or closures), and the following behavior values (treated as closures too), in which w, w' are equality values:

$$a \text{ /\ } b, a \text{ \/ } b, a < b, a \text{ \{/p\}}, a \text{ \{p/q\}}, a \text{ \{p\#w/q\#w'\}},$$
$$p\#w!e\text{=>}a, p\#w?x\text{=>}a, \text{do } e\text{=>}a.$$

Rules (r1) to (r3) are standard; they define an applicative order reduction for parameter passing. In rule (r3), e is either a lambda abstraction or a behavior expression (this results from syntactical constraints on the form of LCS declarations). Rules (r4) to (r6) are also standard: they specify the effects of the store primitives. F-reduction of an input, output, or aliasing expression amounts to F-reduction of the ports these constructions use (rules (r7) to (r9)). Note that reduction of the message sent in an output expression is not required to produce a behavior value. Similarly, reducing a commitment expression does not force reduction of the expression encapsulated by do (to be evaluated for its side-effects).

The B-reductions $\Rightarrow$ transform a thread expression so that actions are possible (by rules (i1) to (i3), then propagated by (i5) and (i6)). B-reducing a thread first makes it a behavior value (by rule (e1.1)). Then B-reduction is applied to the thread components of that behavior value. It is not required, however, that all members of a behavior value are B-reduced to make actions or interactions possible within it; it is actually sufficient that B-reduction is propagated to the particular sub-threads involved and that these are turned into suspensions. Actions typically yield new threads, which are in turn expanded, etc.

The reason for distinguishing the relation $\Rightarrow$ from $\rightarrow$ is that we do not want threads to be created or actions to be performed when evaluating a behavior expression in an argument position (of some function), or in a message position (of an output expression). A behavior expression found in such positions is just F-reduced. Rules (i1) show B-reduction of output threads (consisting of F-reduction of their messages) and of commitment threads (consisting of F-reduction of the enclosed expression).

The B-reduction relation shown in Figure 4.3 is clearly a simplified version of what is actually implemented, omitting exceptions, stream input/output, and most primitives of the language. Exceptions are briefly discussed in the following section. Rigorous treatment of side-effects relies on the specification of an evaluation order, which is specified in Figure 4.3.

4.4.4 Exceptions, Divergence, and Message-Passing Strategies

Exceptions are handled as in Standard ML, except that their scope stops at thread boundaries. As explained earlier, an uncaught exception makes the thread it was raised within signal a specific event EXN passing the exception as message. This has no further consequences if no enclosing handler has been specified for event EXN.

A thread diverges when it infinitely performs $\Rightarrow$ transitions or silent $\xrightarrow{\tau}$ actions. As for exceptions, divergence has a local effect and is not considered catastrophic. Diverging threads just unnecessarily consume computing and storage resources, but should not prevent other threads from progressing. In practice, the scheduling strategies provided by the implementation prevent a diverging process from blocking the whole system of processes (as if the simple threads were each run by distinct physical processors). Divergence, however, might lead to a failure of the whole system of threads by exhausting the available storage. So, programming with divergence (e.g., using infinite choice expressions) should not be considered good practice.

The main reason for adopting the "semi-eager" evaluation strategy of Figure 4.3 for message passing, rather than lazier strategies delaying evaluation of messages until received or used by some process, was the desire to achieve control over the reasons for failure. It may be argued that this strategy is costly since it may lead to reducing messages that will not necessarily be used, or even input, by other processes. That problem is similar to, and not worse than, that of using applicative order evaluation rather than a lazier technique for functional parameter passing.

Further, the operational semantics does not forbid clever B-reduction strategies for minimizing reductions of messages. An implementation may, for instance, delay B-reduction of output constructions (which forces reduction of the message to be sent) until some thread is willing to receive that message. In such "partner-search first" communication strategies, however, care must be taken of the preemptive effects of actions: evaluating messages between partner selection and actual passing of the message makes communications, nonatomic transitions potentially interruptible by another thread.

4.4.5   Light and Strong Processes

The experimental strong processes discussed in Subsection 4.2.7 were omitted from Figure 4.3, in which all threads are assumed to operate on the same store. We now refine that system to accommodate them. Threads that are part of the same system will be allowed to operate on different stores; the store assigned to a thread is determined from the inherited store and from the parallel and choice composition operators. The intended meaning of a /\\ b, for instance, is that subthread a resumes B-reduction with the current store, while subthread b resumes B-reduction with a separate copy of the current store. Operator //\ behaves symmetrically, and //\\ makes both its subthreads operate on distinct copies of the current store.

We will use the word *segment* to mean a captured store. Store capture is expressed operationally by adding to the language of threads an auxiliary construction, noted $[\_, s]$, in which s is a store. The side-effects of B-reductions are limited in scope to the innermost captured store, if any. Strong compositions are B-reduced as follows:

$$a \mathbin{//\backslash} b \Rightarrow b \mathbin{/\backslash\backslash} a \qquad\qquad a \mathbin{\backslash\backslash/} b \Rightarrow b \mathbin{\backslash//} a$$

$$a \mathbin{//\backslash\backslash} b \Rightarrow (\texttt{stop} \mathbin{/\backslash\backslash} a) \mathbin{/\backslash\backslash} b \qquad a \mathbin{\backslash\backslash//} b \Rightarrow (\texttt{stop} \mathbin{\backslash//} a) \mathbin{\backslash//} b$$

$$a \mathbin{/\backslash\backslash} b, s \Rightarrow a \mathbin{/\backslash} [b, s], s \qquad\qquad a \mathbin{\backslash//} b, s \Rightarrow a \mathbin{\backslash/} [b, s], s$$

$$\frac{a, s \Rightarrow a', s'}{[a, s], s'' \Rightarrow [a', s'], s''} \text{ (added to (e2))}$$

As in SML, two reference values are equal if they can be reduced to the same location. If capture of store locations in messages or port values is disallowed, as was assumed in [25], then the above rules are all the changes needed to accommodate strong processes. As discussed in Section 4.2.7, enforcing this restriction conveniently is difficult, however. Combining that check with type checking seems feasible but requires quite important changes to the existing type system (types should distinguish functions or behaviors having side-effects from those not having any); enforcing the constraint dynamically would be easier to implement but obviously less satisfactory.

The benefits of accommodating locations in messages and port values are negligible in terms of expressiveness, but desirable in avoiding the need to enforce the above restriction. It adds some complications of its own, though: To handle references within port values, it is sufficient to consider locations belonging to different segments as different locations, even if they result from copies of the same location. Allowing locations within messages significantly complicates message passing, in general. When sender and recipient share the same segment, then message passing is unchanged. When this is not the case, then the message must be copied into the context of the recipient. To express this, we may add new elementary actions, in addition to (i1) to (i3), as follows. These actions handle the case where a thread accepts a message originating from a thread not operating on the same store; a copy of the originating store decorates the actions.

$$\eta?x{=}{>}a, s \xrightarrow{[\eta?v]s'} clone\ s'\ v\ x\ a, s \quad (i2')$$
$$\eta!v{=}{>}a, s \xrightarrow{[\eta!v]s} a, s \quad (i3')$$

Operator $clone$ is reduced as follows: Let $\{r_1, \ldots, r_n\}$ be the set of locations occurring in value v, $\{v_1, \ldots, v_n\}$ their contents in store s', $\{l_1, \ldots, l_n\}$ n locations not in the domain of s, and let ϕ be the substitution $\langle l_1/r_1, \ldots, l_n/r_n \rangle$. Then $(clone\ s'\ v\ x\ a, s)$ reduces to $(a\langle \phi v/x \rangle, s + (l_1, \phi v_1) + \ldots + (l_n, \phi v_n))$.

The other observation rules should be updated too to accommodate store decorated actions and store capture. This can be done satisfactorily, but we will omit it here. The revised observation rules should allow simple message passing (without cloning) only between threads sharing the same segment, and cloning message passing only between threads not operating in the same segment.

From the definitions of equality of references and of the $clone$ operator follows that twice passing a message from a process to another not using the same segment produces in general two unequal copies of the message into the recipient process. This missatisfaction seems unavoidable.

4.4.6   Equality of Programs

The observation relation $\xrightarrow{\mu}$ of Figure 4.3 defines interaction steps for a process, but does not say when two programs may be considered equal (or when one may be used in place of the other). There is a full spectrum of definitions for equivalence of programs definable from observation relations, including the well-known bisimulation-based equivalences [108, 1] and failure/testing equivalences [74, 69]. All these equivalences amount to indistinguishability of programs under testing, for various abstract testing apparatus.

Related to program equivalences and important for implementations is the question of which program optimizations compilers should be allowed to perform. Consider, e.g., the program p?x=> q?y => A \/ p?x=>r?z=> B, clearly exhibiting local nondeterminism. This program may not be optimized at all (delegating the resolution of nondeterminism to the abstract machine, at run-time), or it might be implemented as either p?x=> q?y=> A or p?x=> r?z=> B (solving local nondeterminism at compile-time), or it might be implemented as p?x=> (q?y=> A \/ r?z=> B) (leaving resolution of nondeterminism to the context at run-time). Under quite sensible testing hypotheses, replacing the first program by any of the last three is undetectable, though these clearly exhibit different interaction or deadlock capabilities. Such ideas are conveniently captured by the idea of implementation preorders discussed in the literature.

We will not discuss further equality of LCS programs, except to note the potential problems brought about by its additional features, compared to CCS. Astesiano and Zucca [13] have shown that adding parameterized communication ports to CCS could be accommodated by its observational semantics. Thomsen extended in [165] the notion of observation equivalence to that of high-order observation equivalence to accommodate behavior passing. The adjunction of the interrupt combinator would not add any specific difficulties. So, not taking side-effects and exceptions into account, a suitable concept of observation or testing equivalence can undoubtedly be formalized for the core calculus of LCS; the additional B-reduction steps would not cause any additional trouble in that case, since absence of side-effects, and thus of interferences between processes, makes the B-reductions threadwise confluent.

In the presence of side-effects, however, B-reductions are no longer confluent. In general, the actions a process may offer, and/or the way they are organized, depend on the nonobservable B-reductions preceding the actions. Fortunately, however, there are large syntactic classes of interference-free LCS programs for which the observation relation provides a useful notion of program equivalence.

4.5   The Implementation Model

4.5.1   From Observations to Reduction

What does it mean to "evaluate a concurrent program"? From Section 4.4, a concurrent program describes interaction capabilities; it computes by performing internal actions (preemptive ($\xrightarrow{\tau}$) or not ($\Rightarrow$)) and interacting (performing a local $\xrightarrow{\mu}$) with the programs connected with it until no internal activity or interactions are possible (it does not terminate then, unless reduced to stop, but rather waits for further external stimuli).

Though the observation relation in Figure 4.3 properly captures this notion of computation, it does not do so in a form readily suitable for implementation. Figure 4.3 clearly defines the elementary steps of computations, but action transitions are defined globally on the whole system of threads, rather than in an expected thread-distributed manner, coinciding with the intuition one has of parallel evaluation. As a step towards implementation, we refine in this section the transition relation so that it has the properties below:

- First, rather than a system of threads considered in a monolithic way, we would prefer to handle the system as a bag of threads, as in the Gamma paradigm [16] or the Chemical Abstract Machine [19], and deduce the transition relation for a system of threads from transitions of its indivisible constituents. This property will be referred to as *thread-locality*.

- Next, we are interested in *effective* transition systems. Both for pragmatic and theoretical reasons, the thread-local transition relation should be a function (deterministic), and evaluating a system of threads should be possible using a bounded amount of computation and storage resources.

The reduction system we describe in the sequel was first discussed in [22]; we give here a slightly simpler presentation. The starting point is the system in Figure 4.3, without the stores (they will be reintroduced later, together with the strong compositions discussed in Subsection 4.4.5).

4.5.2   Channels

Rendezvous communication involves two conditions summed up in the observation relation but that may be separated: a port-matching condition (determined by the port values in output and input expressions and by the port-scoping constructs) and a structural condition (determined by the composition operators enclosing the communicating threads). The former can be handled by using aliases for port values, which we call *channels* here. Threads are augmented by *communication environments*, noted λ, mapping port values into channels. The state is augmented by a set L of *channels*, used as a channel allocator. Initially, L is assumed to hold a countably infinite number of channels, and the local communication environment bijectively maps port values into channels in L.

The restriction, relabeling, and aliasing update the local communication environments, extending the shared channel set when needed. Rules (e2) in Figure 4.3 are replaced by the following local rules (V is the set of all values). Restriction of a label makes the local communication environment map new channels to the ports built from this label. Relabeling and aliasing, in addition to restriction of the target labels, maps their origin ports to the channels previously mapped to their destination ports. In essence, this treatment amounts to a dynamic binding of channels to port values, as noted in Subsection 4.2.2:

$$(a \{/p\}, \lambda), L \Rightarrow \{(a, \lambda + (p\#v, \nu_v)_{\forall v}\}, L \cup \{\nu_v\}_{\forall v} \qquad ((\nu_v)_{\forall v \in W} \notin L),$$
$$(a \{q/p\}, \lambda), L \Rightarrow \{(a \{/q\}, \lambda + (p\#v, \lambda(q\#v))_{\forall v})\}, L,$$
$$(a \{q\#v'/p\#v\}, \lambda), L \Rightarrow \{(a \{/q\}, \lambda + (p\#v, \lambda(q\#v')))\}, L.$$

In actions, port values are replaced by the channels they refer to. Rules (i2) and (i3) are replaced by

$$(\eta?x => a, \lambda), L \xrightarrow{\lambda\eta?v} (a\langle v/x\rangle, \lambda), L,$$

$$(\eta!v => a, \lambda), L \xrightarrow{\lambda\eta!v} (a, \lambda), L.$$

When attempting to adapt this treatment to CCS, one should note that the structure of actions needed to achieve a similar treatment is much more complex than here. Actually, important simplifications are brought about by the particular interpretation of relabelings in LCS. Their restrictive effects make them distribute over all composition operators, which is not the case for CCS relabelings (the equality $(P/\backslash Q) \phi = P \phi /\backslash Q \phi$ holds in LCS).

Note that we did not reach the desired locality property yet, both because we still need the context rules (i6) and because the interaction rules (i7) involve a simultaneous transition of two threads. The next steps are to localize the remaining structure of threads, and then to localize the communication transitions.

4.5.3 Flattening the Structure of Threads, Preemption

Let us say that a thread is *persistent* with respect to another when it is not preempted by an action of the latter. The structure of the system of threads (now reduced to constructions $/\backslash$, $\backslash/$, and $<$) is used for two purposes: first, to remove from a system of threads those that are nonpersistent with respect to a thread having performed an action, and next, to determine when two threads offering matching actions may indeed interact. The latter condition, referred to as *synchronizability* in the sequel, is in general independent from persistence. In the particular case of LCS, however, it is not: Two threads are synchronizable if either one is persistent with respect to the other. So, the persistence predicate here captures all the necessary structural information.

The structural information necessary to compute persistence may be distributed in the threads themselves, with the help of some additional shared information to encode which threads are active at some point. Seeing compound threads as trees with nodes labeled $/\backslash$, $\backslash/$, or $<$, the basic idea is to attach to each thread an encoding of the path from the root of that tree to that particular subthread; the relative persistence of any two threads is then clearly computable from these paths. The global information needed to determine active threads is an encoding of the set of paths of the threads having performed an action since the beginning of computation. We now discuss a possible encoding of this scheme.

Let us add to each thread a component π, called the *position* of the thread, and to the global state an information P, called the *accumulator*. Intuitively, π locates that particular thread in the tree discussed above (it encodes its access path), and P records which threads performed preemptive actions.

Both the local positions π and the shared accumulator P map *preemption tokens* to *accesses*, defined as follows: Preemption tokens are primitive objects in a set K, ranged over by κ, κ', etc; an access is an element of the set $\{-, 0, +\}$.

We define then the predicates $\mathcal{P}$ (read *persistent with respect to*) and $\|$ (read *synchronizable with*) by

$$\pi \, \mathcal{P} \, \pi' \Leftrightarrow \forall \kappa \in dom(\pi). \, \pi\kappa \leq \pi'\kappa \ , \text{ where } a \leq a' \Leftrightarrow a = a' \ \lor \ a = 0;$$

$$\pi \parallel \pi' \Leftrightarrow \pi \mathcal{P} \pi' \lor \pi' \mathcal{P} \pi.$$

Compound threads may now be seen as a bag of simple threads; the context rule (e3) is replaced by the following set including a simpler context rule and new B-reduction rules for the composition operators. @ denotes bag union (associative and commutative, with neutral element $\{\}$), and B, B', etc. are some bags of threads. The relation $\Rightarrow$ now links bags of threads associated with the L (channels) and P (accumulator) information. Global progress of the system of threads ($\triangleright$) is distinguished from progress of its subsystems ($\Rightarrow$):

$$\frac{B, L, P \Rightarrow B', L', P'}{B@B'', L, P \triangleright B'@B'', L', P'},$$
$$\{(a \wedge b, \lambda, \pi)\}, L, P \Rightarrow \{(a, \lambda, \pi), (b, \lambda, \pi)\}, L, P,$$

and, assuming $\kappa \notin Dom(P)$,

$$\{(a \vee b, \lambda, \pi)\}, L, P \Rightarrow \{(a, \lambda, \pi+(\kappa, -)), (b, \lambda, \pi+(\kappa, +))\}, L, P+(\kappa, 0),$$
$$\{(a < b, \lambda, \pi)\}, L, P \Rightarrow \{(a, \lambda, \pi+(\kappa, 0)), (b, \lambda, \pi+(\kappa, +))\}, L, P+(\kappa, 0).$$

The local preemption and shared accumulator information are computed from the current ones and the composition operators. Parallel compositions change neither the local π nor the shared P; the other compositions introduce a new preemption token, mapped to 0 in the accumulator (to mean that no process having that token has made a preemptive action yet) and mapped to particular accesses in the local positions.

In an interaction, all processes involved *commit* their position, which consists of overriding the accumulator by their position. The committed pairs with nonzero accesses could be subsequently removed from the local π; this is not expressed in the rule below though this helps in practice to keep the size of the accumulator at the minimum necessary. The preempted threads are prevented from performing actions; this is expressed by the persistence side-conditions. Persistence is also used to determine synchronizability in the communication rule. Rules (i1) and (i7) are replaced by the following:

$$\{(\text{do } v\text{=>}a, \lambda, \pi)\}, L, P \Rightarrow \{(a, \lambda, \pi)\}, L, P+\pi \qquad (\pi \mathcal{P}P);$$

$$\{(\eta?x\text{=>}a, \lambda, \pi), (\eta'!v\text{=>}a', \lambda', \pi')\}, L, P \qquad (\pi \mathcal{P}P \wedge \pi'\mathcal{P}P \wedge \pi \| \pi')$$
$$\Rightarrow \{(a\langle v/x\rangle, \lambda, \pi), (a', \lambda', \pi')\}, L, (P+\pi)+\pi'.$$

Besides localizing structural information, an additional advantage of this treatment is that removal of the preempted threads resulting from an interaction can be delayed; removing those threads after each interaction, as suggested in Figure 4.3, would be costly in practice. Preempted threads are removed by a special pruning rule:

$$(a, \lambda, \pi), L, P \Rightarrow \{\}, L, P \qquad \neg(\pi \mathcal{P}P).$$

Should all B-reduction transition rules have a persistence side-condition $(\pi \mathcal{P}P)$ attached too, like the do rule above? This would be costly in practice. In the absence of side-effects, B-reducing preempted threads is semantically harmless as long as they are not allowed to interact; but this is clearly useless. There are various practical solutions to make a thread aware, sooner or later, that it has been preempted by another; the issue is discussed in [22] in more detail. In the presence of side-effects, however, reducing preempted threads might violate causality in an observable way, and a persistence test must be added to the transitions modifying the shared state information.

The actual implementation is close in spirit to this description; the coding details are left out, as well as optimizations (preemption tokens are encoded as references; many fewer tokens would be created by giving them an arity to handle embedded choice compositions, etc). The solution described above is also close in spirit to that used in implementations of Poly/ML (discussed in Chapter 3 of this monograph), though the symmetry of the persistence predicate there allows some simplifications (Poly/ML has no interrupt combinator). In practice, the pruning operation is combined with garbage collection; it also removes useless tokens from the local positions, and persistence side-conditions are combined as often as possible with scheduling.

4.5.4   Store Segments

The scope of side-effects in a thread is limited to the innermost store captured by the thread. Some additional structure must be added to the store to take into account local captures of parts of the store: The store now maps *segment identifiers*, written σ, σ', etc., to *store segments*, each segment mapping locations to values. Threads are associated with a segment identifier. Strong compositions introduce new segment identifiers, bound in the store to a copy of the current segment; e.g., the strong parallel composition transition is expressed as

$$(a \mathbin{/\backslash} b, \lambda, \pi, \sigma), L, P, S \qquad\qquad (\sigma' \notin Dom(S))$$
$$\Rightarrow \{(a, \lambda, \pi, \sigma), (b, \lambda, \pi, \sigma')\}, L, P, S + (\sigma', S\sigma).$$

In addition, the assignment rule should be given a persistence side-condition, as explained in Section 4.5.3. In practice, there are several alternatives for efficiently handling that side-condition in conjunction with scheduling and preemption.

4.5.5 Localizing Communications

The last rules to localize are those expressing simultaneous transitions of two threads (the interaction transitions, rule (i7)). There is a well-known technique for localizing rendezvous communication: that of using channels as suspension holders.

Let us associate with each channel ν of Section 4.5.2 a pair of bags of threads I, O. The bag O holds the threads having earlier offered a message on channel ν but that could not find a matching partner at that time, and symmetrically for bag I and input threads. The resulting reduction system is shown in Figure 4.4. It is obtained as follows from the system of Subsection 4.5.4:

- Local transitions ($\Rightarrow$) transform a thread into a bag of threads.

- Each channel now refers to two bags of suspended threads, initially empty. The restriction transition is updated accordingly.

- A thread willing to interact on some channel ν suspends itself in the adequate suspension bag if no matching partner is found (rules (14) and (15)). Otherwise, a partner is selected, interaction occurs (committing the accumulator), and both threads are resumed (rules (12) and (13)).

- Finally, two new pruning rules remove preempted threads from the suspension bags (rules (18) and (19)). The pruning rule (17) applies when the current thread has been preempted. These three rules, as well as the clean-up rule (16), could be considered global rules as well (handled by a dedicated mechanism).

We now have a trivial global transition rule (1), expressing that the progress of a system of threads just results from the progress of its individual constituents, fulfilling in a satisfactory way our locality requirement of Section 4.5.1. If the choice of a partner in rules (12) and (13) is made deterministic, then the local transition relation ($\Rightarrow$) is indeed a function.

(1) $$\frac{a, L, P, S \Rightarrow B, L', P', S'}{B'@\{a\}, L, P, S \rhd B'@B, L', P', S'}$$

(2) $$\frac{(e, \lambda, \pi, \sigma), L, P, S \to \{(e', \lambda', \pi', \sigma')\}, L', P', S'}{(e, \lambda, \pi, \sigma), L, P, S \Rightarrow \{(e', \lambda', \pi', \sigma')\}, L', P', S'} \quad (\pi\mathcal{P}P)$$

$(\text{do } e\texttt{=>}a, \lambda, \pi, \sigma), L, P, S \Rightarrow \{(\text{do } e'\texttt{=>}a, \lambda', \pi', \sigma')\}, L', P', S'$

$(\eta!e\texttt{=>}a, \lambda, \pi, \sigma), L, P, S \Rightarrow \{(\eta!e'\texttt{=>}a, \lambda', \pi', \sigma')\}, L', P', S'$

(3) $(a \land b, \lambda, \pi, \sigma), L, P, S \Rightarrow \{(a, \lambda, \pi, \sigma), (b, \lambda, \pi, \sigma)\}, L, P, S$

(4) $(a \land\land b, \lambda, \pi, \sigma), L, P, S \qquad (\sigma' \notin Dom(S))$
    $\Rightarrow \{(a, \lambda, \pi, \sigma), (b, \lambda, \pi, \sigma')\}, L, P, S+(\sigma', S\sigma)$

(5) $(a \lor b, \lambda, \pi, \sigma), L, P, S \qquad (\kappa \notin Dom(P))$
    $\Rightarrow \{(a, \lambda, \pi+(\kappa, -), \sigma), (b, \lambda, \pi+(\kappa, +), \sigma)\}, L, P+(\kappa, 0), S$

(6) $(a \lor/ b, \lambda, \pi, \sigma), L, P, S \qquad (\kappa \notin Dom(P), \sigma' \notin Dom(S))$
    $\Rightarrow \{(a, \lambda, \pi+(\kappa, -), \sigma), (b, \lambda, \pi+(\kappa, +), \sigma')\}, L, P+(\kappa, 0), S+(\sigma', S\sigma)$

(7) $(a < b, \lambda, \pi, \sigma), L, P, S \qquad (\kappa \notin Dom(P))$
    $\Rightarrow \{(a, \lambda, \pi+(\kappa, 0), \sigma), (b, \lambda, \pi+(\kappa, +), \sigma)\}, L, P+(\kappa, 0), S$

(8) $(a\texttt{\{/p\}}, \lambda, \pi, \sigma), L, P, S \qquad ((\nu_v)_{\forall v \in W} \notin Dom(L))$
    $\Rightarrow \{(a, \lambda+(\texttt{p\#}v, \nu_v)_{\forall v}, \pi, \sigma)\}, L+\{(\nu_v, \emptyset, \emptyset)\}_{\forall v}, P, S$

(9) $(a\texttt{\{q/p\}}, \lambda, \pi, \sigma), L, P, S$
    $\Rightarrow \{(a\texttt{\{/q\}}, \lambda+(\texttt{p\#}v, \lambda(\texttt{q\#}v))_{\forall v}, \pi, \sigma)\}, L, P, S$

(10) $(a\texttt{\{q\#}v\texttt{/}\eta\texttt{\}}, \lambda, \pi, \sigma), L, P, S \Rightarrow \{(a\texttt{\{/q\}}, \lambda+(\eta, \lambda(\texttt{q\#}v)), \pi, \sigma)\}, L, P, S$

(11) $(\text{do } v\texttt{=>}a, \lambda, \pi, \sigma), L, P, S \Rightarrow \{(a, \lambda, \pi, \sigma)\}, L, P+\pi, S \qquad (\pi\mathcal{P}P)$

(12) $(\eta?x\texttt{=>}a, \lambda, \pi, \sigma), \qquad\qquad (\pi\mathcal{P}P \land \pi'\mathcal{P}P \land \pi \parallel\pi')$
     $L+(\lambda\eta, I, O@\{(\eta'!v\texttt{=>}a', \lambda', \pi', \sigma')\}), P, S$
     $\Rightarrow \{(clone\ (S\sigma')\ v\ x\ a, \lambda, \pi, \sigma), (a', \lambda', \pi', \sigma')\},$
     $L+(\lambda\eta, I, O), (P+\pi)+\pi', S$

(13) $(\eta!v\texttt{=>}a, \lambda, \pi, \sigma), \qquad\qquad (\pi\mathcal{P}P \land \pi'\mathcal{P}P \land \pi \parallel\pi')$
     $L+(\lambda\eta, I@\{(\eta'?x\texttt{=>}a', \lambda', \pi', \sigma')\}, O), P, S$
     $\Rightarrow \{(clone\ (S\sigma)\ v\ x\ a', \lambda', \pi', \sigma'), (a, \lambda, \pi, \sigma)\},$
     $L+(\lambda\eta, I, O), (P+\pi)+\pi', S$

(14) $(\eta?x\texttt{=>}a, \lambda, \pi, \sigma), L+(\lambda\eta, I, O), P, S \qquad (\pi\mathcal{P}P \land Wait(\pi, P, O))$
     $\Rightarrow \{\}, L+(\lambda\eta, I@\{(\eta?x\texttt{=>}a, \lambda, \pi, \sigma)\}, O), P, S$

(15) $(\eta!v\texttt{=>}a, \lambda, \pi, \sigma), L+(\lambda\eta, I, O), P, S \qquad (\pi\mathcal{P}P \land Wait(\pi, P, I))$
     $\Rightarrow \{\}, L+(\lambda\eta, I, O@\{(\eta!v\texttt{=>}a, \lambda, \pi, \sigma)\}), P, S$

where $Wait(\pi, P, E) \Leftrightarrow \forall(a', \lambda', \pi', \sigma') \in E.\neg((\pi'\mathcal{P}P) \land (\pi' \parallel\pi))$

(16) $(\texttt{stop}, \lambda, \pi, \sigma), L, P, S \Rightarrow \{\}, L, P, S$

(17) $(a, \lambda, \pi, \sigma), L, P, S \Rightarrow \{\}, L, P, S \qquad\qquad \neg(\pi\mathcal{P}P)$

(18) $a, L+(\nu, I@\{(e, \lambda, \pi, \sigma)\}, O), P, S \Rightarrow \{a\}, L+(\nu, I, O), P, S \qquad \neg(\pi\mathcal{P}P)$

(19) $a, L+(\nu, I, O@\{(e, \lambda, \pi, \sigma)\}), P, S \Rightarrow \{a\}, L+(\nu, I, O), P, S \qquad \neg(\pi\mathcal{P}P)$

FIGURE 4.4. The global ($\rhd$) and local ($\Rightarrow$) transition relations

That relation is still expressed inductively in Figure 4.4, due to rule (2) expressing F-reductions, but there are known techniques for replacing this rule by a set of premise-free transitions; a solution based on Landin's SECD machine (see, e.g., [40] or [142] for a description), with expressions compiled into abstract code, was discussed in [22]. The persistence side-condition of rule (2) is only needed for transitions updating the store.

4.5.6   Abstract Machines

The threaded reduction system in Figure 4.4 can be considered an abstract machine, with one virtual processor attached to each nonsuspended thread. To be of practical interest, that abstract machine needs to be refined to express sharing of evaluation of the many possible threads of a program by a finite number of physical processors. This can be done by adding a "virtual processor" layer to the reduction system, intermediate between the "thread" layer and the "global" layer, as was done in [22]. Each virtual processor would reduce a thread and maintain locally a set of ready threads waiting for the processor. The issues involved are those of determining scheduling techniques both to allow a reasonably fair reduction of a system of threads and to use in an efficient way the physical computing resources associated with the virtual processors. The abstract machine may be instantiated in a number of ways, towards sequential, parallel, or distributed implementations, and the issue will be briefly discussed in the next section.

We conclude the subsection by a short comparison with existing work on abstract machines for concurrent computations. Two obvious candidates for comparison are the Gamma paradigm discussed in [16] and the Chemical Abstract Machine (CHAM) of [19]. Both served as a constant source of inspiration for the work described here.

- The thread-locality property aimed at here also plays a central role in Gamma, but the comparison cannot be made much more precise. Gamma is a computing paradigm more than a programming notation, and it is not of direct help for implementing a particular concurrent programming language. It did influence us, however, in emphasizing the importance of locality.

- The CHAM effort is aimed at similar goals. It also emphasizes locality by separating local transitions (reactions) from global transitions (operating principles). However, it does not yield an effective reduction system for the calculi that were investigated, so we do not quite agree with [19] on what should be an abstract machine. Another point of disagreement is that the authors of [19] rule out preemption from the operating principles of abstract machines, while we clearly do not. Nevertheless, the CHAM effort also deeply influenced us, notably in making clear how observation of processes and evaluation are related.

4.5.7   Implementations

The actual implementations of LCS are closely based on the rules shown in Figure 4.4, with some additional enhancements discussed in [22] and many optimizations. Several implementations have been investigated, and these are reviewed in the sequel.

A sequential implementation, running the many threads of an LCS application inside a single Unix process, had been implemented by 1988 [21] and continuously improved since then [23]. It allows one to use concurrency and communication as powerful structuring principles for complex applications, but obviously, no advantage is taken of explicit concurrency to speed up applications. This implementation also served as a workbench to help us develop and improve the language, its compiler, and its abstract machine. The SML subset of the language has been locally developed too as part of the project. The abstract machine is implemented as a byte-code interpreter.

Parallel implementations, with all the LCS threads sharing a single store, have been investigated in depth in [87]. This thesis discusses an architecture for parallel virtual machines, easily cast into the framework presented here, that allows parallel reduction of LCS applications on a variety of parallel and distributed targets. The parallel abstract machine stands on a shared memory abstraction provided on distributed targets by a Distributed Shared Virtual Memory layer embedding also distributed memory allocation and garbage collection services. That memory layer was first described in [88]; it was later improved and implemented conjointly with the Poly/ML group of Edinburgh LFCS to yield the LEMMA layer described in [102, 101]. The LEMMA memory management layer currently constitutes the ground on which parallel implementations of Poly/ML are built, as well as the forthcoming parallel implementations of LCS. Other aspects of parallel abstract machines have been investigated in detail, notably distributed scheduling and load-balancing techniques [87, 89]. All these components are currently being integrated.

Our short-term goals include distributed implementations of the language and of its abstract machine, combining in a single framework the capabilities of the parallel implementation described above with the capability of making several LCS applications operating on different address spaces cooperate. The simple idea is to allow them to share all or part of their communication environment. The language is already equipped with a notion of strong process to accommodate processes operating on different stores. A minimal linguistic support will be added to let LCS applications establish connections with others dynamically; such extensions are being designed and evaluated.

4.6   Conclusion

4.6.1   Related Work

LCS benefited from the results of the PFL experience, an early attempt to add CCS capabilities to ML [76]. PFL required a "continuation-passing" style of programming together with channels passed as parameters to the behaviors. LCS managed to keep the original CCS combinator set and concept of port, and more closely integrates behaviors with other features of the language.

CML [150] and Poly/ML [100] are based on different principles from LCS; they provide a strictly functional interface for concurrency and communication. One of the difficulties with that approach is delaying communications while keeping an applicative order evaluation. This often leads to the addition of dummy parameters to processes, just for the sake of delaying their evaluation. LCS uses a layered evaluation method for achieving transparently the same effects. Like LCS, the language FACILE [59] uses behavior expressions to describe processes, though restricted there to the termination behavior and compositions. However, the FACILE treatment is overall closer to that of languages offering a functional interface.

Among the parallel-functional languages designed for similar purposes, LCS is the sole one strictly based upon CCS for its naming aspects. In terms of expressiveness, CCS naming forbids label passing, but LCS allows one to approximate it by parameterized ports and behavior passing. On the other hand, one never has to declare communication ports or pass them as parameters; this greatly simplifies programs, and the basic set of CCS combinators is fairly easily understood. There are also good perspectives for verification tools for large subsets of LCS, based on the many available methods for proving process equivalences in CCS-style calculi (see, e.g., the work around the LOTOS specification language).

In terms of implementation, communication in LCS is certainly more difficult to implement than in languages having "first-class" channels, and typechecking requires more sophisticated techniques. The LCS treatment amounts to a dynamic binding of channels to communication ports. This could be costly at run-time if naively implemented; among other optimizations, LCS implementations use a software cache for speeding access to channels (not described here). Channels are searched when first accessed and then found directly in the cache; the code generated by the compiler helps management of the cache.

4.6.2   Conclusion and Further Work

LCS allows one to comfortably experiment with the concurrent programming concepts introduced by CCS and related behavioral formalism, and to gain experience in using these paradigms. It is also a valuable teaching tool for these concepts. LCS includes all capabilities of CCS and inherits most of its theory. Concurrent applications can be written abstractly so that users may reason about their programs, and they can be refined to run with good performance. The fact that sufficiently abstract specifications and sufficiently efficient implementations can be written in a single framework is certainly an advantage for formal development of programs.

Among the spinoffs of the experiment is the original technique for typing behavior expressions; the so-called tagged types used by LCS could be used to type a variety of other features in programming languages, including extensible records and some object-oriented features. The fairly general implementation model described in Section 4.5 is another important result of the experiment; its flexibility and richness would permit it to be used for implementation of many other process languages.

Our short-term goals include completion of parallel and distributed implementations of the language. In the long term, introduction of some synchrony in the language will be investigated as a convenient approach to some classes of reactive applications such as cooperative multimedia.

5
FACILE—From Toy to Tool

Bent Thomsen, Lone Leth, and Tsung-Min Kuo

with contributions by
P.-Y. Chevalier, P. Cregut, A. Giacalone, F. Knabe, A. Kramer,
S. Prasad, and J.-P. Talpin

ABSTRACT The FACILE system combines language, compiler, and distributed system technology into a programming environment supporting the rapid construction of reliable and sophisticated end-user applications operating in distributed computing environments. In particular, FACILE is well suited for construction of systems based on the emerging and increasingly popular "mobile agents" principle.

FACILE distinguishes itself from other distributed systems by providing a simple and coherent formally well-defined conceptual model of computations, both sequential and distributed, through which programmers access services provided by "middleware" such as OSF/DCE, CORBA, ANSA, and traditional operating systems. Using a special language for distributed programming makes the distance from the programmer's mental model to the actual program shorter. It also gives other advantages such as readability, portability, static typing, dataflow analysis, program transformations, and optimisations. The FACILE language combines a predominantly functional programming language, Standard ML (SML), with a model of concurrency based on CCS and its higher-order and mobile extensions (CHOCS and the π-calculus). Furthermore, constructs for distributed computing are based on recent results from timed process algebra and true concurrency theory. These models are integrated with the fundamental philosophy of SML that all values in the language are first-class values. This means that any value—simple, complex, user-defined, even functions, process scripts, and communication channels—may be placed in data structures, given as arguments to functions, and returned as results of function invocations or communicated between processes possibly residing on different machines. In addition, FACILE brings the notion of strong, fully polymorphic typing known from SML into the world of distributed computing. In fact, this integration yields the fundamental building blocks for supporting programming of mobile agents in a secure and reliable manner.

Since the beginning of the FACILE project at ECRC in 1991, FACILE has been developed from the state of a calculus or a toy language to a full-fledged, industrial strength, distributed programming environment. Currently the FACILE system runs on loosely connected, physically distributed, and heterogeneous machines with distributed memory. The system may operate on both local area and wide area networks. Furthermore, support for mobile computing has been integrated into the system.

FACILE has been used to develop significant components of a number of systems, including Calumet—a cooperative work application that provides a distributed slide presentation and teleconferencing system; Einrichten—a teleworking application that presents virtual collaborative interior design at a distance; and Mobile Service Agents—a mobility application that enables access to agents that operate in an open, distributed environment.

The FACILE project represents a vehicle of industrial exploitation of major theoretical results that have been developed over many years. Many of these results have been developed in the context of the European Union ESPRIT research program, in particular in the Basic Research Actions and Working Groups in which ECRC participated: CONFER (6564), LOMAPS (8130), CONCUR 2 (7166), SEMAGRAPH 2 (6345), and COORDINA-TION (9102).

This chapter focuses on some issues in the design of the FACILE language, its implementation, and (informal) semantics. In particular, this chapter describes the state of FACILE somewhere between its first official release—the FACILE Antigua Release—and its second formal release—the FACILE Barbados Release. We shall also describe some of its applications and discuss the future evolution of FACILE.

Acknowledgment This work is partially supported by ESPRIT BRAs 6454 CONFER and 8130 LOMAPS.

5.1   Introduction

With the diffusion of communication networks, in particular the development of the Global Information Infrastructure and the increasing integration of computing and communication devices, distributed computing is one of the great challenges and at the same time one of the great opportunities faced by the developers of information technology products and services.

The explosive growth of the Internet and the emerging commercial information infrastructures, such as AT&T PersonaLink, American Online, and CompuServe, are proof that roadwork on information superhighways has already begun. There is now a rapidly growing number of services from businesses and governments being made available electronically. Millions of users have started to access this information and use services such as electronic shopping.

Characteristic for distributed computing is that it is an order of magnitude more complex than sequential programming. Furthermore, distributed systems are usually massive, meaning that they contain millions of lines of source code. They are long lived; thus the technology used now will have to interact with older software and with new technology turning up now and in the future. Systems have to be robust and sustain the potential for failure of part of the system—both software and hardware—and it must be possible to recover quickly. Many distributed systems are "nonstop" systems; hence it must be possible to correct bugs or add or remove software while the system is running. Often distributed systems will have to react in real time or at least in a timely manner. Furthermore, with the tendency to global interconnection, distributed systems are becoming very heterogeneous. This trend is further fueled by the fact that cheap and powerful mobile devices with wireless communication capabilities are starting to reach the market. In the near future a large number of people will be carrying such devices and connecting to the global information infrastructure when necessary. The trend towards mobile users will further stimulate the use of dynamically evolving systems, both in structure and in functionality. This again is calling for new methods in the construction of distributed systems—e.g., mobile agents are currently being proposed as one such solution.

Traditionally, when constructing distributed systems it is often necessary to use multiple programming styles with incoherent programming models, and very often it is necessary to resolve conflicts by low-level methods, reverting to the lowest common denominator. Historically, application developers split their system so that application-specific subsystems depend upon the operating system directly. However, application implementers often experience difficulties with their applications' not being portable because each operating system has its own distinct application programming interface, and different versions of the applications employ different subsystem architectures due to the fact that distinct operating systems provide services that differ in kind and semantics.

Current technology is working to solve these historical problems by introducing a concept called "middleware." Here, an application interfaces with the middleware and normally does not access the underlying operating system directly. Middleware service providers distinguish themselves by implementing a particular collection of services that they advertise as useful. For example, OSF/DCE [81] offers communication, naming, and security services; COMANDOS [42] defines and implements a virtual machine that hides distribution to the programmer; while ANSA [8] provides support for federated client-server applications. Existing middleware is mainly a collection of useful services, but most often not a very coherent collection. This is essentially due to the fact that existing middleware was developed following a bottom-up approach; from low-level services to language support.

5.1.1   The FACILE Approach

In contrast to the mainstream approach to middleware for distributed systems mentioned above, FACILE follows a language approach. This means that a strong emphasis is put into the definition of a programming model that cleanly integrates low-level services for distribution. Using a special language for distributed programming will make the distance from the programmer's mental model to the actual program shorter. It also gives other advantages, such as readability, portability, static typing, dataflow analysis, program transformations and optimisations, normally not present in distributed computing environments.

FACILE may be characterized as a tight integration between a language with formal foundations, sophisticated compiler technology, and a set of sophisticated middleware services. The FACILE system integrates components from run-time systems, such as automatic memory management; from operating systems, such as process management; and communication subsystems, such as message passing and synchronization, as well as name management.

The FACILE language combines a predominantly functional programming language, Standard ML (SML), with a model of concurrency based on CCS and its higher-order and mobile extensions (CHOCS [164, 165, 168, 170], LCCS [92] and the π-calculus [109]). Furthermore, constructs for distributed computing are based on recent results from timed process algebra and true concurrency theory.

In addition to FACILE being suitable for constructing reliable transactional or client/server systems, FACILE is particularly well suited for programming systems based on the emerging "mobile agents" principle. This is no coincidence. Since the FACILE model of concurrency is based on higher-order mobile processes (i.e., processes and communication links as first-class objects), this provides the necessary linguistic means for programming mobile agents. In fact, the multiparadigm nature of FACILE allows a mixture of styles such as combinations of agent-based and client-server-based applications.

Special care has been given to developing the formal foundations of the FACILE model. The basic philosophy of the FACILE project has been to develop a language comprising a basic set of primitive constructs that are intuitive for programming, have a clear semantic formalization, and have a quite efficient implementation. These primitives are powerful enough for defining a variety of abstractions commonly employed in concurrent and distributed computing. Since FACILE has been constructed by combining SML with a model of higher-order concurrent processes based on CCS, special care has been taken in preserving the semantic model of SML and thus making constructs from SML behave naturally, or as expected, in a distributed environment.

The basic computational model of FACILE consists of one or more nodes, or virtual processors, on each of which there are zero or more processes. Processes execute by evaluating expressions in a functional style, and they can communicate values between each other by synchronizing over typed channels.

FACILE is well suited for running on loosely connected, physically distributed systems with distributed memory. It is possible to execute FACILE programs on both local area networks (LANs) and wide area networks

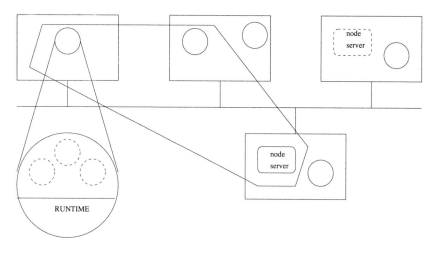

FACILE NODE

FIGURE 5.1. A FACILE system

(WANs). A FACILE system under Unix[1] consists of a collection of FACILE nodes and a node server. Each FACILE node, as well as the node server, runs in a separate Unix process. The FACILE nodes and the node server may all be running on different machines. Each FACILE node consists of a collection of FACILE processes[2] managed by one run-time system. FACILE processes communicate over channels, and they may communicate with FACILE processes running on different nodes. Communication between processes on different machines goes via the network, but appears almost transparent to the user. The system's node server keeps track of nodes and implements some bootstrapping functions.

A FACILE system is depicted in Figure 5.1. This system consists of two nodes and a node server. This is sketched by encapsulating two nodes and a node server in a polygon. We have "zoomed in" on a FACILE node in order to show its contents, namely a number of FACILE processes, a heap, and a run-time system.

This chapter focuses on some issues in the design of the FACILE language, its implementation, and (informal) semantics. In particular, this chapter describes the state of FACILE somewhere between its first official release in the summer of '94—the FACILE Antigua Release—and its second formal release—the FACILE Barbados Release. We shall also describe

---

[1]Unix is a registered trademark of UNIX Systems Laboratories, Inc.

[2]FACILE processes are lightweight and should not be confused with the Unix processes hosting FACILE nodes. FACILE processes may be thought of as threads sharing an address space.

some of its applications and discuss the future evolution of FACILE.

The outline of this chapter is as follows: Section 5.2 describes the design and development of FACILE, Section 5.3 contains details about the language features, Section 5.4 describes the implementation of FACILE Antigua, Section 5.5 focuses on applications using FACILE, and Section 5.6 contains conclusions and some directions for future work.

5.2   Design and Development of FACILE

The original work on FACILE (done at SUNY Stony Brook 1988–90) focused on the formal foundations of the functional/concurrent language integration [140, 139] and on abstract implementation models [58, 59]. The operational semantics of the core language is formalized in the structural style using labeled transition systems. Based on the operational semantics, a notion of equivalence of programs with respect to an interface of observation was proposed using an extension of the bisimulation technique. This work was influenced by research on the semantics of higher-order processes [164, 165, 168, 170] and mobile processes [54, 92, 109].

Since the start of the FACILE project at ECRC in 1991, the main objective has been to provide a higher level of distributed programming support. We have tried to address all three aspects of it—investigating semantic issues of distribution, defining suitable language constructs for programming, and developing an efficient distributed implementation. Although the formal semantics is not the subject of this chapter, we stress that the design of the language has evolved by seeking a good balance between what is considered useful for programming, what can be formalized cleanly, and what can be implemented with reasonable efficiency. For further details see [172, 93, 167, 7].

Albeit a suitable research vehicle, FACILE as it stood at the end of 1990 was evidently not suitable for practical programming. Among the most obviously missing components were a flexible type system and appropriate abstraction mechanisms. Hence, to achieve its original objective, the first major task of the FACILE project, before addressing distributed programming issues, was to bring FACILE from a calculus to a programming language.

Standard ML (SML) [112] was chosen as a platform for various reasons. It was the model for the sequential part of the original FACILE design, and thus represented the closest fit with the functional component of FACILE. SML has a well-developed semantic foundation and provides a rather simple and clean programming model. Furthermore, it brings a sophisticated polymorphic type inference system that supports user-defined and abstract data types; and a rich set of abstraction mechanisms from the basic function abstraction up to a very powerful module system. The choice was also motivated by the availability of the SML system developed by AT&T Bell

Laboratories, commonly referred to as SML/NJ. SML/NJ provides one of the most advanced, robust, and efficient implementations of SML. The accessibility of the full SML/NJ implementation also gives us a potential strategy, which was eventually chosen, for the FACILE implementation: to modify an existing language platform rather than develop a full implementation from scratch.

The implementation of the FACILE Antigua Release is based on SML/NJ version 0.93 since this was the most recent SML/NJ release at the time of completing the FACILE Antigua Release. Thus, sequential computation in FACILE, or rather FACILE Antigua, resembles programming in SML, in particular it resembles programming in SML/NJ version 0.93.

FACILE enriches SML with primitives for distribution, concurrency, and communication over typed channels. The additional data types provided in the language include node identifiers, process scripts, and communication channels. All of these are first-class values that can be manipulated in an applicative style and in particular be communicated. New nodes and channels can be created dynamically, and processes executing a given script can be spawned dynamically on a given node.

In the rest of this section we shall discuss some of the most fundamental principles underpinning the design of FACILE. Many of these principles exist for SML already. During the design of FACILE, great care has been taken to preserve them. In essence, we can say that they served as the most important guidelines throughout the design process.

5.2.1   Integration of Programming Paradigms

One of the major design principles of FACILE is its approach to integration of different programming paradigms. It is widely accepted that each programming paradigm has its own merits and is more suitable for expressing certain classes of computation than others. A language that supports many programming paradigms often enables a more direct expression of the design, since many problems and solutions consist of various components that are more natural and easier when viewed in different ways. Allowing more direct expression of the design in the implementation helps to avoid many unnecessary encodings that often are great sources of software errors and maintenance complication.

In this light, FACILE attempts to encompass four different programming paradigms—functional, imperative, concurrent, and distributed—in a single programming language.

FACILE takes a symmetric integration approach, which means that every programming paradigm can use any other paradigm as a subcomponent for its expression. For example, a function can have a part described using concurrent computation and communication. And naturally, concurrent processes can use function applications for describing their computations and use expressions to specify the values used in communication. In summary, the granularity of a programming paradigm is a single concept; thus, there is no visible programming unit that admits only one paradigm but excludes all the others.

Symmetric integration further enhances the benefit of multiparadigm programming languages in the sense that different paradigms can be used for different levels of abstraction, and programmers have full control over when to use which paradigm. It also provides an avenue to simplify the language. This is quite evident in FACILE, where reusing the very rich set of abstraction mechanisms of SML avoids introducing another set for the concurrent and distributed paradigms. For example, we can limit channel access to send-only or enforce a certain communication protocol using function abstraction.

Actually, FACILE has gone one step further. Its view of paradigm integration is integration of concepts rather than merely putting together all the language constructs. Each programming paradigm is broken up and its essential concepts are extracted. Then a single coherent framework, which incorporates all the concepts, is constructed. During this process, redundancy is removed. Certain concepts are merged together, and some are expressed using similar ones from other paradigms. For example, channel creation and communication all become function application; and one scoping rule applies uniformly to all language constructs. This follows the tradition of SML on integrating functional and imperative paradigms, in which the concept of state change from the imperative paradigm is blended into the concept of value in the functional paradigm by introducing mutable values. Such a merging of concepts allows all the language constructs from the functional paradigm to remain usable for manipulating stateful objects and hence renders the additional language constructs for the imperative paradigm unnecessary. One important advantage, for example, is to allow only one parameter-passing mechanism and only one binding mechanism. Moreover, by treating variables as values, we can eliminate the complications arising from the distinction between l-value and r-value, and the distinction between pass-by-value and pass-by-reference, which plague all imperative programming languages.

To some extent, one can argue that FACILE has only one programming paradigm, which employs all the essential concepts from the four programming paradigms in a coherent framework. This is one programming paradigm that supports programming in four different styles in any combination that one might want to have. This is significant for programmers because at almost any point in a program and within any context, the most appropriate programming paradigm that the design calls for can be used, and used without much worry about interference with the surrounding context simply because it happens to be expressed with a different paradigm.

5.2.2 Simplicity and Coherence

It is of ultimate importance for a programming language to provide programmers with an easy-to-comprehend conceptual framework to base their work on. This is essential for making the language easy to understand and easy to master, and thus facilitating its effective use. To make such a framework possible, the language must be designed to be simple and coherent. To be simple, there must be relatively few (language-level) concepts. To be coherent, there must be no unexpected interaction when they are combined.

Similarly, language constructs should also be simple and coherent. The meaning and proper usage of each language construct should be easy to describe, both formally and informally, and should not be too sensitive or have many subtle restrictions to the surrounding context. Every language construct should be designed to support a single concept or a simple combination of concepts.

In terms of language constructs, there are only a few additional ones for FACILE, mostly related to the new concept of behavior. Most of the new functionalities are expressed using the mechanism for specifying computation in SML, namely expression, through the use of value, function, and function application. This is in the spirit of the λ-calculus that all the computational power is embedded in constants, leaving only one language construct—function application. Here, λ-abstractions are considered as constant objects encoding computation since they denote primitive objects—functions.

5.2.3 Uniformity of Values

One of the most important characteristics of SML is its uniform treatment of values. All computations are expressed as manipulation of values, and all values are treated equally. For example, functions and structured values, such as tuples and records, are all given the same status as values of primitive types. In particular, there is no distinction between the concepts of expressible, denotable, and storable values. The consequence is that any kind of value can be used as a function argument, as the returned value of function invocation, as a component of structured value, as referred value of a mutable object, or as the denotation of an identifier. This makes a uniform and simple function invocation and parameter-passing mechanism possible. Uniformity of values also makes parametric type definition very simple and separates the concern of data composition from the data components, thus laying the foundation for a usable polymorphic type system.

For programmers this means that the concern of whether a particular way of describing a computation process in our mind is acceptable by the language in a certain context is largely removed. This basically avoids an additional layer of complexity in the solution on top of the inherent complexity in the problem we are solving.

During the design of FACILE, such a fundamental principle is carefully preserved. When the new concepts from the two new programming paradigms, concurrent and distributed, are integrated into SML, they are mapped into types, values, and functions whenever possible. For example, script, channel, guard, node, and library are all first-class values. And almost all functionalities to support concurrent/distributed programming are provided as functions/values, and all computations involved are realized through expression evaluation.

Such a design practice not only keeps the language simple and preserves the uniformity of values, which relieves us from worrying about the potential interference with the sophisticated polymorphic type system of SML, but it also brings us a great deal of flexibility in programming. For example, channels being first-class values naturally gives us the support for dynamic communication interconnections. Furthermore, scripts as first-class values gives mobile processes. Just as in SML, treating functions as first-class values gives us higher-order functions for free; these are primary examples of getting more by worrying less.

5.2.4 Object Lifetime

While the scoping rule is intended to control the lifetime of name bindings, many conventional programming languages also use it to control the lifetime of (static) objects. Meanwhile, many of these languages also provide language features that make references to objects independent of name binding possible, e.g., the address-of operator. Often the end result is the nasty bugs of referring to objects that do not really exist. Even for a well-disciplined programmer, this could still present a minor nuisance and a constant distraction of the mental effort of programming. A subtle consequence of such coupling is that in many languages, it is rather tricky to make a function return a compound object, e.g., a tuple or record. Since such a task is inevitable, it seems natural to have functions returning results through input rather than through output. That, in turn, gives the absolute requirement for all kinds of fancy and complex parameter-passing mechanisms.

In contrast, SML defines the object lifetime as being the same as the accessibility, i.e., an object is alive as long as it is accessible. This completely takes one factor of consideration away from programmers. It allows programmers to concentrate more on the problem they are trying to solve, rather than paying a lot of attention on how to manage the memory correctly; and at the same time it eliminates a whole class of hard-to-find software errors. FACILE keeps the tradition by, for example, not having explicit open-close or disposal of channels. Thus, all the communication facilities, process scripts, and communication guards are managed automatically by the system just as are all the other objects. This also ensures that all programming paradigms are equally easy to exploit and encourages straightforward implementation rather than excessive encoding of the design.

5.2.5 Concurrency and Distribution

FACILE is conceived to support the construction of reliable distributed applications. A number of design considerations derive directly from this focus. The nature of distributed computing has been characterized as follows in [15]:

> Distributed systems are characterized by multiple autonomous processors that do not share primary memory but by sending messages over a communication network.
>
> Distributed systems are potentially (but not necessarily) more reliable than sequential systems because they have the so called partial failure property, i.e., a failure in one processor does not affect the correct functioning of other processors.

As a consequence distributed computing is different from sequential programming in at least the following three points:

- The use of multiple processors,

- Cooperation among the processors,

- The potential for partial failures.

Many distributed platforms, such as ANSA [8] and CORBA [128, 127, 115], try to make distribution and failure transparent. By not recognizing the fundamental nature of distributed systems, which makes them different from sequential (and even multi-threaded) systems, these object-based approaches are bound to create confusion and in the end are bound to leave the application programmer with no other option than to program around the problem.

The approach taken in FACILE is in sharp contrast with the popular object-based approaches. A programming language for distributed programming must satisfy the following requirements:

- Ability to assign different parts of a program to be run on different processors,

- Communication and synchronization,

- Ability to detect and recover from partial failure.

In many applications the programmer needs to control where a process executes, e.g., the code for user interactions and displaying a screen image should run on the user's workstation rather than on some other machine. Also, an application may require that a process perform some recovery in case of failure of remote components. For example, the programmer may wish to free a process blocked while attempting to communicate by timing out the communication attempt.

A direct design goal for FACILE was that such issues should be addressed within the language model, not compelling the programmer to exit it and work at an operating-system level, where type safety is lost and the complexity of working with a different framework is introduced.

Clearly, while the details of physical distribution and concurrency in the computational model are made explicit by language constructs, in certain scenarios one may wish these hidden, to various extents, from the user. For example, concurrency may be used to gain parallelism in multiprocessing environments and distribution for increasing reliability or availability of resources, but these details may be transparent to the programmer. A more abstract programming model via some fault-tolerance mechanism can be obtained by building suitable abstractions, e.g., physical distribution or concurrency can be hidden to the desired extent. However, the programmer should never be misled to believe that the problems of physical distribution and partial failure have gone away. They have just been slightly better hidden.

To support locality of processes a notion of *node* is introduced, which corresponds to a virtual processor with an address space. A FACILE system typically executes as a collection of nodes, each hosting concurrent FACILE processes. Nodes are dynamically created and may reside on different workstations, and processes may be spawned at specific nodes. The model of concurrency remains essentially unchanged. Processes do not have identity, other than the set of channels through which they communicate. Arbitrary data structures may be communicated, over FACILE channels, between processes on different nodes. At the semantic level we follow a model based on [35] and [2].

For partial failures, no single mechanism seems adequate to cover all the various scenarios of what applications require to be reported as failures and how these may be detected and handled. There seems to be an endless spectrum of potential failures in a distributed system, so trying to list them and propose solutions for each would be impossible. Instead we will try to provide language constructs that could allow the programmer to handle at least some foreseeable failures. The approach being followed in FACILE is to provide a combination of mechanisms. First of all, the notion of exceptions from SML provides a clean and well-defined model for reporting exceptional outcomes of computations, and the mechanism for capturing and handling raised exceptions allows the programmer to define the appropriate actions to be taken.

Furthermore, the handshake communication discipline may block processes when failures occur, e.g., in remote processors or physical networks. In a distributed application, on the other hand, one often wishes to avoid blocking an entire system when some component fails. A partial solution often adopted in distributed programming is to use time-out mechanisms. Rather than introducing directly "time-out-able" send-and-receive constructs we introduce some more general/primitive constructs that will allow us, among other things, to implement the mentioned constructs. This requires the introduction of a notion of time. To define a semantics for the time constructs in FACILE we follow some recent developments in timed process algebra surveyed in [120].

As mentioned before, the model of concurrency and communication in FACILE is based on abstract models such as CCS and CSP. However, it has been necessary to adjust these to the reality of physical distribution.

Seen from a conceptual point of view, a channel in FACILE is an interaction point in the sense of CCS [108]. However, from an implementational point of view a channel has a physical manifestation as a data structure or even a thread of control. If the implementation uses primitives provided by traditional operating systems, such as Unix, channels have to be declared and connected to processes using links (e.g., sockets). There are several implementation choices for channel management. Two such alternatives that we shall discuss are centralized and decentralized channel management.

Centralized channel management means that one manager takes care of matching senders with receivers for the entire FACILE system. Clearly the centralized channel management approach is very vulnerable to node failure. If the node where the channel manager resides fails, all communications in the system will be blocked since communication requests cannot be enqueued.

One way to improve this situation is to replicate the channel manager on each node and keep the replicas consistent. Consistency can be achieved by group communication protocols such as ISIS [27, 26]. The ISIS protocols rely heavily on broadcast communication. Experiments using ISIS for implementing the channel communication mechanism of FACILE in a distributed environment have shown that it is very expensive in terms of the number of low-level messages needed to ensure consistency between replicated channel managers.

As an alternative to replicating channel managers a different approach has been taken for FACILE. Instead of letting the implementation take care of replicating the channel manager as suggested above, we give the programmer control over where channels are created. This is easily facilitated in a decentralized channel management scheme or in a per channel management scheme. Thus, decentralized channel management implies that there is one channel manager per FACILE channel. Each such manager takes care of matching senders and receivers using a particular channel. Some further work is needed by the channel managers to coordinate communications that stem from choices.

In the face of node failure it is obvious that channel managers may disappear when a node fails, just as in the case of centralized channel management. However, only the channels created on a node disappear when that particular node fails, and the system may still communicate over channels created on other nodes. The programmer can therefore safeguard an application by placing channels on different nodes. Clearly, processes may be blocked when attempting communications over channels residing on failed nodes. This seems unavoidable, and only a time-out mechanism for unblocking communications can solve this problem (or rather provide means by which the programmer may program around the problem of blocked communications).

In a distributed system a process potentially has to be ready to communicate with several other processes; hence a number of alternative actions are possible. Depending on the actual communication partner, the corresponding action is performed. Here the problem is how to select one of the alternatives, and several possible choice operators can be considered. In general, choice operators impose a cost on distributed value communication, and this cost seems to increase with the generality of the operator. FACILE as described in [58, 59] offers a choice operator on behavior expressions for selecting one out of a number of alternatives of execution, the operator being inspired from the CCS choice operator "+" [108]. However, even though this semantics is possibly the simplest, most general, and compact at the level of a formalism for specification [108, 52], it poses severe implementation problems once it is integrated into a programming language that allows the specification of distributed executions. The semantics specifies that the choice may be triggered by both external communications and internal transitions in either branch, and each branch might contain activations of concurrent processes and nested choices. This requires some bookkeeping on "child" processes until the choice has been resolved, maybe even freezing their computations temporarily. From an implementation point of view this is difficult and expensive, especially in a distributed setting.

Another source of complexity is that in any alternative branch, internal transitions, caused by function application, channel creation, or process spawning, may trigger the choice. In an implementation of FACILE, computational steps specified by the top-level semantics generally require the execution of several low-level instructions. However, internal transitions arising from bookkeeping activities should not trigger the choice. Hence it is necessary to distinguish the different types of internal transitions.

Based on these considerations, we have experimented with a choice operator that is easier and more efficient to implement in a distributed setting, yet that preserves as many of the essential mathematical properties as possible. The operator has a deterministic evaluation strategy for evaluating its options. Nondeterminism in the choice is based on the nondeterminism of the underlying system and the presence of potential communication partners. More details about the choice operator can be found in Section 5.3.1.

The experiments with various choice operators have been performed by casting the FACILE semantics in the CHAM framework [19, 20, 34] and introducing various semantic interpretations for the choice operator [93]. This has allowed us to justify design issues and implementation decisions before carrying out a full-scale implementation effort. We have used the formal CHAM semantics to give informal arguments about implementability of various constructs based on the observation that the more complicated the CHAM machinery needed to describe the semantics of certain constructs, the harder it is to give an implementation.

5.2.6 Design Alternatives and Tradeoffs

In this section we discuss various design alternatives that have been considered during the design and implementation of FACILE. We look at how to treat mutable objects in a distributed environment and how to deal with exceptions.

Copy semantics for mutable objects is adapted in FACILE for several reasons. Compared with the virtual shared memory alternative, it allows a much more efficient distributed implementation (see Section 5.4.5). Furthermore, when true sharing is needed, communication can be used easily to provide the service. But the most important reason for adapting copy semantics for mutable objects is to keep the semantics of pattern matching simple. The constructor `ref` in SML is a data constructor, and hence it can be used for pattern matching. If copy semantics were not used, pattern matching could potentially result in delay or even failure. Since `ref` is the only constructor that would get into such a situation, it does not seem to be an attractive solution to add blocking and exception raising into the model of pattern matching. Clearly one can argue that `ref` has no role to play in pattern matching. However, we have decided that such subtle changes to SML are not to be pursued for the moment.

Despite having some good reasons for adapting copy semantics, there are some pitfalls that programmers should be aware of, mainly because there are many ways of communicating a mutable object across the node boundary and thus turning it into a different object, and some of them may be rather implicit and subtle. Other than being sent directly via a channel, a mutable object can also be embedded in other values, e.g., functions or scripts, that are moved to another node. Not only channel communication can make this possible, but remote spawning can also move a script from one node to another. Furthermore, since it might not be apparent whether a node identifier is denoting the local node or a different node, we cannot always be sure that `r_spawn` will spawn a process remotely. Or, due to the multiparty nature of channel communication, we can never be sure where the other communication partner is located. Hence, it might not always be obvious from a program whether certain mutable objects will be copied.

Mutable objects should therefore be used with great care.

Another example of careful design is the interaction between exceptions and concurrency and distribution. There are many ways in which computation can go wrong. In addition to the situations that arise from normal sequential computation, FACILE introduces many others that result from the nature of distributed computation, such as communication, remote spawning, access to library, etc.

SML already provides a very good exception-handling mechanism. Since most primitive operations for concurrent/distributed computing are designed to be values and thus can be used in expressions, the exception handling mechanism for SML expressions carries over to FACILE nicely. However, this still leaves the problem of how to deal with uncaught exceptions in a process. The SML way of catching an uncaught exception with a universal exception handler that prints a message in the top-level loop does not work well when many processes are executing concurrently.

One solution could be to propagate uncaught exceptions to the "parent" process. However, this is problematic since it will require a change to the semantics of FACILE processes, since they would have to have a parent-child relation affiliated with them.

We have opted for a simple, but crude, approach that avoids tangling with semantics of processes. Exceptions raised inside a process will not propagate to other processes. In fact, the expression being evaluated in an individual process may be thought of as surrounded by a default handler `handle _ => script(terminate)`. Thus, an uncaught exception in the expression being evaluated will result in the process terminating. This essentially puts all responsibility on the shoulders of the one who constructs the script, since the user can only start the script by spawning it and accept whatever it does and not influence the behavior of a script.

An alternative approach, where each locally spawned process implicitly inherits the exception handlers of its creator, has been experimented with in early implementations of FACILE. In this way, one can specify an exception handler for a process when the process is spawned. Although not really solving the aforementioned problem, this approach does provide a lot of flexibility for the programmers to manage it. One significant advantage of this approach is that it provides better support for the script abstraction, since it essentially gives the power of wrapping an exception handler around any given script without the need for the knowledge of how the script is constructed. Unfortunately, there are quite a few semantic and pragmatic problems associated with such an approach. First of all, this strategy renders a rather special semantics to `spawn`, which can no longer be considered as a normal function since the wrapping of exception handlers becomes implicit and depends on the exception handlers in the scope of the spawn construct. There is also the question of how to handle the situation where the exception handler raises another exception. The problem is whether it should be caught by the outer scope handler, and when should that stop. On the typing issue the question is what the type of the exception handler should be. Clearly it needs to conform to the expression it covers, but it should also conform to the type of the script, i.e., be of type `src`. More seriously, on the pragmatic side, programmers writing any exception handler now have to worry about whether it would fit all spawned processes besides the expression itself. This seems to turn the relatively simple exception-handling mechanism of SML into a mind-boggling one.

A more explicit alternative to exception handling for process scripts could be provided by adding a primitive operator for explicitly adding an exception handler to the FACILE language:

```
fun handling : scr * (exn -> scr) -> scr.
```

In fact, this is just one example of a whole class of operators that could be introduced on process scripts (or values of type `scr`). Other operators include preemption operators, as found in LOTOS; or restriction and renaming operators, as found in CCS and other process calculi. The main motivation for not including them in FACILE is that the effect of such operators can be programmed using combinations of the other primitives in the language, and they may thus be considered derived operators or syntactic sugar. However, operators on process scripts become very important when programming open systems based on the mobile agent principle, since agents are just process scripts. Thus, the recipient no longer has access to the internals of the agent, since somebody else might have programmed it. Currently the only thing that can be done with a received agent is to spawn it and interact with it. Clearly the agent can not do anything really harmful due to static scoping and type safety, but it may be able to "steal" clock cycles and use memory as well as network bandwidth by remote communications. Thus, operators that can be wrapped around a process script may be very useful for constraining the behavior of agents.

5.3   Language Features

In the previous section we have described the design principles underpinning the development of FACILE. In this section we go into more detail with the language features. Sequential programming in FACILE resembles programming in SML (in particular it resembles programming in SML/NJ version 0.93). Hence we will not review SML-specific features. Instead we focus on distributed programming, looking at topics related to concurrency, distribution, modules, and dynamic connectivity.

5.3.1   Concurrency

First we describe the concurrency part of the FACILE language; processes, channels, guards, and time.

In FACILE, a process executes essentially by evaluating expressions. The behavior of a process is syntactically described by a behavior expression. Behavior expressions are a distinct syntactic category in FACILE. They are not expressions, and thus do not denote values or possess types. They cannot be directly bound to an identifier.

The simplest behavior expression is `terminate`, which can be thought of as describing a process that does nothing. The other basic form of behavior expression is `activate exp`, where `exp` must be of type `src`. This expression describes a process that will first evaluate `exp` to a process script, and then behave as specified by the script. To treat behaviors as values, FACILE provides a construct called `script`, which can convert a behavior expression into a value. For any behavior expression b, $script(b)$ is a value of type `scr`. As opposed to the `script` construct, the `activate` construct provides an avenue from expressions to behavior expressions. Since we can easily make a value out of any given behavior expression using `script`, `activate` enables us to construct a behavior expression from a simpler one by going through the expression world. Combining this construct with recursive functions, it is also possible to construct recursive behavior expressions using `activate`.

Process scripts are (first-class) values; they can be used just like any other FACILE value. The only primitive function operating on scripts is spawn:

```
val spawn : src -> unit,
```

which when applied to a script will create a new process with the behavior described by the script and start the execution of the process. After the process is created, the function invocation returns a unit value and the evaluation continues.

The example below shows the use of a recursive function in FACILE:

```
- proc fibo_serv (inc,outc) =
  let
      fun fib n = if (n=0) orelse (n=1)
                      then 1
                      else fib(n-1) + fib(n-2)
  in
      send(outc,fib(receive inc)) ;
      activate fibo_serv(inc,outc)
  end ;
val fibo_serv = fn : int channel * int channel -> scr
- val in_ch : int channel = channel() ;
val in_ch = channel : int channel
- val out_ch : int channel = channel() ;
```

```
val out_ch = channel : int channel
- spawn(fibo_serv(in_ch,out_ch)) ;
val it = () : unit
- send(in_ch,8) ;
val it = () : unit
- receive out_ch ;
val it = 34 : int
```

There are three language constructs in FACILE that allow composition of behavior expressions to make a more complex behavior expression. One such construct is the semicolon, which is a sequencing operator just as in the expression world, hence as in SML. For any behavior expression b,

     exp ; b

is a behavior expression that describes a process that first evaluates exp then behaves like b. The second construct is the let construct

    let *decs* in b end.

The intended meaning is again similar to the let construct for expressions, again as in SML. The declarations are processed and used in the enhanced environment for the behavior expression b. These two constructs are provided only for the convenience of programming, and can be expressed using activate. For example,

     exp ; b

can be written as

    activate (*exp* ; script(b)),

and

    let *decs* in b end

can be written as

    activate let *decs* in script(b) end.

A behavior expression can also describe the behavior of two or more concurrent processes. The concurrent composition construct, ||, takes two behavior expressions and makes one behavior expression that indicates that they are to be executed concurrently. This extends to more than two behavior expressions in an obvious way. In general, we can write a concurrent composition of a sequence of behavior expressions separated by ||, in the form

$$b_1 \; || \; \ldots \; || \; b_n,$$

where $b_1, \ldots, b_n$ are behavior expressions. Again, concurrent composition can be expressed using `activate`. For example,

$$b_1 \; || \; b_2$$

can be written as

```
activate (spawn(script(b_1)) ; script(b_2)).
```

Another language construct is available for making abstraction of process scripts. The `proc` keyword provides a convenient notation for defining process abstraction. It is used in the same way as the `fun` keyword, except that the body is a behavior expression instead of an expression. The `proc` construct actually defines functions, just as the `fun` construct does, which, when fully applied, always yield scripts. Thus the definition

```
proc f pats = b
```

is equivalent to

```
fun f pats = script(b).
```

Although these keywords may be viewed as syntactic sugar, they are important for the touch and feel of the language, giving the programmer constructs to express intentions in terms of process structures.

FACILE processes interact with each other by communicating values over typed channels. Communications in FACILE are two-party, hand-shake communications with one value exchanged. That is, there are exactly two different processes, one sender and one receiver, involved to make a communication happen, i.e., two processes synchronize when communication occurs. Therefore, a process will block in an attempt to communicate until there is another process ready to participate in a communication. When two processes synchronize, a value is transmitted from the sender to the receiver.

FACILE channels are typed in the sense that all values communicated over a channel must be of the same type. This ensures that the receiver always knows the type of the values it receives without looking at the values, and thus makes the static type checking over communication possible. However, for any type, a channel can be created to communicate values of that particular type. As a consequence, any value in FACILE can be used in communication, including scripts, channels, guards, and nodes.

In FACILE, channels are first-class values of type t `channel` for some type t. The type constructor `channel` is of unary arity, the type parameter t indicates the type of values that can be communicated over that channel. A fresh channel is created each time the function

```
val channel : unit -> '1a channel
```

is called. As one might expect, channels are stateful just like the reference objects. Since the current implementation of FACILE is obtained by extending SML, in particular modifying the run-time system of SML/NJ and tailoring its front-end to FACILE, it was quite natural to adapt MacQueen's weak polymorphic typing scheme [73, 63] for the FACILE implementation (we say more about typing of channels in the conclusion). Also note that channel is not an equality type, thus = and <> cannot be used for comparing channels. However, a function equal is provided to test whether two channels are identical.

For communication, two primitive functions are provided:

```
val send : 'a channel * 'a -> unit,
val receive : 'a channel -> 'a.
```

The function send takes a channel and a value of a type that can be sent on the channel and returns the unit value. Before it returns the unit value, a call to send has the external effect of sending the given value on the specified channel. The send function call does not return until there is another process willing to receive the value on the channel. If there is no receiver process, the call to send blocks until there is one. The function receive takes a channel and returns some value, i.e., the value that is sent by another process on that channel. The function call returns only when another process sends a value on the channel. The value returned can be any value of the type that is transmittable on the particular channel.

Since channels are values, and send and receive are merely functions, anyone who has access to them can initiate communications. Therefore, channels in FACILE can potentially support multiparty, two-way communication. This is a very powerful and flexible paradigm for communication, but it also makes outsiders who have access to the channel capable of interfering with the communication protocol. Obviously, limiting access to only those parties that adhere to a communication protocol is vital for guaranteeing correctness of the protocol. In the view of such need, the fact that channels and communication primitives are first-class values becomes very convenient. Being first-class values, accessibility of channels can be governed by the usual scoping rules of FACILE. Using function closures, one can also limit the use of a channel to be send-only or receive-only. Furthermore, an entire communication protocol can be represented as a function to ensure that users always adhere to the protocol; or, a channel can be created at run-time and communicated over another channel to ensure the privacy of communication.

It is often the case that a process must be ready to communicate with one of several possible processes, or more precisely, communicate over one of several possible channels and consequently select one of several alternative courses of action. In FACILE, one such operator, alternative, is supported that bases its selection on readiness for synchronization upon channel communication. This is captured in FACILE with the concept of guards, making `alternative` an operator that chooses one among a list of guards based on the above criteria.

FACILE provides two basic forms of synchronization, sending and receiving. Thus, there are two forms for constructing guards. One corresponds to `send` and the other to `receive`.

```
val sendguard : 'a channel *  'a * (unit -> 'b) -> 'b guard,
val recvguard : 'a channel * ('a -> 'b) -> 'b guard.
```

These are normal functions, where all arguments are evaluated using the usual strict, call-by-value discipline of SML, and the function is invoked and returns a guard value. Generally speaking, a guard value indicates the requirement for synchronization and the computation to be performed upon synchronization. We can also wrap a function around a guard to compose the computation using

```
val wrapguard : 'a guard * ('a -> 'b) -> 'b guard.
```

The resulting guard has the same requirement for synchronization and the same computation as the original guard but with an additional step to apply the function on the result of that computation.

The primitive type constructor `guard` is a unary type constructor, with a type parameter to indicate the resulting type of continuing computation. Containing the encoding of a computation, `guard` obviously is not an equality type.

The function

```
val alternative : 'a guard list -> 'a
```

takes a list of guard values and selects one nondeterministically. As mentioned before, the selection is driven by the availability of synchronizations. If none of the guards can synchronize immediately, the process calling `alternative` will be blocked until at least one of the guards can synchronize.

Note that actions with possible external effects (e.g., communication or process creation) performed during the evaluation of a list element to a guard value do not trigger the selection of that alternative. This is again following the usual strict, call-by-value discipline of SML. The argument to `alternative` is first evaluated to a list of guards; then `alternative` is invoked and the selection of one guard is done afterwards. In its simplest and perhaps safest usage, i.e., without external effects during guard evaluation, `alternative` can be viewed as a "guarded choice" operator. One can certainly argue that the semantics allows possibly undesirable "side effects" during the evaluation of guards. However, these external effects may play a useful role in certain situations. The FACILE programmer should consider the `alternative` operator to be a guarded choice over guard values, and consider the external effects obtained while evaluating the guards to be part of the preceding sequential evaluation performed by the process.

FACILE processes attempting communications on channels for which there are no communication partners will be blocked. This is well known from operating systems where processes may be blocked on communication. Most operating systems provide mechanisms for unblocking processes. Instead of providing mechanisms that directly unblock processes, the programmer may safeguard the application by introducing some timeout mechanism on communications. In the following we describe the time-dependent constructs of FACILE.

Time in FACILE is represented simply by an integer for counting the number of time units. The time unit currently used is one hundred milliseconds.

The most general primitive function is

```
val delay : int -> unit
```

The effect of calling `delay` is to suspend the execution of the invoking process for (at least) the number of time units specified by the integer argument. The actual delay duration depends on the accuracy of the machine clock as well as the operating system.

Combining the notion of time with that of synchronization, we get the time-out mechanism for all operations that involve synchronization and thus can potentially be blocked. FACILE provides three primitive functions:

```
val timeout_send : 'a channel * 'a * int -> unit,
val timeout_receive : 'a channel * int -> 'a,
val timeout_alternative : 'a guard list * int -> 'a,
exception EXN_TIMEOUT
```

corresponding to `send`, `receive`, and `alternative`, respectively. When these functions are used, and the specified synchronization does not happen within the specified time limit, then the exception `EXN_TIMEOUT` is raised and the invoking process continues.

The notion of time in the FACILE Antigua Release is rather crude. In future releases we expect to have a more abstract notion of time.

5.3.2 Distributed Programming

In this section we describe the distributed part of the FACILE language: nodes and mutable objects.

A typical FACILE application consists of a collection of nodes. The notion of node corresponds to that of a virtual processor with an address space. Each node hosts a number of FACILE processes that execute concurrently. Moreover, during its lifetime, every FACILE process must execute on a single node that is determined when the process is created. Similarly for the channels. It is the choice of the programmer whether to place new processes (or channels) at specific nodes or to place them locally. The model of concurrency remains essentially unchanged, but the communication model needs a slight adjustment due to potential network failures.

The nodes may be dynamically created and placed on a specific workstation on a network. This is done by calling the function `node` with a character-string argument identifying a host name. The function attempts to create a new node on the specified host. If successful, it returns a node identifier, a value of type `nodeid`, that corresponds to the created node. Otherwise, the function invocation raises the exception `EXN_NODE_OUTCOME`. When this exception is raised it may or may not be the case that a Unix process has been created, and it may thus be necessary to check at the Unix level and take appropriate action. For the node created at the Unix level, there is also a corresponding node identifier. Thus, every node has a distinct corresponding node identifier. The function `current_node` can be used to obtain the node identifier corresponding to the node that hosts the invoking process. In addition, there is a special node identifier that does not correspond to any specific node but denotes the concept of "local node," i.e., the node on which the process using this node identifier is executing. This special node identifier can be retrieved by calling the function `this_node`.

For the normal node identifiers (returned by `node` or `current_node`), all built-in functions that use node identifiers will interpret them as the corresponding nodes. In contrast, the special node identifier (returned by `this_node`) is always interpreted as the node that hosts the process that uses it. In either case, we say that the node is denoted by the node identifier. The difference between `current_node` and `this_node` is not apparent unless the values returned are transmitted to another node. In that case, the value from `current_node` will denote the node on which `current_node` was executed, while the value from `this_node` will denote the local node.

Note that `nodeid` is not an equality type. However, a function `equal` is provided that when given two node identifiers will compare the nodes they denote. Note that it compares the denotation of the node identifiers rather than the node identifiers themselves.

Given a node identifier, the following functions,

```
val r_spawn : nodeid * scr -> unit,
val r_channel : nodeid -> '1a channel,
```

can be used to create a new process or channel on the node denoted by the node identifier. Except for the location aspect, they have the same semantics as the `spawn` and the `channel` functions. Due to the potential network failure (or node killed), the creation of a process or a channel on a remote node may not succeed. In that case, the exception `EXN_NODE_OUTCOME` is raised.

Three other functions on node identifiers are provided for use in constructing distributed applications. They all operate on the node denoted by the input node identifier:

```
val host_name : nodeid -> string,
val ping : nodeid -> bool,
val kill : nodeid -> unit.
```

The identifier host_name gives the string name for the host machine where the node is located; ping returns true if the machine where the node is located is up and running and it returns false otherwise; kill forces the node to exit. All processes executing on that node will be terminated. This function may be used to simulate a machine failure. This can be very useful when testing the fault tolerance of a distributed application.

In FACILE, the semantics for communication does not change when used for distributed programming except for the aspects of performance and failure. In general, local communication within a node is more efficient. This is why sometimes r_channel is useful to place a channel on a specific node for more efficient communications.

As mentioned earlier, the physical reality of distributed programming requires that we adjust the communication model slightly. Failures may occur when FACILE processes attempt communications over channels that are shared by processes on different nodes. These failures are reported via the exceptions EXN_CHANNEL_UNAVAIL, EXN_OUTCOME, and EXN_VALUE. These exceptions are raised by the run-time system to the invoker of the corresponding (failed) communication primitive. EXN_CHANNEL_UNAVAIL is raised if the node where the channel is located is unreachable; EXN_OUTCOME is raised if a failure occurs during the protocol implementing FACILE's handshake communication; and EXN_VALUE is raised if a message is too large to be transmitted.

If a failure is detected in trying to close any branch of an alternative expression, the alternative expression raises the exception to the invoking process even if some other branch could, or could eventually, have succeeded.

The time-out variants of send, receive, and alternative may raise the same exceptions as the base communication primitives as well as the exception EXN_TIMEOUT. Time-outs might be delayed while communications are being attempted and the communication exceptions are reported in preference to the time-out exception.

Failure detection is performed on a per-communication basis. Thus it is possible for a retry communication attempt to succeed after the previous attempt raised an exception (e.g., if a partitioned network is repaired).

FACILE retains the mutable objects of SML, i.e., references and arrays, to support the imperative programming paradigm. Since they are first-class values, they can be shared by many processes just like any other values in FACILE.

Naturally, in the context of concurrent execution, there is the usual problem of multiple observers and mutators. In FACILE it is the responsibility of the designers and programmers to ensure appropriate access control of shared mutable objects. The communication/synchronization primitives in

FACILE can be used for this purpose.

Within a single node, i.e., one address space, this would be enough. However, in a distributed environment, there are additional issues of latency, failure, and in general getting a coherent view of the state. To avoid the complication of these issues and the potentially high performance penalty of using reference and array, FACILE uses copy semantics for mutable objects, i.e. they are copied when communicated across the node boundary. (Please refer to Section 5.2.6 for a more detailed discussion). Therefore, whenever a mutable object is transmitted to a remote node (by whatever means), a new and independent object with the same state will appear on the remote node. Afterwards, the two objects can change state independently and are essentially two unrelated objects. Note that the creation of copies is done per transmission, hence sharing of components within a compound object will be preserved. For example, supposing r is a reference, sending (r,r) via a channel to a remote node will result in a pair that has the same reference object in both components with an initial state being the same as the initial state of r. On the other hand, if we send r twice via a channel and construct a pair at the receiving end with the two received values, the result will be a pair with two different objects.

5.3.3 Modules in FACILE

FACILE inherits and conservatively extends SML's sophisticated modules facility for "programming in the large." Modularization lets the programmer organise a program in terms of smaller units, each with a well-defined interface. These units, or modules, may be manipulated relatively independently of one another. The modules facility also provides mechanisms for connecting different modules together, for specifying dependence of modules on others, and for specifying the interfaces of modules. Thus the facility supports the incremental construction and the maintenance of large programs as a collection of interdependent program units.

FACILE's modules facility consists of (a) Constructs present in SML's module language; (b) Certain extensions to SML's modules language that have been proposed by various researchers [176, 9]. These have been included in FACILE to experiment with them, study their usefulness, and better understand their semantics. We mention some of these features below; (c) Features for dynamically linking independent programs by exchanging modules [47].

We briefly summarize SML's module facility. Structures, in both FACILE and SML, are basically heterogeneous reified environments, e.g., sequences of type and value declarations, encapsulated as program units. The declarations of types in a structure may employ any types and type constructors supported in FACILE, e.g., int, list, channel, and scr, and value declarations may be in terms of any permitted FACILE expression. In particular, a value declaration may entail the creation of processes and interprocess communication. Structures may also be nested as substructures of other structures.

The example below shows that processes may be defined and created in a module and also that a process may use module components during its execution:

```
- structure S =
  struct
     type int_chan = int channel
     structure B = struct
                        proc sender (c,i) =
                           (
                            send(c,i) ;
                            activate sender(c,i+1)
                           )
                    end
     val rd_ch : int_chan = channel()
     val r = (
                spawn(B.sender(rd_ch,7)) ;
                receive rd_ch
              )
  end ;
  structure S :
    sig
      structure B : ...
      type int_chan
      val r : int
      val rd_ch : int_chan
    end
- S.r ;
val it = 7 : int
- receive S.rd_ch ;
val it = 8 : int
```

A structure is not a first-class value and thus may not be the argument or result of a function. However, the modules language supports parameterized modules, called functors, that are based on the idea of functional abstraction. Functors are used to "glue together" different structures to form a complex program.

A signature is a (static) description of an interface to a structure, specifying which named components are visible, together with the specifications of these components, e.g., the types of value components, the interfaces for substructures, and whether an identifier is used as a type name. FACILE inherits SML's ability to infer the signature of a given structure. A key notion is that of a structure S matching a given signature Σ, i.e., that the inferred signature of the structure S is consistent with the specification expressed by signature Σ. An example of a signature that matches the above structure is

```
signature SIGMA = sig
                    type int_chan
                    val r : int
                    val rd_ch : int_chan
                  end
```

One may use a signature to coerce a structure, limiting the accessible part of the structure to only those components mentioned in the given signature. For example, coercing S using signature SIGMA renders the substructure B of S inaccessible.

Coercion by signatures provides only a limited form of information hiding, but does not support abstraction from representational forms. For instance, the fact that type int_chan is int channel may be evident outside the structure S. We use an abstraction, rather than a structure, to suppress all information about a structure other than what is specified by a given signature.

Another important mechanism by which different structures can interact is sharing. Sharing specifications declared in a signature may be used to enforce that two separate modules employ the same implementation for what are intended as common components.

FACILE being a research vehicle, the Antigua Release of the language contains several experimental features that loosen various restrictions on signatures, functors, and structures imposed in the definition of SML. Some of these experimental features are also found in recent releases of SML/NJ. The most significant of these features are

- Declaration of type abbreviations in signatures, which lets us specify that a particular type identifier in the signature is an abbreviation for another type;

- Functor signatures, which allow us to provide specifications of parameterized modules independent of their definitions (these are the functor-level analogues of signatures for structures);

- "Module-class signatures," which permit signature declarations inside structures. This feature lets us group together a set of signature declarations, and to locally constrain a substructure. It also allows signatures to appear as parameters of functors.

- Higher-order functors, which allows functors to be arguments and results of functors. This extension yields a more uniform treatment of parameterized and nonparameterized modules. Together with module-class signatures, we have a way of making functors explicitly polymorphic.

We refer the reader to [174] for some simple examples of the use of these experimental features.

The integration of communication and concurrency primitives into SML has only a minor impact on the module-level language, i.e., that we have a few additional types and type constructors available, and that a richer language of expressions may be used. Changes to the formal semantics are restricted to those arising from the changes in the expression language semantics. One reason for this is that in SML the core expression language and the modules language are not tightly coupled, and there are few "points of contact" between the two layers.

The major reason, however, is that the notion of modules is related to how we organize the internal structure of a program when we create and elaborate it, rather than a notion dealing with the dynamics of a program during execution.

However, there is an experimental feature in FACILE where the notions of structures, functors, and signatures are employed in the dynamic connection of two independently created distributed applications. This feature, the subject of the next section, entails modifications to the module-level language and integration with a suitable model of communication and concurrency.

5.3.4 Dynamic Connectivity

In a concurrent programming language all the processes launched by an application come from a single environment in which the application has been compiled. The process that was initialized when starting the application is the common ancestor shared by all processes. Because of this common ancestor it is easy to establish communication links between two processes. Communication channels can be initiated at this level and can be passed along until they reach both processes (communication partners). Channels are typed upon declaration, and because both processes will see the same specification of the channel objects, they will have to send and receive compatible values, hence avoiding safety problems.

In a distributed environment these assumptions are no longer guaranteed since applications are independent programs. Without a common ancestor the two processes ready to communicate have to post to the network information about their communication potentials. One of the applications creates a channel and publishes it on the network by giving it a name (the supplying mechanism described below), and the other application retrieves this information from the net by searching for a channel of the corresponding name (the demanding mechanism described below). Of course this only works if the applications have agreed on the type of the channel to be exchanged.

The remainder of this section describes FACILE constructs that allow for type safe dynamic connectivity between applications that may have been created and compiled independently. The constructs described here are particularly useful for connecting FACILE nodes started from the Unix level, i.e., nodes not having a common ancestor. The constructs can also be used for dynamically obtaining new services at run-time. The constructs and their implementation are rather experimental in nature.

As discussed earlier, the FACILE module system is a conservative extension of the SML module system [97]. The extension discussed in this section contains constructs for storing and retrieving modules (structures) from repositories on a network. The mechanism may be seen as an extension of the import/export mechanism described in [67]. Currently the service simulates object persistence by storing modules in Unix files.

The mechanism is based on the principle that applications may store modules by *supplying* them to servers on the network. These modules may be retrieved by other applications by *demanding* them based on an interface specification (a signature). Since signatures are rather weak specifications, several modules may match the same signature. To solve conflicts between modules matching the same interface a notion of *library* is introduced. Servers may contain several libraries, and modules matching the same interface can be stored in different libraries.

A library is a logical collection in which any number of modules can be stored (only subject to operating-system limitations on the number of files a user may create). Each library is attached to a module server, and a library is identified by a FACILE value of the primitive type `library`. New libraries can be created at any point of execution by any FACILE process. Furthermore, there is a mechanism for supplying and demanding signatures from a server on the network.

The structure `Connect` with the following signature forms the interface to the structure and signature servers and libraries:

```
signature CONNECT =
sig
  type library
  val new_library : string -> library
  val initial_library : string -> library
  val forget : string -> unit
  val structure_server : string -> unit
  val signature_server : unit -> unit
end
```

The function `structure_server` creates a new structure server. The function takes a string argument that serves as an identifier for the structure server. The string argument identifies a subdirectory in the current directory. The directory is used to store the physical representation of structures. This directory must have been created by the user before the call to `structure_server`.

A structure server is implemented as a special FACILE process. When the function `structure_server` is executed it will create a FACILE process on the node where the function is executed. Currently there is no way of stopping a structure server from within an application, but if a node dies all the servers created on this node will also die.

A structure server may be unreachable due to network failure or because the node on which it is running has been killed. On restarts, structure servers reinitialize their states from their persistent directory, making the libraries created in previous server incarnations available to their clients together with the structures registered previously.

Each structure server has an initial library that can be obtained by calling `initial_library` with a string argument identifying the server (i.e., the name of the structure server directory). Similarly, new libraries can be created by calling `new_library` with a string argument that identifies the structure server. If the structure server is unreachable these functions will raise the exception `EXN_CONNECT`.

Supplying (storing) a structure is an operation at the module declaration level, i.e., at the same level as declaring structures and signatures. It has the following syntactic form:

$$sdec ::= \texttt{supplying}\ exp\ \texttt{with}\ str,$$

where *exp* must evaluate to a value of type `library`.

Applications can retrieve modules from libraries by specifying a signature. The last module stored matching the interface is sent back after coercion by the signature. Since demanding a structure from a library returns a structure, demanding is a construct at the structure level. It has the following syntax:

$$str ::= \texttt{demanding}\ exp\ \texttt{with}\ sign,$$

where *exp* must evaluate to a value of type `library`.

If there is no structure matching the signature in a library when the command is executed, the execution will block until some other application supplies a matching structure. The construct `demanding exp with sign` will fail if the server holding the library identified by *exp* is not running. Failure of `demanding` is reported in the top-level loop.

Figure 5.2 demonstrates the above example from the top-level loop of two machines. In this example `host A` and `host B` are two different machines. First, `host A` starts a structure server identified as `"server"`. Then a string channel is created and a signature is specified. This signature matches the structure s, which is declared to contain a value of type `string channel`; in fact it will be the channel ch created just before. Then this structure is supplied to the structure server and the string `"hello"` is sent on the channel ch.

Then `host B` starts by demanding a structure from the initial library of the structure server identified by `"server"`. It will match the structure supplied by `host A`, and the obtained channel `s.ch` may now be used in

```
(* host A *)
- open Connect ;
open Connect
val new_library = fn : string -> library
val initial_library = fn : string -> library
val forget = fn : string -> unit
val structure_server = fn : string -> unit
val signature_server = fn : unit -> unit
- structure_server "server" ;
val it = () : unit
- val l = initial_library "server" ;
val l = - : library
- val ch : string channel = channel() ;
val ch = channel : string channel
- signature S =
  sig
      val ch : string channel
  end ;
signature S = sig val ch : string channel end
- structure S : S =
  struct
      val ch = ch
  end ;
structure S : S
- supplying l with S ;
supplying <str>
- send(ch,"hello") ;
val it = () : unit
(* host B *)
- open Connect ;
open Connect
val new_library = fn : string -> library
val initial_library = fn : string -> library
val forget = fn : string -> unit
val structure_server = fn : string -> unit
val signature_server = fn : unit -> unit
- val l = initial_library "server" ;
val l = - : library
- structure S = demanding l with
                   sig
                       val ch : string channel
                   end ;
structure S : sig val ch : string channel end
- receive S.ch ;
val it = "hello" : string
```

FIGURE 5.2. Dynamic connectivity

local computations. In this example a communication over channel ch will take place and the string "hello" will be received on host B.

The above example shows how it is possible to create a channel on one node and "export" it to another node. This mechanism may be used for bootstrapping communication between independently created nodes.

Another use of the supplying and demanding mechanism is in exchanging user-defined data types. This is particularly important since in SML and thus in FACILE data types are generative (i.e., two identical datatype definitions produce different types, even though they have the same name).

Structures can contain user-defined data types; hence an application does not always know the specific signature for a supplied structure. For this purpose there is a mechanism for creating a signature server that can be used to exchange signatures between independently created applications. The signature server is launched by executing the function signature_server on a unit argument. Signatures are stored under names (identifiers) and retrieved on the basis of lookup for a signature stored under some identifier. Supplying (storing) and demanding (retrieving) a signature has the following syntactic form:

supplying signature *sign* as *id*,

demanding signature *id*.

Since there is only one signature server per FACILE system, supplying a signature with a key (an identifier) that already exists will overwrite the previously supplied signature. Thus, demanding a signature will return the last supplied signature under the requested key. If no signature is stored under the requested key, demanding signature will block until a signature gets supplied under the requested key.

Signatures stored on the signature server are not persistent. When the signature server exits, all stored signatures are forgotten. A signature server may exit because the node from which it was created dies. Finally, note that supplying signature and demanding signature will fail if the signature server is not running.

The above operations have been presented at the top-level loop. Thus, one may get the impression that dynamic connectivity only happens at link time since there is a clear separation between the module-level language and the core language in SML. However, this separation has been relaxed in the FACILE Antigua Release. Here, structures may be declared in local declarations, for example inside functions, and so we allow expressions of the form

let structure *ident* = *str* in *exp* end.

Using structure expressions declared inside the let construct it is possible to retrieve new structures at run-time, i.e.,

```
fun get_new_string_ch () =
let
   val l = initial_library "server"
   structure S = demanding l with
                   sig
                       val ch : string channel
                   end
in
   S.ch
end
```

This piece of FACILE code queries the initial library of the structure server "server" for a module matching the signature discussed above and thus dynamically obtains the most recently supplied structure matching the signature. In the above example a structure containing a string channel is obtained. This could be very useful for fault-tolerant programming since a channel may be unreachable due to network failures, but new connections may be established through the above mechanism.

If demanding in a let construct fails, the exception EXN_CONNECT will be raised. This exception can be handled by an exception handler surrounding the let construct.

Currently there is a syntactic restriction that forbids supplying structures in the let construct. Thus, modules can only be supplied at the module level (i.e., at link-time), making it impossible to supply new modules at run-time. The distinction between link-time and run-time is not so apparent in the interactive environment. However, the syntactic restriction ensures that modules can only be supplied at the top level in the interactive environment.

In general it should be mentioned that demanding and supplying structures give more computational power to the module language. (The interested reader may have fun constructing a recursive functor using a combination of demanding, supplying, and higher-order functors.) The module language may be viewed as a strongly typed λ-calculus enriched with broadcast communication. An interesting future development would be to add more computational power, such as branching, exception handling, and time-dependent computations, to allow more control of the configurations of systems. A related issue is that there is no garbage-collection procedure for structures supplied to structure servers. The FACILE Antigua Release provides a function forget that may be used to erase supplied structures.

The function forget has the following type:

```
val forget = fn : string -> unit.
```

Calling the forget function has the effect of erasing all structures supplied from the node where the forget function is called. Future structure demandings might block.

5.4   Implementation

In the previous sections we have described the major design philosophy of FACILE, and we have looked at the language features that go beyond those of SML.

We devote this section to describing some details about and strategies used in the implementation of the FACILE Antigua Release. Due to the research nature of our work on FACILE, we are well aware that some of the described implementation choices are not optimal, but as they stand they are part of the FACILE Antigua Release. Some of these implementation details are likely to be revised in future releases of FACILE. In this section a brief overview of how a FACILE system maps onto a network of workstations is given. Furthermore, support for dynamically connecting multiple applications is discussed.

As already mentioned the implementation utilizes a modified version of SML/NJ. In summary, SML/NJ consists of an interactive environment, a native code SML compiler whose back-end is based on continuation passing style (CPS), and an associated run-time system[10]. The run-time system provides a single heap for tagged allocation of all structured run-time values including argument records, function closures, and continuations. It also provides an operating system interface for SML and support for signal handling.

5.4.1   Nodes

A typical FACILE application consists of a collection of nodes, possibly situated on different networked workstations (see Figure 5.1 in Section 5.1). Within a node, FACILE processes are implemented in a shared virtual address space and execute concurrently under the control of a preemptive scheduler. A node constitutes a notion of a virtual processor and a shared address space. It could in principle map directly onto a physical processor or could be implemented utilizing such operating-system constructs as Unix processes or Mach [3] tasks. In the FACILE Antigua Release, a FACILE node is implemented by a modified SML/NJ system running in a Unix process.

Nodes may be created dynamically, and a node may or may not run a top-level interactive loop. If it does, a FACILE process handles the interaction with the user. The user is thus viewed as incrementally providing an expression that is evaluated in that process. In particular, the user may define and create processes and channels or perform communications.

5.4.2   Concurrent Processes

The run-time system of SML/NJ has been augmented with a lightweight processes package used to preemptively multiplex the execution between the FACILE processes. Control is switched to the run-time system on each invocation of a concurrency primitive (communication, process creation, process termination, node creation), on preemption of currently executing processes, and on remote interaction such as the arrival of messages or transmission timeouts. The state of a process is defined by the set of machine registers in which roots for values in the heap are maintained (including the continuation of the process). This state is saved when control switches to the run-time system and restored on exit, possibly switching to another process. This is in contrast to stack-based implementations where both registers and the stack need to be swapped when control switches.

Within a FACILE system, processes have globally unique identifiers, which are outside the scope of a node's local garbage collector.

The implementation of the FACILE Antigua Release takes advantage of the CPS-based implementation of SML/NJ, especially its stackless nature. The approach differs from language-level, continuation-based concurrent extensions of SML/NJ (e.g., [150]). These use the *callcc* and *throw* operators to capture computations and perform queue manipulation in SML. There are several reasons for choosing to implement concurrency in the run-time system. This strategy ties the implementation more consistently with the management of the distribution aspects, in particular the internode communication protocols. It gives closer control over memory allocation and garbage collection, essential for transmission of run-time data structures between nodes. Furthermore, the implementation of the FACILE Antigua Release shows a significant increase in performance within a node compared to an early FACILE implementation that was based on language-level continuations, especially for programs requiring a large number of concurrent processes.

5.4.3 Channels

Channels are represented as data structures that manage two sets of communication requests for `send` and `receive` operations. Each process attempting to communicate over a channel leaves a request on it. The handshake across different nodes, which implements the FACILE synchronized communication scheme, is realized by a request/propose/transmit-value protocol between nodes, which in turn uses a simple datagram-based request/reply protocol. The situation is more complex for the implementation of the `alternative` operator, which allows a process to communicate with one out of several possible partners. To attempt a communication, a channel forwards a matching request pair to a potential sender process. The latter tentatively commits and notifies the proposed receiver, which decides whether or not to commit to the communication. The protocol uses back-off to break overlapping choices. An alternative protocol for FACILE choice, which is live-lock free but not free from starvation, is presented in [83].

A more detailed discussion on possible implementation strategies may be found in [93].

Like processes, channels and structures representing communication requests reside in the modified run-time system. Neither channels nor their communication requests contain SML/NJ values and are therefore outside the local garbage collector's scope. They are manipulated by the local run-time system on behalf of local processes and by code that performs protocol processing of messages from other nodes. Channel identifiers are passed to SML as opaque values. On creation, FACILE channels are assigned globally unique identifiers from a sparse global name space. In the FACILE Antigua implementation, this name space is partitioned among nodes, and channel structures reside in the node where they were created. Structures representing idle channels, that is, channels on which no process is attempting to communicate, may be reclaimed. The channel access mechanism utilizes location hints in channel identifiers and as a fall-back mechanism, a hash table that maps each channel identifier to its current structure.

5.4.4 *Transmission of Values*

Transmission of values is handled in the following way: Once a handshake is established, a value is copied from the environment of the sending process to the environment of the receiving process. When both processes are located at the same node, this is done by simply copying a pointer to the value. If processes are on different nodes, the run-time data structure to be transmitted is linearized directly into several noncontiguous buffers for internode transmission. Arbitrarily complex values of any FACILE type may be communicated, and large structures are transmitted in several fragments. The receiving node waits for all the pieces, and once the transmission is completed, the structure is deposited directly into the heap and relocated— since pointers must be converted from offsets within the message to heap locations.

The packaging of run-time data structures utilizes a modified version of code extracted from the SML/NJ garbage collector—the code that computes the transitive closure of a structure to generate a linearized copy. This strategy avoids the overhead of starting a full garbage collection.

In the FACILE Antigua Release, functions and processes are transmitted between nodes in their binary representation. For this reason, only networks of homogeneous processors are supported by the FACILE Antigua Release. In future versions of FACILE, functions and processes will be transmitted between heterogeneous machines in a machine-independent intermediate representation and compiled to native code on receipt [84]. When transmitting functions and processes, both of which are represented as closures, it is desirable to reduce the size of the closure that may be transmitted. For a functional language targeted at a single address space it is perfectly reasonable to optimize space usage, access to functions, and compilation time by letting functions share closures. Furthermore, since most functions need to access the pervasive environment, it is sensible to include extra pointers to it in closures. However, this conflicts with efficient transmission of functions and processes where small closure representations are desired. The problem is reduced by producing smaller closures when compiling and adding a phase to the marshalling of functions and processes that trims closures for pointers to "omnipresent values" such as functions in the pervasive environment. A satisfactory solution will inevitably involve dataflow analysis and a restructuring of the pervasive environment in order to (selectively) minimize the size of closures.

5.4.5   Object Sharing

When moving into a distributed setting, maintaining a semantically consistent view when objects are shared among various parts of the system becomes a very delicate issue. There are basically two categories of problems in FACILE—state consistency and object identity.

The potential problem with state consistency is quite apparent when it is possible to share stateful objects across node boundaries. Channels, libraries, and nodes are all addressed nicely in our distributed implementation since their states are centralized. However, the implementation of mutable objects that already exists in SML, such as reference and array, cannot be carried over to a distributed environment easily. Using the same implementation technique as for channels will impose an unbearable runtime cost for sequential computation and add more complications to the fault-tolerance issues. As described in Section 5.3.2, FACILE uses copy semantics for mutable objects instead when they are transmitted between nodes. This is a simple consequence of the strategy for marshalling values for transmission. By not treating mutable objects differently in marshalling, we have correctly implemented copy semantics. As mentioned in Section 5.2.6, this is one of the reasons why we opted for copy semantics.

On the other hand, the problem with object identity, although easier to deal with, is much more critical to the integrity of the semantics. In FACILE many objects have, in addition to the mutable ones, a sense of object identity, which is used for equality testing. For example, type constructors have identities for type checking, and similarly, data constructors for pattern matching. Since they contain information that is immutable after the objects are constructed, there is no work needed for maintaining state consistency. However, when these objects are communicated to other nodes, by whatever means, the identity needs to be preserved. The identities of data constructors are normally implemented as integer tags; hence the checking amounts to integer comparison, which poses no difficult problem.

However, exceptions are implemented using references in SML/NJ, and equality testing is done by comparing the memory addresses. Due to the fact that we have adapted copy semantics for references, exceptions will lose their identities when communicated across node boundaries. Imagine that an exception that is sent to another node through a channel and then comes back suddenly becomes a different exception. This could create a rather confusing situation for programmers. The solution we have taken is to use global identities for exceptions. In addition to the old reference to a string representing its name, there are two more components—the node number and a local counter. Testing equality of exceptions is now done by comparing both these numbers. Implementing exception handling this way adds a small performance penalty even when no distribution is involved. However, this is acceptable compared with the semantic chaos otherwise. For the type constructors, the same approach has been taken.

5.4.6 Node Server

Several FACILE applications may execute within a FACILE system. In the implementation of the FACILE Antigua Release, a system is controlled by a node server, which is implemented as a server process on some machine. Several systems may execute independently over a network under the control of different node servers.

Node servers perform two main functions. One is to manage a system's dynamically evolving collection of nodes and in particular, to guarantee the uniqueness of node identifiers within a system. The other is to provide a simple name service for channels that supports the dynamic connection of applications that were started independently. This service is only used internally for implementing the safe dynamic connection of independently started applications via the supplying and demanding constructs.

5.4.7 Demanding and Supplying of Modules

In this section we sketch the implementation of demanding and supplying modules (described in Section 5.3.4). Remember that applications may store modules by supplying them to servers on the network, and these modules may be retrieved by other applications by demanding them based on an interface specification (a signature).

Here we limit ourselves to describing the implementation of demanding, the description of supplying being very similar (for further details see [47]).

The signature specifying the interface is transformed into its internal representation. From this a template structure matching the signature is extracted. This process is called instantiation and is a regular part of module elaboration [48]. The structure obtained from this instantiation will be the result of demanding, and this structure is added to the static environment. The static representation is then enhanced with information about this particular instance of demanding. The enhanced representation is given as argument to the code that will perform the demanding during the execution of the program.

During execution of the program some actions are performed on the client demanding a particular module and the module server. First the demanding client releases the frozen static representation and related information. The structure, together with the adequate environment, is sent to the server. On the module server itself a number of things happen. First the signature of the template structure is specialized, i.e., the renaming environment is applied. (The server understands the internal representation of signatures). The server then searches in the corresponding library to see if the static representation of a module matches the requested signature. A match is assumed. Then the server extracts the necessary information about the structure, also matching template data with actual data in the matching (supplied) structure. Finally, the server sends the code of the supplied structure to the demanding client, which then adds the code to the dynamic environment. As the interface may restrict the contents of a supplied module, it might be necessary to reorganize the record representation of the module.

The final consequence of enhancing the module system is that the implementation of functors (functions operating on modules) has to be modified accordingly. If a functor contains either of the new commands, demanding or supplying, the template structure transmitted to the server is not the structure used during the elaboration of the functor, but the structure that can be computed when the functor is applied. The code of a functor takes a new argument comprising the list of static representations of the requested or sent objects. Upon elaboration of the functor application the static representations are extracted and given to the code of the functor.

Links between the server and the client nodes are regular FACILE channels. The code of the server reuses as much as possible of the SML/NJ compiler front-end.

5.5 Applications

The general objective of the FACILE project is to offer an effective solution for application developers by developing a formally well-founded programming language and environment that integrates a high-level and well understood model of concurrent computation and communication with desirable features of advanced, declarative programming languages and services normally found in middleware and traditional operating systems. The environment provides the ability to structure applications as compositions of autonomous communicating processes and to configure them to operate in a physically distributed environment without having to deal with low-level details that have to do with the underlying hardware or operating system. The combination of these characteristics has all the potential to render possible a leap of orders of magnitude in several dimensions—development costs, reliability, maintainability—with respect to programming languages and tools currently used by industry.

The focus of the FACILE project is on supporting the development of end-user applications rather than so-called system software, e.g., operating systems or generic platforms. The strategy is thus to develop implementation techniques that enable FACILE-based applications to operate on state-of-the-art hardware and software platforms. In fact, a significant amount of work is being devoted to enabling the FACILE implementation to operate across networked hardware and across possibly different operating systems. Interfaces have also been developed with foreign environments, thus allowing a system implemented in FACILE to be used as a component of a larger application that may include other components implemented, for example, in C, C++, Lisp, or Prolog.

In the following subsection we shall review three of the medium-scale applications developed by the FACILE project, and we shall discuss the use of the FACILE programming language in the applications.

5.5.1 Calumet

Calumet is a cooperative work application that supports teleconferencing [161]. This tool is a distributed, multiuser, multimedia application that implements distributed slide presentations. The Calumet paradigm mimics a colloquium in which a speaker presents a lecture to a collection of attendees, where no two people need be present in the same room. At any time during the lecture, the speaker may relinquish his or her right to talk to any attendee. The attendee may either continue in the role as speaker or the attendee may ask a question and return control to the original speaker. At any time, an attendee or the speaker may interactively annotate the visual presentation.

Underlying the Calumet user interface is an implementation partially built in FACILE. The software architecture takes advantage of FACILE's distribution features to produce highly structured, easily understandable code. This implementation provides advanced, reusable distribution features, e.g., fault tolerance, dynamic group membership, and reliable broadcast [159]. The Calumet software architecture comprises three components that demonstrate interoperability between code implemented in FACILE and C, respectively. The most significant component is the control program, implemented in FACILE, which orchestrates distributed interaction between the speaker and the attendees. The other components are a centralized name server and a graphical user interface. Calumet can display LaTeX style slides with graphics in TIFF format. Furthermore, telephone-quality voice interaction is supported.

Calumet differs from commercially available slide presentation software because the system integrates a sophisticated human interface with distribution. Currently, ECRC uses Calumet on its own local area network to provide in-house presentations, and it has been demonstrated on wide area networks at AT&T (Murray Hills, New Jersey) and between ECRC (Munich), CWI (Amsterdam), and CMU (Pittsburgh).

5.5.2 Collaborative Interior Design

Einrichten is a collaborative design system developed at ECRC. It is a demonstration of interactive graphics and real-time video for the purpose of interior design [6]. The system combines the use of a heterogeneous database system of graphical models, an augmented reality system, and the distribution of 3-D graphics events over a computer network. This application shows how improvements in computing and communication hardware can be combined with sophisticated software platforms to produce powerful results for end users.

The scenario for this application consists of an office manager who is working with an interior designer on the layout of a room. The office manager intends to order furniture for the room. On a computer monitor the pair see a picture of the room from the viewpoint of the camera. By interacting with various manufacturers over a network, they select furniture by querying databases using a graphical paradigm. The system provides descriptions and pictures of furniture that are available from the various manufacturers who have made models available in their databases. Pieces or groups of furniture that meet certain requirements such as color, manufacturer, or price may be requested. The users choose pieces from this "electronic catalog," and 3-D renderings of this furniture appear on the monitor along with the view of the room. The furniture is positioned using a 3-D mouse. Furniture can be deleted, added, and rearranged until the users are satisfied with the result; they view these pieces on the monitor as they would appear in the actual room. As they move the camera they can see the furnished room from different points of view.

The users can consult with colleagues at remote sites who are running the same system. Users at remote sites manipulate the same set of furniture using a static picture of the room that is being designed. Changes by one user are seen instantaneously by all of the others, and a distributed locking mechanism ensures that a piece of furniture is moved only by one user at a time. In this way groups of users at different sites can work together on the layout of the room. The group can record a list of furniture and the layout of that furniture in the room for future reference.

The 3-D graphics and augmented vision components of the system are built with GSP [5], a software platform that combines interactive 3-D graphics and computer vision technology to calibrate, align, and display 3-D models and real-time video.

The system also provides a means of distributing graphics events in a transparent manner. The communication of these events to multiple GSP applications, the locking, and the management of users joining and leaving the group are achieved through FACILE, which provides the tools for reliable connections, disconnections, and multicasts.

The FACILE environment includes group communication mechanisms and conferencing services that facilitate the construction of the distributed parts of shared, group-based applications. One of the aims of the environment is to enable developers, who are not necessarily experts in distributed systems, to construct a shared application. The environment provides more than simply communications, as would be provided for example by a message bus between the distributed parts. The environment may maintain its own representation of parts of the global state of the application based on the history of interactions that are forwarded from the various connected user interfaces.

The construction of an application is made easier by isolating an application's distribution concerns into a separate component (the conferencing component). This is especially true if an environment is available where the programmer can use generic services including lock-based concurrency control and conferencing functions. Special features can be implemented without much effort, such as transparent initialization of models as they connect to a distributed session to be supported.

Furthermore, the FACILE environment provides a reliable atomic broadcast protocol that facilitates the replicated maintenance of the application's global state using the state machine approach. The environment also provides a group abstraction that allows the transmission of ordered broadcasts between group members, which are processes that may join (and later leave) multiple application-level groups. Furthermore, a group also provides its members with notifications of the joining and leaving of other members, possibly due to a processor crash.

5.5.3   Mobile Service Agents

One emerging approach to providing the technology to go beyond the access methods to and services on the information highway of today is called agent-based computing. To study and demonstrate the potential of agent-based computing, researchers at ECRC have developed a technology called *Mobile Service Agents* (MSAs) [85, 171, 173].

MSAs are self-contained pieces of software that can move between computers on a network. Agents can serve as local representatives for remote services, provide interactive access to data they accompany, and carry out tasks for a mobile user temporarily disconnected from the network. Agents also provide a means for the set of software available to a user to change dynamically according to the user's needs and interests.

To implement the MSA architecture we have used the FACILE Antigua Release. FACILE is conceived to support the development of systems exhibiting a high degree of mobility, that is, systems that may evolve dynamically in terms of structure, communication, and computation capabilities.

Furthermore, we have constructed user interfaces using an advanced user interface tool kit (TK).

As proof of concept we have developed an application scenario to demonstrate MSA support for the mobile person and new ways of accessing information on the information highway. The demonstration is centered on a person from ECRC going to a meeting in Brussels. It shows which services ECRC and the meeting center in Brussels may provide. Connecting to "ECRC," you will get an "electronic front-door" giving you access to services offered by ECRC. You are going to a conference in Brussels so you want to prepare yourself by connecting to "Brussels" and accessing the services at the conference domain (via the global information highway). You may retrieve a map of the conference site and the agenda for the meeting. You may interact with the map of the conference site, even if you disconnect to travel from Munich to Brussels. When you arrive at the conference site you can plug in and get notified if the agenda has changed. You may see that an interesting presentation is taking place in a parallel session, so you start up the slide presentation system (Calumet) to attend remotely. Then you may start attending the Calumet presentation (which happens to be about FACILE and MSA and the potential of agent technology).

Mobile agents offer compelling advantages for constructing flexible and adaptable distributed systems, and their further development appears inevitable. Ten or even five years ago the Internet did not offer enough in the way of services to justify mobile agents. With the Internet's dramatic expansion in the last few years, it now appears that agents can provide a significant contribution as an underlying structuring technology.

There are still a number of technological developments needed for realizing the full potential of mobile agents. For example, solutions for mobile information processing have to be put in place for supporting physically mobile users on the Internet. Furthermore, the coverage of mobile networks, such as GSM, will have to be expanded and the data bandwidth should be increased if multimedia is to be supported. These developments are already in progress. Standardized access to user interfaces should be provided as part of the pervasive environment. This will lead to agents being able to assume the same access functions no matter what their location and the particularities of the underlying platform.

We expect to continue to expand the current application scenario by adding further services. An interesting extension is adding navigation capabilities, possibly based on a physical metaphor such as "walking down the street," and 3-D virtual reality when "meeting people or agents downtown." Building up abstractions that will make construction of mobile agents easy has been identified as a very important precondition for the success of the approach [116].

5.6   Conclusion

The FACILE system is a combination of language, compiler, and distributed systems technology, based on strong formal foundations, that places an emphasis on reliability of software, as well as flexible (and reliable) management of applications that need to evolve over time in terms of architecture, interfaces, and functionalities.

These requirements are common to different application domains, such as industrial automation, air traffic control, telecommunications, and financial markets. Extensive experiments and demonstrative applications show that FACILE will be an especially valid candidate for the implementation of the infrastructures that support applications in these domains. Several organizations in all these domains have expressed a strong interest in the FACILE technology. These include divisions of ECRC's shareholder companies—Bull, ICL, and Siemens—organisations that are customers of these companies, and other organizations.

In addition to FACILE being suitable for constructing reliable transactional or client/server systems, FACILE is particularly well suited for programming systems based on the emerging "mobile agents" principle. This is no coincidence. Since the FACILE model of concurrency is based on higher-order mobile processes (i.e., processes and communication links as first-class objects) this provides the necessary linguistic means for programming mobile agents. In fact, the multiparadigm nature of FACILE allows a mixture of styles such as combinations of agent-based and client-server-based applications.

FACILE as it stands now is mature enough to be used for sizable applications. However, FACILE is not in a frozen state. In fact we hope that FACILE will continue to play the role of a research vehicle where theoretical results will be applied and transferred into real usage. There are several extensions to the FACILE system underway or planned. Furthermore, we anticipate adjustments and new features being added as the "real" needs from users start to provide feedback to the further development.

In the following sections we will describe some of these extensions. Some of them are "obvious extensions;" others are user or application demanded.

5.6.1   Type System Based on Effect Analysis

In the original definition of FACILE [59, 140] the language was given a monomorphic type system. Since the current implementation of FACILE is obtained by extending the SML language, in particular modifying the run-time system of SML/NJ and tailoring its front-end to FACILE, it was quite natural to adapt MacQueen's weak polymorphic typing scheme for the FACILE implementation. However, there is a price to be paid in two respects. Firstly, the semantic foundation of MacQueen's weak polymorphic typing scheme is not so well understood, though recent research has shed some light on this aspect [73, 63]. Secondly, and more important to the design of the FACILE language, MacQueen's weak polymorphic typing scheme assigns different types to programs considered equivalent at the operational level. From a programmers point of view this is very unfortunate.

Recently a different approach to polymorphic typing of mutable objects in SML has been proposed. It may be characterized by attempts to associate with every expression a conservative approximation to the set of reference cells that the expression allocates [95, 82, 91, 183, 160]. In this approach an expression is not only assigned a type, but also an "effect" (named after the FX system [95]). In [160] the authors conjecture that their effect system may be easily adapted to cater for effects in concurrent functional languages like CML [149, 18] and FACILE. Over the past few years several authors have proposed effect based type systems for CML [28, 30] and FACILE [167] (some are presented in other chapters of this book).

Recently an effort has been made to design and implement an effect system for the full FACILE language extended with object oriented features based on sub/super types. An algorithm for type inference is being implemented. Subtleties relating to the interaction between effect analysis and user-defined datatypes, including disjoint union, subtypes and supertypes, have been identified. These relate to inferring effect analysis related information from the type definitions, in particular when the type constructors are mutual-recursively defined. It seems hard to achieve a good balance between completeness and complexity. A better understanding of what effect analysis actually is getting at in this context will be necessary.

5.6.2   Effect-Based Analysis

Apart from providing information for safe polymorphic generalization, effect-based systems may be of independent interest since they capture essential static information about a program's potential dynamic behavior.

An interesting avenue to explore is to adapt (adopt) the behavior system presented in Chapter 7 and investigated in [122, 125, 123]. Behavioral descriptions will capture essential static information about a program's potential dynamic behavior, in particular its potential for communication and for dynamic creation of processes. This information may impact

1. compile-time optimizations of run-time placement of processes and channels in distributed environments such as networks of workstations or parallel processors.

2. fault-tolerance in distributed environments, e.g., dead-lock detection and static approximation (for reduction) of resource replication.

3. safety in communication of mobile agents (i.e., higher-order functions and processes) in distributed applications, e.g., an application may receive an agent that was compiled elsewhere. The application

may want/need to check the potential external effects of the incoming agent in the applications environment. Thus, behavior inference may provide a level of safety, since only agents satisfying a behavior specified by the receiving side are accepted.

5.6.3 Interoperability

Future plans for the development of the FACILE programming language include porting the software to other hardware platforms (such as Intel x86 processors) and possibly other operating systems (such as WindowsNT). Related to this is work in progress on interoperability between FACILE systems on different platforms. We currently use a system called the contract mechanism, developed at ECRC, for connecting systems written in FACILE with systems written in different languages. We expect to address questions such as interoperability with systems implemented in different programming languages (such as C, C++, prolog) via industrial standards such as XDR, ASN.1, or possibly the emerging CORBA standard. This may replace the contract mechanism in future releases.

A critical issue when operating in a multiplatform environment is the efficient transmission of code (functions and processes) across different processors. In essence, machine code cannot generally be communicated, and source code would have to be recompiled and further suffers from not preserving static binding. So a natural approach is to send closures in a machine-independent representation.

Functions and processes that may be sent to a foreign environment must be kept in an intermediate representation. Since it is not desirable to keep all functions and processes in machine-independent representation, it is necessary to specify which are kept and which are not. The initial approach will be based on program annotations, where the programmer explicitly specifies which objects are transmissible and which are not [84]. It is hoped that at some point in the future these annotations can be eliminated and that program analysis can detect which objects should be kept and which need not be kept in machine-independent representation.

5.6.4 New Communication Paradigms

The communication paradigm in the FACILE Antigua Release is based on handshake (synchronous) communication over typed channels. On top of this primitive one may build more elaborate communication protocols (e.g., group communication [159]). However, in some applications it is more natural to think directly in terms of point-to-point streams (video and audio are good examples) or multicasts or transactions. It is clear that other such paradigms can be "simulated" by implementing them using synchronous channels. However, it may also be advantageous to have these communication paradigms as primitives since some may be implemented directly in hardware or supported directly by communication sublayers.

At first one may use the "SML approach" by giving an implementation in terms of channels and define this as the semantics, but have the implementation use the actual hardware or communication sublayer. However, this should be considered a temporary solution. A challenging long-term goal is to integrate such paradigms and have them coexist, both in terms of semantics and in terms of implementation.

5.6.5   The Future of ML with Concurrency

Languages combining functional languages with concurrency and communication have been an area of research for quite some years, and FACILE is related to a class of such languages, such as Amber [43], Hope+ [134], PML [149], CML [150], Erlang [11], ML with threads [46], LCS [25], and PFL [76].

This book gives a good overview of the proliferation of approaches; a function view of concurrency and communication as in CML, a process view of concurrency and communication as in for example, LCS, and a combination of the two approaches as found in FACILE. Looking deeper into CML, LCS, and (at least the functional concurrent core of) FACILE, it is evident that there are quite a few commonalities among them, not really surprising taking the motivations and background for these languages into account. The goal of future research might be to join these various research efforts and aim at a language for ML with concurrency and communication based on experiences from earlier language development research at different sites. Maybe the result of this joint effort could be some kind of standard for the functional and concurrent programming paradigm. In the next release of FACILE we expect to take one step in this direction by adopting the CML communication primitives, or more precisely, the SML concurrency primitives as defined in [18], as interface to handshake, channel-based communication.

To ensure that the new integrated programming paradigm has an impact in the relatively near future, we need to encourage everybody to try out the usefulness and the limitations of our new approach(es). Obviously this requires development of "real" applications that benefit from the advanced features of our language(s), especially if programmers can be convinced that our approach is a good alternative to well established programming platforms. One concrete measure of the success of our approach would be that people outside of the "ML community" take the programming language(s) with concurrency and communication seriously, i.e., it is seen as a good—or maybe even better—alternative to the conventional programming languages such as C or C++ combined with middleware systems such as OSF/DCE, CORBA, or ANSA.

6
A Semantic Theory for ML Higher-Order Concurrency Primitives

Mourad Debbabi and Dominique Bolignano

ABSTRACT We present a semantic theory for concurrent, functional and imperative programming languages that consists mainly in a static semantics together with a dynamic semantics. The static semantics is inspired by the type and effect discipline. More precisely, we present a generalization of this discipline in order to deal with concurrency. The generalization consists in an inference type system that propagates the communication effects that result from channel creation, sending, and receiving. Hence, the static evaluation of an expression in our type system yields as a result not only the principal type, but also all the minimal communication effects. The dynamic semantics presented is denotational. It is based on an extension of the acceptance trees model. The main novelties of the model described are its construction and its expressiveness. The construction is not classical and relies on an established dependency between the static and the dynamic spaces. The dynamic spaces are typed according to the hierarchy laid down by the static spaces. The dynamic semantic domains are then generated in a compositional and systematic way thanks to an induction on the static information. A significant advantage of this method is that it provides a semantic treatment for polymorphism at the dynamic level by handling suitably free type and effect algebras. The expressiveness of the model is exemplified by the fact that it provides a semantics for communication, value-passing, return of results, dynamic creation of channels and processes, sequencing, and higher-order objects.

6.1 Motivation and Background

The intent of this chapter is to provide theoretical foundations for the unification of three computational paradigms that we refer to as concurrent, functional, and imperative programming. A great deal of interest has been expressed in each of these programming styles, and the underlying models have been deeply investigated, though generally separately.

Concurrency models have been a focus of interest for a great number of researchers. Accordingly, this gave rise to plenty of calculi and models. Among the most prominent calculi, one can cite process algebras such as CCS (Calculus for Communicating Systems) [107, 108] and CSP (Communicating Sequential Processes) [75, 74], for which mathematically well-behaved models have been advanced. One can cite the failure-sets model of Brooks, Hoare, and Roscoe [36, 37, 38] or the acceptance trees model of Hennessy [68, 69]. However, in spite of the large activity of the concurrency community, it remains that formalisms and techniques devised for concurrent and distributed systems are generally relevant to pure processes; in other words, they focus only on control aspects. Thus, in such frameworks, there is no data, no communication, no states, etc. These simplifications are generally adopted in order to put the emphasis on the difficulties inherent in concurrent systems, for instance nondeterminism, the semantics of combinators, etc.

On the other hand, functional programming has been extensively studied. Consequently, many powerful, general-purpose programming languages have been devised. For instance, one can cite ML dialects. These rest on secure theoretical foundations that are demonstrated by the large body of results on pure and typed λ-calculus. Generally, functional languages are endowed with imperative features for efficiency reasons. Also, programming without such facilities becomes quickly tedious and cumbersome in many situations.

The motivations underlying the integration of these computational styles are many. Both distributed applications and multiprocessor machines are becoming more common nowadays. To simplify the programming of these applications and to take advantage of the high computing power of such machines, appropriate programming languages are needed. Furthermore, any application has naturally two aspects: data and control. Thus, having a concurrent and functional language seems to be appropriate for a natural, comfortable, and elegant programming of these aspects.

The intent of this work is to bridge the gap between theory and practice. In other words, the aim is to establish a connection between real-life concurrent programming languages and formal concurrency models. In particular, the intention is to accommodate some of these theoretical models, so as to use them in the semantic definition of a concurrent and functional programming language.

This chapter is written mainly for the exposition of the new semantic traits. So the intention is to provide an easy-to-understand presentation of the main ideas, and so conciseness will prevail over completeness. Accordingly, the presented work deals only with the semantics of higher-order concurrency primitives of ML. The lifting of the presented theory to a real-life language is presented in Debbabi's Ph.D. thesis [51], where a full account of the involved aspects is provided. The problems addressed here are relevant to any integration of concurrent and functional computational styles. In such an integration, one has to find the appropriate type system, to design the appropriate dynamic models, and to provide useful and intuitive preorders. The main complication here comes from the fact that a real integration is needed and not a simple cumulation.

The work that will be presented hereafter is meant to explore whether programming styles and conveniences that have evolved as part of concurrent, functional, and imperative programming could be somehow brought together to coexist in a single language. More accurately, the intention is to experiment with our ideas on an ML-like language extended with concurrency features. Thus, the language described here supports polymorphic types and both functional and process abstractions as in CML [145, 150, 147] and FACILE [59]: functions may be used to describe internal computations of concurrent processes. Functions, processes, and communication channels are first-class values and thus can be passed along channels. Consequently, the mobility of these values is supported.

At the theoretical level, we will present the static semantics of this language as well as the dynamic semantics. The type inference system is based on an extension of the type and effect discipline: a new approach to implicit typing that can be viewed as an extension of the ML-style type discipline. In addition to that, as shown in [160], effect-based type disciplines are more appropriate for integrating safely and efficiently functional and imperative programming. In this chapter we will show that it contributes also significantly to the integration of concurrency features. The dynamic semantics presented here is denotational. It is based on an accommodation of the acceptance trees model [68, 69].

The rest of this chapter is organized as follows. A comparison with related approaches is given in Section 6.2. Then an informal description of the language is presented in Section 6.3. Section 6.4 is devoted to the presentation of the static semantics. The dynamic denotational semantics is presented in Section 6.5. A few concluding remarks and a discussion of further research are given in Section 6.6.

6.2   Related Work

During the last decade, many proposals have been advanced for concurrent programming languages. OCCAM [129] is a parallel imperative programming language that is a concretization of the pioneering work of Hoare on CSP [75]. Lately, the idea of unifying concurrent, functional, and imperative programming paradigms has been the focus of interest of many theoretical and practical researchers. This active research has resulted in a wide variety of languages. Some of them use a LISP dialect as a functional kernel and extend it with concurrency primitives. We can cite CDScheme [141], QLISP [61], and MULTILISP [66] as representatives of this category of languages. Recently, modern languages emerged from the idea of using a Standard ML-like [112, 111] language as a functional core and extending it with CSP-like [75, 74] or CCS-like [107, 108] process algebras. Representatives of this approach are PML [149], Concurrent ML (CML) [145, 146, 150, 147], FACILE [59], and LCS [25].

These languages are quite expressive, and as reported in [18], there is a need to have a semantic theory that enables one to reason about the programs and to grasp the meaning of sophisticated constructions. A structural operational semantics has been proposed for both CML [147, 124] and FACILE [59]. Another description of FACILE semantics has been developed using the CHAM [20] (CHemical Abstract Machine) framework [93]. In [29] we presented a structural operational semantics for the concurrency primitives presented here.

6.2.1   Typing

The static semantics (typing semantics) in CML, FACILE, and LCS rests on the type inference discipline. It is well known that this discipline is problematic in the presence of nonreferentially transparent constructs. More precisely, the problem is relevant to type generalization in the presence of mutable data. Therefore, many extensions of the initial work of Milner [106] have been proposed.

The classical way to deal with this issue is the imperative type discipline [175]. An extension of this approach has been used in the implementation of Standard ML of New Jersey. It is based on weak type variables: these type variables have an attached strength information, denoting the number of applications needed to get a nontrivial effect. In [91], another method is proposed that consists in detecting some so-called dangerous type variables (the ones occurring in the types of imperative objects) and labeling function types accordingly.

Later, in [160], the type and effect discipline is introduced. The latter yields as a result of the static evaluation of an expression not only its principal type, but also all the minimal side effects. It should be noted that the idea of considering the effects as part of the static evaluation of an expression has been suggested in [96] and adopted in the FX project [60, 95].

In [51, 29] we proposed a new inference typing system that computes in addition to the principal types of expressions and their side effects the minimal communication effects generated by the concurrent constructs. We have also presented an adequate operational semantics for our language, and we proved that our typing system is consistent with respect to the operational semantics. Similar results have been established independently by Nielson and Nielson [124] and Thomsen [167], respectively, on CML and FACILE. Both proposed a static semantics based on the type and effect discipline [160] together with an operational semantics.

6.2.2   Denotational Models

We are not aware of the existence of any denotational model for the previously mentioned languages, except for OCCAM. A denotational description of the latter is presented in [154]. However, we are interested here in some issues such as polymorphism, implicit typing, and higher-order aspects that are not supported by OCCAM. Furthermore, we are interested in giving a semantics to a language that provides both process and functional abstractions.

Denotational models are important first to get a well understood foundations of the language. They also allow the semantics designer to extract a proof theory for the language. Once such a theory devised, denotational models can serve as a model for it.

As pointed out before, the two prominent denotational models for concurrency are the failure sets model [36, 37, 38] and the acceptance trees model [68, 69]. The failure sets model has been designed as a semantic theory for a quite abstract version of CSP usually referred to as TCSP (Theoretical CSP). It supports only pure processes. The acceptance trees model is very similar to the failure sets model and has been devised as a model for TCSP- or CCS-like abstract languages.

To deal with data aspects that are value-passing, assignment, return of results, and store sharing, as well as some control aspects such as sequencing, Robert Milne proposed an extension of the acceptance trees model [103] as part of the RSL models. The whole RSL denotational semantics is presented in [104]. Inspired by [103], Hennessy and Ingólfsdóttir investigated value-passing and proposed a fully abstract model [70]. The same authors [71] proposed a semantic theory for an imperative language referred to as VPLA that supports value-passing and assignments. In both [70] and [71] the authors presented three semantic approaches (i.e., denotational, axiomatic, and operational) and proved their equivalence. The foundations as well as the algebraic properties of the RSL denotational models presented in [104] are detailed in [28].

The main contribution of this chapter is the presentation of a semantic theory for ML higher-order concurrency primitives that consists of the following:

- A static semantics is provided as an effect-based type system that reconstructs not only the type of an expression but also the communication effects that may be induced by its execution.

- A dynamic denotational semantics is built upon an accommodation of the acceptance trees model. The main novelties of the model presented here are its construction and its expressiveness. The construction is not classical and relies on an established dependency between the static and the dynamic spaces. The dynamic spaces are typed according to the hierarchy laid down by the static spaces. The dynamic semantic domains are then generated in a compositional and systematic way thanks to an induction on the static information. A significant advantage of this method is that it provides a semantic treatment for polymorphism at the dynamic level by handling suitably free type and effect algebras. The expressiveness of the model is exemplified by the fact that it provides a semantics for communication, value-passing, return of results, dynamic creation of channels and processes, polymorphism, sequencing, and higher-order objects.

6.3   Informal Presentation

In this section we present the syntax of the language considered in this work. The syntactic constructions allowed are close to those allowed in FACILE and CML. We consider

- Literals such as integers, booleans true and false, a distinguished value (), and a constant skip that models an expression that immediately terminates successfully by returning the trivial value ().

- Three binding operations that are the λ-abstraction, the recursion rec, and the let definition.

- Expressions that may communicate through typed channels. The expression channel() means to allocate a new channel. The expression send(e, e') means to evaluate e', evaluate e, and then send the result of the e' evaluation on the channel resulting from the evaluation of e. The whole expression evaluates then to (). The expression receive(e) evaluates to any value received on the channel resulting from the evaluation of e. Notice that the communications are synchronized as in CCS and CSP.

- Three concurrency combinators are allowed:

  _[]_: Nondeterministic (internal) choice.

  _[]_: External choice.

  _||_: Parallel composition of two expressions.

- A sequencing operator: "_;_".

More formally, the BNF syntax of the core language is presented in Figure 6.1.

Notice that we have three syntactic categories. The category of expressions ranged over by e, the category of values ranged over by v, and the category of constants ranged over by c.

We will consider a minimal core syntax so as to provide a more compact and complete description of the static and the dynamic semantic traits.

Notice also that the imperative aspects, supported usually through the notion of reference, are not part of the core language. We decided to do so in order to provide a more compact and complete description of the static

$$e ::= x \mid v \mid \texttt{let } x{=}e_1 \texttt{ in } e_2 \mid e_1\ e_2 \mid e_1\ ;\ e_2 \mid \texttt{rec } x \texttt{ => } e$$
$$v ::= c \mid \texttt{fn } x \texttt{ => } e$$
$$c ::= () \mid \texttt{true} \mid \texttt{false} \mid \texttt{skip} \mid \texttt{channel} \mid \texttt{receive} \mid \texttt{send} \mid \lceil \rceil \mid \lceil \rceil \mid \|$$

FIGURE 6.1. The core syntax

and the dynamic semantic traits. Furthermore, imperative aspects can be simulated using servers that communicate through channels as shown in [18, 147]. A full treatment of references, stores, and imperative aspects is provided in [51], which generalizes and improves the work done in [32, 29].

6.4   Static Semantics

As we pointed out before, we decided to adopt the type and effect discipline as a starting point in giving a static semantics to our language. This choice is motivated by the following reasons:

- First, the intention is to control safely the type generalization in the presence of polymorphic channels. Actually, types and effects are used to control the generalization of type and effect variables. As shown in [90, 160], effect-based type systems compete very well with the other type systems when typing in the presence of mutable data.

- Second, the communication effect information together with the principal type captures valuable static information on the dynamic behavior of a program. The latter information may be of great interest in the static analysis of programs.

- The third and the main motivation for our use of an effect type system is due to the construction of the denotational model presented in [51, 33, 30] and its foundations. In fact, the technique used establishes a dependency between the static and the dynamic spaces. More accurately, the dynamic spaces are typed according to the hierarchy laid down by the static spaces. The dynamic semantic domains are then generated in a compositional and systematic way thanks to an induction on the static information.

The type and effect discipline reported in [160] does not support communication effects. Thus the work reported hereafter is an extension of this discipline to concurrency. We define the following static spaces:

- The space of *communication regions*: Communication regions are intended to abstract channels. Their space consists of the disjoint union of a countable set of constants ranged over by c and variables ranged over by γ. We will use $\rho, \rho', \ldots$ to represent values drawn from this space.

- The space of *communication effects*: It is defined inductively by

$$\sigma ::= \emptyset \mid \varsigma \mid chan(\rho, \tau) \mid in(\rho, \tau) \mid out(\rho, \tau) \mid \sigma \cup \sigma'.$$

We use ς to stand for a communication effect variable. The basic communication effect $chan(\rho, \tau)$ represents the creation of a channel of type τ in the communication region ρ. The term $in(\rho, \tau)$ denotes the effect resulting from an input of a value of type τ on a channel in the communication region ρ, while $out(\rho, \tau)$ denotes an output of a value of type τ on a channel in the communication region ρ. We write $\sigma \sqsupseteq \sigma' \Leftrightarrow \sigma = \sigma' \cup \sigma$. Equality on effects is modulo ACUI (Associativity, Commutativity, and Idempotence with $\emptyset$ as the neutral element).

- The space of *types*: It is inductively defined by

$$\tau ::= Unit \mid \alpha \mid chan_\rho(\tau) \mid \tau \xrightarrow{\sigma} \tau.$$

Unit is the type with only one element "()," α a type variable; $chan_\rho(\tau)$ is the type of channels in the communication region ρ that are intended to be media for values of type τ; the term $\tau \xrightarrow{\sigma} \tau'$ is the type of functions that take parameters of type τ to values of type τ' with a *latent* communication effect σ. By latent effect, we mean the effect generated when the corresponding expression is evaluated.

In this chapter, given sets A and B we will write $A \xrightarrow{m} B$ to denote the set of all mappings from A to B. A mapping (map for short) $m \in A \xrightarrow{m} B$ could be defined by extension as $[a_1 \mapsto b_1, \ldots, a_n \mapsto b_n]$ to denote the association of the elements b_i to a_i. We will write $dom(m)$ to denote the domain of the map m and $ran(m)$ to denote its range (codomain). We will write m_x for the map m excluding the associations of the form $x \mapsto \_$. Given two maps m and m', we will write $m \dagger m'$ for the overwriting of the map m by the associations of the map m', i.e., the domain of $m \dagger m'$ is $dom(m) \cup dom(m')$ and we have $(m \dagger m')(a) = m'(a)$ if $a \in dom(m')$ and $m(a)$ otherwise. We will use $\mathcal{P}_f(E)$ to denote the finite power set of a given set E.

The static semantics manipulates sequents of the form:

$$\mathcal{E} \vdash e : \tau, \sigma,$$

which state that under some typing environment $\mathcal{E}$, the expression e has type τ and communication effect σ. We also define type schemes of the form $\forall v_1, \ldots, v_n.\tau$, where v_i can be type, communication region, or communication effect variable. A type τ' is an instance of $\forall v_1, \ldots, v_n.\tau$ denoted

(cte)	$$\frac{\tau \prec TypeOf(\texttt{cte})}{\mathcal{E} \vdash \texttt{cte} : \tau, \emptyset}$$
(var)	$$\frac{\tau \prec \mathcal{E}(x)}{\mathcal{E} \vdash x : \tau, \emptyset}$$
(abs)	$$\frac{\mathcal{E}_x \dagger [x \mapsto \tau'] \vdash e : \tau, \sigma}{\mathcal{E} \vdash \lambda x.e : \tau' \xrightarrow{\sigma} \tau, \emptyset}$$
(app)	$$\frac{\mathcal{E} \vdash e : \tau \xrightarrow{\sigma} \tau', \sigma'' \quad \mathcal{E} \vdash e' : \tau, \sigma''}{\mathcal{E} \vdash (e\ e') : \tau', \sigma \cup \sigma' \cup \sigma''}$$
(seq)	$$\frac{\mathcal{E} \vdash e : \tau, \sigma \quad \mathcal{E} \vdash e' : \tau', \sigma'}{\mathcal{E} \vdash e\ ;\ e' : \tau', \sigma \cup \sigma'}$$
(rec)	$$\frac{\mathcal{E}_x \dagger [x \mapsto \tau] \vdash e : \tau, \sigma}{\mathcal{E} \vdash \texttt{rec}\ x.e : \tau, \sigma}$$
(let)	$$\frac{\mathcal{E} \vdash e' : \tau', \sigma' \quad \mathcal{E}_x \dagger [x \mapsto Gen(\sigma', \mathcal{E})(\tau')] \vdash e : \tau, \sigma}{\mathcal{E} \vdash \texttt{let}\ x\texttt{=}e'\ \texttt{in}\ e : \tau, \sigma \cup \sigma'}$$
(obs)	$$\frac{\mathcal{E} \vdash e : \tau, \sigma \quad \sigma' \sqsupseteq Observe(\mathcal{E}, \tau, \sigma)}{\mathcal{E} \vdash e : \tau, \sigma'}$$

FIGURE 6.2. The static semantics

by $\tau' \prec \forall v_1, \ldots, v_n.\tau$ if there exists a substitution θ defined over $v_1, \ldots, v_n$ such that $\tau' = \theta\tau$. Static environments ranged over by $\mathcal{E}$ map identifiers to type schemes. Figure 6.2 presents the static semantics of our core language.

Type generalization in this type system states that a variable cannot be generalized if it is free in the type environment $\mathcal{E}$ or if it is present in the observed communication effect. The first condition is classical while the other is due to the fact that types are bound to regions in the effects. The reader should refer to [160, 29] for a detailed explanation of this issue. The formal definition is as follows

$$Gen(\sigma, \mathcal{E})(\tau) =$$
$$\textbf{let}\ \{v_1, \ldots, v_n\} = fv(\tau) \backslash (fv(\mathcal{E}) \cup fv(\sigma))$$
$$\textbf{in}\ \forall v_1, \ldots, v_n.\tau$$
$$\textbf{end},$$

where $fv(\_)$ denotes the set of free variables

$$fv(\mathcal{E}) \quad = \quad \cup \{fv(\mathcal{E}(x)) \mid x \in dom(\mathcal{E})\},$$

$$fv(\forall v_1, ..., v_n.\tau) = fv(\tau)\backslash\{v_1, ..., v_n\},$$
$$fv(\emptyset) = \emptyset,$$
$$fv(\varsigma) = \{\varsigma\},$$
$$fv(\langle chan|in|out\rangle(\rho, \tau)) = fv(\rho) \cup fv(\tau),$$
$$fv(\sigma \cup \sigma') = fv(\sigma) \cup fv(\sigma'),$$
$$fv(\gamma) = \{\gamma\}.$$

Let S_Type be the space of types. The observation criterion was introduced in order to report only effects that can affect the context of an expression. The formal definition is as follows

$Observe(\mathcal{E}, \tau, \sigma) =$

   $\{\varsigma \in \sigma | \varsigma \in fv(\mathcal{E}) \cup fv(\tau)\} \cup$
   $\{chan(\rho, \tau') \in \sigma | \rho \in fr_r(\mathcal{E}) \cup fr_r(\tau) \wedge \tau' \in$ S_Type$\} \cup$
   $\{in(\rho, \tau') \in \sigma | \rho \in fr_r(\mathcal{E}) \cup fr_r(\tau) \wedge \tau' \in$ S_Type$\} \cup$
   $\{out(\rho, \tau') \in \sigma | \rho \in fr_r(\mathcal{E}) \cup fr_r(\tau) \wedge \tau' \in$ S_Type$\},$

where $fr_r(\mathcal{E})$ stands for the set of free communication regions in the static environment $\mathcal{E}$:

$$fr_r(\mathcal{E}) = \cup \{fr_r(\mathcal{E}(x)) \mid x \in dom(\mathcal{E})\},$$
$$fr_r(\forall v_1, ..., v_n.\tau) = fr_r(\tau)\backslash\{v_1, ..., v_n\},$$

$fr_r(\tau)$:

   $fr_r(Unit) = \emptyset,$
   $fr_r(\alpha) = \emptyset,$
   $fr_r(chan_\rho(\tau)) = \{\rho\} \cup fr_r(\tau),$
   $fr_r(\tau \xrightarrow{\sigma} \tau') = fr_r(\tau) \cup fr_r(\tau') \cup fr_r(\sigma),$

$fr_r(\sigma)$:

   $fr_r(\emptyset) = \emptyset,$
   $fr_r(\varsigma) = \emptyset,$
   $fr_r(chan(\rho, \tau)) = \{\rho\} \cup fr_r(\tau),$
   $fr_r(in(\rho, \tau)) = \{\rho\} \cup fr_r(\tau),$
   $fr_r(out(\rho, \tau)) = \{\rho\} \cup fr_r(\tau),$
   $fr_r(\sigma \cup \sigma') = fr_r(\sigma) \cup fr_r(\sigma'),$

The function *TypeOf* allows the typing of built-in primitives as defined in Figure 6.3. Below we present an example on the static evaluation of expressions.

$$
\begin{array}{lll}
[& \text{channel} & \mapsto \quad \forall \alpha, \gamma, \varsigma. Unit \xrightarrow{\varsigma \cup chan(\gamma, \alpha)} chan_\gamma(\alpha), \\
& \text{receive} & \mapsto \quad \forall \alpha, \gamma, \varsigma.\ chan_\gamma(\alpha) \xrightarrow{\varsigma \cup in(\gamma, \alpha)} \alpha, \\
& \text{send} & \mapsto \quad \forall \alpha, \gamma, \varsigma.\ chan_\gamma(\alpha) \times \alpha \xrightarrow{\varsigma \cup out(\gamma, \alpha)} Unit, \\
& \| & \mapsto \quad \forall \alpha, \varsigma.\ \alpha \times \alpha \xrightarrow{\varsigma} \alpha, \\
& \sqcap & \mapsto \quad \forall \alpha, \varsigma.\ \alpha \times \alpha \xrightarrow{\varsigma} \alpha, \\
& [] & \mapsto \quad \forall \alpha, \varsigma.\ \alpha \times \alpha \xrightarrow{\varsigma} \alpha \\
]
\end{array}
$$

FIGURE 6.3. The initial static basis

Example 6.4.1. Let us consider the process that creates a channel c and then performs in parallel an output of the value () together with an input on the same channel c:

```
let c = channel ()
in receive(c) ‖ send(c,())
end
```

Let us denote by P the above process. Without using the observation criterion, the type of the previous expression under an empty typing environment is

$$[\,] \vdash P : Unit, chan(\gamma, Unit) \cup in(\gamma, Unit) \cup out(\gamma, Unit).$$

After the application of the observation criterion, the type of P becomes

$$[\,] \vdash P : Unit, \emptyset.$$

$\square$

As we have seen above, the cumulative effect $chan(\gamma, Unit) \cup in(\gamma, Unit) \cup out(\gamma, Unit)$ has been abstracted to the empty effect after the application of the rule **(obs)** since these effects are neither free in the type of P nor in the environment, and so there is no need to propagate them.

Example 6.4.2. Now let us consider an expression similar to the previous one that returns the created channel value c after the parallel composition:

```
let c = channel ()
in (receive(c) ‖ send(c,()) ) ; c
end
```

Let us denote by Q the above process. Without using the observation criterion, the type of the previous expression under an empty typing environment is

$$[\,]\vdash Q : chan_\gamma(Unit), chan(\gamma, Unit)\ \cup\ in(\gamma, Unit)\ \cup\ out(\gamma, Unit).$$

After the application of the observation criterion, the type of P becomes

$$[\,]\vdash Q : chan_\gamma(Unit), chan(\gamma, Unit)\ \cup\ in(\gamma, Unit)\ \cup\ out(\gamma, Unit).$$

□

The last example illustrates the case where the inferred communication effect is observable.

6.5   Dynamic Semantics

The intention hereafter is to provide a denotational model for the core language introduced previously. The model will be devised so that it can be easily adapted to any other concurrent functional language such as FACILE or CML. The technique considered here takes advantage of the existing work on more abstract process algebra. More accurately, our starting point will be the acceptance trees model [68, 69], which is known to be mathematically well-behaved in the world of pure process algebra. The intention is to extend this model for handling input, output, communication, value-passing, return of results, dynamic creation of channels and processes, polymorphism, sequencing, and higher-order objects.

The presentation of our dynamic denotational semantics will come in four steps. First, we present the principles underlying our dynamic semantics. More accurately, we describe the method used in the generation of semantic domains. This method has been devised within Debbabi's Ph.D. thesis [51]. It establishes a dependency between the static and the dynamic semantics. More accurately, the dynamic domains are typed according to the hierarchy laid down by the static domains, i.e., the type and effect algebras. A significant advantage of this method is that it provides a semantic treatment for polymorphism at the dynamic level by handling suitably free type and effect algebras. Second, we recall briefly the acceptance trees model. Third, we present the extended concurrency model that will be the basis of the semantic definition. Finally, the technique used in the semantic description is presented. The semantic rules as well as the semantic functions are given in the appendixes at the end of this chapter.

6.5.1   Typed Dynamic Semantics

The dynamic semantics that will be presented here is said to be typed, i.e., it is made dependent on the static semantics. The reasons underlying such a dependency are motivated by the desire to get rid of some domain theory limitations such as the restriction to continuity of domain operators in reflexive domain equations. Such limitations are really problematic especially when we know that the ultimate goal of our work is the definition of a wide-spectrum specification language that supports both data and concurrency descriptions. The idea is to follow the same approach as the one used in the design of Extended ML [157]. The starting point will be the design of an implicitly typed, polymorphic, concurrent, and functional programming language. Specification aspects will be supported by allowing axioms to appear in signatures and structures as in Extended ML. The resulting specification language is thus highly expressive though it embodies a restricted number of concepts. Generally, specification languages are not executable and many of them advocate formality. So, there is a natural need for their formal definition. The nonexecutability of these languages makes denotational semantics the unique alternative for their semantic definition. At this level, the use of domain theory to devise the semantic domains may be problematic especially if the language incorporates discontinuous objects. Recall that continuity is a crucial mathematical condition for the applicability of domain theory resolution methods.

One major contribution of the work presented here is to show how to benefit from an established dependency between the static and the dynamic semantics to construct safely some sophisticated dynamic domains in denotational semantics. Furthermore, we will take advantage of such a dependency to provide a semantic treatment for CML polymorphism at the dynamic level.

In the sequel, we propose an inductive construction method of the dynamic domains. This method has been devised by the first author in [51]. The construction of the dynamic spaces is done thanks to a strong typing of the dynamic domains. The latter are constructed by structural induction on static types and effects. This means that the type and effect algebras must be restricted so that the induction is well-founded. For instance, no function accesses a variable, accesses a channel, or accepts a parameter that has a type that might include the type of the function. Such a requirement is fulfilled in the case of our type and effect algebras since types and effects are restricted to be finite.

To construct the dynamic spaces, we generate, in a compositional and systematic way, the dynamic spaces from a static information that range over type and effect domains. The construction principle is illustrated by Figure 6.4.

Starting from a static information "s_z" drawn from a static space "S_Z", we construct a dynamic domain in the same manner as [104, 105], a dynamic domain "D_Z(s_z)". This is done via the function "D_Z". The generated dynamic domain "D_Z(s_z)" is said to be typed by the static information "s_z". For instance, given a static information of the form "s_x '→' s_y", drawn from a static domain of the form "S_X × {'→'} × S_Y", the associated

Static element	Static domain	Dynamic domain
s_z=	S_Z=	D_Z(s_z)=
s_unit $\in$	$\{s\_unit\}$	D_Unit
s_bool $\in$	$\{s\_bool\}$	D_Bool
s_int $\in$	$\{s\_int\}$	D_Int
s_x '+' s_y $\in$	S_X $\times$ $\{'+'\}$ $\times$ S_Y	D_X(s_x)+D_Y(s_y)
s_x '$\times$' s_y $\in$	S_X $\times$ $\{'\times'\}$ $\times$ S_Y	D_X(s_x) $\times$ D_Y(s_y)
s_x '$\rightarrow$' s_y $\in$	S_X $\times$ $\{'\rightarrow'\}$ $\times$ S_Y	D_X(s_x)$\rightarrow$D_Y(s_y)
s_set $\in$	$\mathcal{P}_f(S\_X)$	$\prod$ s_x $\in$ s_set . D_X(s_x)

FIGURE 6.4. Relationship between static and dynamic domains

dynamic space is the domain of all functions from D_X(s_x) to D_Y(s_y). Notice that the $\rightarrow$ symbol is quoted in S_X $\times$ $\{'\rightarrow'\}$ $\times$ S_Y while it appears without quotes in D_X(s_x)$\rightarrow$D_Y(s_y). This is to mention that in the first case it is just a tag while in the second case it is the usual function constructor. Quoted symbols or merely tags like '+', '$\times$' and '$\rightarrow$' are subject to interpretation at the construction of the dynamic spaces (they are interpreted as sum, product, and function constructors). The symbol $\prod$ is borrowed from constructive type theory. It stands for the general product of dependent types. Such an operator is finite here and takes some static value to a dynamic domain constructed via the function "D_".

The method above assumes the groundness of the static elements "s_z". In our case, polymorphism is allowed. Thus, the static evaluation may refer to some type and effect variables. Consequently, the type and effect spaces become free algebras that require interpretation.

Given a function "D_Z" such that when "'s_z" is a ground term in a suitable space, "D_Z(s_z)" is a dynamic space, we define in a generic way a polymorphic counterpart to "D_Z", written "P_Z", which acts on all terms "s_z" (whether or not they are ground) by setting

$$P\_Z(s\_z) = \prod \theta \in \mathcal{GS}(fv(s\_z)). \ D\_Z(\theta s\_z),$$

where $\mathcal{GS}(X)$ stands for the set of all ground substitutions whose domains include the variables of X. Thus, given a static information "s_z" not necessarily ground, we generate a dynamic space "P_Z(s_z)". The latter is a dependent type that takes a ground substitution θ that instantiates completely "s_z" to the dynamic space "D_Z(s_z)". Notice that the space "P_Z" is not defined compositionally in Z unlike the case for "D_Z".

6.5.2   Acceptance Trees Model

The intention hereafter is to recall briefly the general model of acceptance trees. Let Σ be a set of events that the processes can perform. In the rest of this section, we need the notion of *saturated sets*. Thus, a set $A \subseteq \mathcal{P}_f(\Sigma)$, is said to be saturated if it satisfies the following closures:

1. $\bigcup A \in \mathcal{A}$ (union closure).

2. $A, B \in \mathcal{A}$ and $A \subseteq C \subseteq B$ implies $C \in \mathcal{A}$ (convex closure).

The set of all saturated finite subsets of $\mathcal{P}_f(\Sigma)$, all saturated sets over Σ, is denoted by $Sat(\Sigma)$. Let $c(\mathcal{A})$ be the saturated closure of a set $A \subseteq \mathcal{P}_f(\Sigma)$, defined as the least set that satisfies

1. $A \subseteq c(\mathcal{A})$,

2. $\bigcup A \in c(\mathcal{A})$,

3. $A, B \in c(\mathcal{A})$ and $A \subseteq C \subseteq B$ implies $C \in c(\mathcal{A})$.

The process space D is then defined as

$$D = \{(m, S) \mid (m, S) \in ((\Sigma \xrightarrow{m} D) \times Sat(\Sigma)). \, dom(m) = \bigcup S\} \cup \{\bot\}.$$

Thus, D is a set of pairs each of which represents a process. The first component of a pair is an association (a map) between finitely many members of Σ and members of D, while the second one is an acceptance set. It should be noted that the definition given above is recursive, but such a space exists and satisfies elegant algebraic properties [68, 69]. Let us consider the preorder $\sqsubseteq$ on D defined by

1. $\forall d \in D. \, \bot \sqsubseteq d$,

2. Let (m, S) and (m', S') be two elements of D. We write $(m, S) \sqsubseteq (m', S')$ if and only if

   (a) $dom(m') \subseteq dom(m) \, \wedge \, S' \subseteq S$,
   (b) $\forall e \in dom(m'). \, m(e) \sqsubseteq m'(e)$.

The space D is a countably-based algebraic complete partial order whose set of compact elements, $K(D)$, is formally defined as the least set that satisfies

1. $\bot \in K(D)$,

2. $S \in Sat(\Sigma)$, $m \in K(D)$ and $dom(m) = \bigcup S$ implies $(m, S) \in K(D)$.

The underlying proofs (existence, algebraicity, and domainhood) are detailed in [68, 69]. Now let us come back to the underlying intuitions. A process can be modeled as a pair (m, S) that stipulates that the process is waiting to engage in one event, say e, chosen from $dom(m)$, and once chosen, the process continues progressing as the process $m(e)$. We will refer to $m(e)$ as the sequel of the process. The choice of the event is governed by the corresponding acceptance set. In fact S stands for the set of the possible internal states that can be reached nondeterministically. The actions in a set A from S are those that the process can perform when in that state.

The special element $\perp$ corresponds to the most nondeterministic process, known in the literature as chaos. In other words, it models divergent processes. We consider here a bounded nondeterminism, so at any given time, a process can be waiting to participate in one of only finitely many events. That is why $dom(m)$ and the relevant internal states of an acceptance set are restricted to be finite.

6.5.3 Dynamic Domains

Now let us start introducing the semantic dynamic domains. As we already mentioned, they are constructed from static spaces, according to the method presented in the previous section. The first space to be introduced is the space of dynamic types. To each ground type we associate a dynamic type, a set of dynamic values, as follows:

$$
\begin{aligned}
\text{D\_Type}(\tau) = \ &\mathbf{case}\ \tau\ \mathbf{of} \\
&Unit \rightsquigarrow \{()\} \\
&Bool \rightsquigarrow \{tt, f\!f\} \\
&Int \rightsquigarrow \mathbb{Z} \\
&chan_\rho(\tau') \rightsquigarrow \{c(\rho, \tau', i) \mid i \in \mathbb{N}\} \\
&\tau' \xrightarrow{\sigma} \tau'' \rightsquigarrow \text{D\_Type}(\tau') \rightarrow \text{D\_Routine}(\tau'', \sigma) \\
&\mathbf{end}
\end{aligned}
$$

The dynamic interpretation of literal types is classical. For instance, $\text{D\_Type}(Unit)$ is a one-set element and $\text{D\_Type}(Bool)$ contains two values: the usual truth values. A channel type is interpreted dynamically as a countable set of dynamic channel values (in order to provide many channel values having the same type). The dynamic interpretation of the static type $\tau' \xrightarrow{\sigma} \tau''$ is the set of all functions from $\text{D\_Type}(\tau')$ to $\text{D\_Routine}(\tau'', \sigma)$. The space $\text{D\_Routine}(\tau'', \sigma)$ is what we call the space of processes. Its elements, called dynamic routines, are structures that record computations, i.e., input/output communications, the values to be returned as results as well as the choices available at each level of the computation. In other words, the elements of such a space capture all the possible behaviors of a given expression in terms of termination, input, output, and the choices available among all these possibilities.

We need to define the following functions on effects:

$$
\begin{aligned}
in(\sigma) &= \{chan_\rho(\tau) \mid in(\rho, \tau) \in \sigma\}, \\
out(\sigma) &= \{chan_\rho(\tau) \mid out(\rho, \tau) \in \sigma\},
\end{aligned}
$$

where $in(\sigma)$ and $out(\sigma)$ stand respectively for the input and output channels of the communication effect σ.

Now let us turn to the space of dynamic routines or merely dynamic processes. This space is based on some accommodations and extensions performed on the acceptance trees model. The first accommodation consists in the fact that processes are able to perform one-to-one communications through typed channels. The adapted model distinguishes between events in order to handle input and output. Thus, events are not simply assumed to range over an alphabet of actions, but are split into two categories according to their direction. So input and output events are distinguished and correspond respectively to inputs and outputs from certain channels.

Another adaptation, due to communication and sequencing handling, consists of two kinds of sequel processes (or just sequels). In fact, sequels are not simply identified, as previously, with processes, but are also classified according to the nature of the event that just occurred. The sequel attached to an input communication is modeled as a λ-abstraction, that maps a value of the associated channel's type to some process that represents the rest of the computation. An output sequel is modeled as a mapping that maps the values that may be communicated to the processes that represent the rest of the computation.

We will consider as a result of a process execution a computable value. But since processes may be nondeterministic, we will consider the set of possible outcomes, i.e., the set of possible results.

A process can be viewed as a 4-tuple, where the first component is the set of the possible results that the process may return when it terminates. The second component, called the input map, maps an input event (input from a channel) to the corresponding sequel process (a λ-abstraction). The third component, called the output map, maps an output event (output to a channel) to the corresponding sequel process. We introduce a special event denoted by "$\sqrt{}$" (pronounced tick) to signal the successful termination of a process. When such an event occurs, the process immediately terminates and then returns some value among those available in the first component of the 4-tuple structure. At any given time, a process can be waiting to participate in one of only finitely many events. The choice of the event is governed by the fourth component, called the acceptance set. In fact, it is a set of subsets of events and stands for the set of possible internal states that can be reached nondeterministically. The formal definition of the process space depends on the spaces of input maps, output maps, and acceptance sets introduced hereafter.

Input maps are containers of input communications. The set of input maps over a ground type τ and a communication effect σ, written

D_Input_Map(τ, σ), is defined as the greatest subset of

$$(\cup \{\text{D-Type}(chan_\rho(\tau')) \mid chan_\rho(\tau') \in in(\sigma)\})$$
$$\overrightarrow{m}$$
$$(\cup \{\text{D-Type}(\tau') \rightarrow \text{D-Routine}(\tau, \sigma) \mid chan_\rho(\tau') \in in(\sigma)\}).$$

which satisfies the following condition:

$$\forall I \in \text{D-Input-Map}(\tau, \sigma).\forall c(\rho, \tau', i) \in dom(I).$$
$$I(c(\rho, \tau', i)) \in \text{D-Type}(\tau') \rightarrow \text{D-Routine}(\tau, \sigma).$$

Similarly, output maps are containers for output communications. The set of output maps over a ground type τ and a communication effect σ, written D_Output_Map(τ, σ), is defined as the greatest subset of

$$(\cup \{\text{D-Type}(chan_\rho(\tau')) \mid chan_\rho(\tau') \in in(\sigma)\})$$
$$\overrightarrow{m}$$
$$(\cup \{\text{D-Type}(\tau') \overrightarrow{m} \text{D-Routine}(\tau, \sigma) \mid chan_\rho(\tau') \in in(\sigma)\}),$$

which satisfies the following invariant:

$$\forall O \in \text{D-Output-Map}(\tau, \sigma).\forall c(\rho, \tau', i) \in dom(O).$$
$$O(c(\rho, \tau', i)) \in \text{D-Type}(\tau') \overrightarrow{m} \text{D-Routine}(\tau, \sigma) \wedge$$
$$dom(O(c(\rho, \tau', i))) \neq \emptyset.$$

The condition above states that for each possible output event, the set of possible values to be output is not empty. Notice that when an output event occurs, one value is selected nondeterministically and is sent along the corresponding channel.

Acceptance sets are triples that dictate the choice strategy between the input communications, output communications, and termination. The set of all acceptance sets over a ground type τ and a communication effect σ, written D_Acceptance_Set(τ, σ), is defined as the greatest subset of

$$\mathcal{P}_f(\ \ \mathcal{P}_f(\ \cup \{\ \text{D-Type}(chan_\rho(\tau')) \mid chan_\rho(\tau') \in in(\sigma)\ \}\ ) \times$$
$$\mathcal{P}_f(\ \cup \{\ \text{D-Type}(chan_\rho(\tau')) \mid chan_\rho(\tau') \in out(\sigma)\ \}\ ) \times$$
$$\mathcal{P}_f(\{\sqrt{}\})$$
$$),$$

which satisfies the following invariant:

$\forall A \in$ D_Acceptance_Set(τ, σ). $A \neq \emptyset \wedge$
$\sqrt{} \in \bigcup\{\pi_3(z) \mid z \in A\} \Rightarrow (\emptyset, \emptyset, \{\sqrt{}\}) \in A \wedge$
$\forall x \in A$. $\forall y \in$ ($\mathcal{P}_f \left(\cup \{ \text{D\_Type}(chan_\rho(\tau')) \mid chan_\rho(\tau') \in in(\sigma) \} \right) \times$
$\qquad\qquad \mathcal{P}_f \left(\cup \{ \text{D\_Type}(chan_\rho(\tau')) \mid chan_\rho(\tau') \in out(\sigma) \} \right) \times$
$\qquad\qquad \mathcal{P}_f(\{\sqrt{}\})$
$\qquad$),
$\qquad (\pi_1(y) \subseteq \bigcup\{\pi_1(z) \mid z \in A\} \wedge$
$\qquad \pi_2(y) \subseteq \bigcup\{\pi_2(z) \mid z \in A\} \wedge$
$\qquad \pi_3(y) \subseteq \bigcup\{\pi_3(z) \mid z \in A\} \wedge$
$\qquad \pi_1(x) \subseteq \pi_1(y) \wedge$
$\qquad \pi_2(x) \subseteq \pi_2(y) \wedge$
$\qquad \pi_3(x) \subseteq \pi_3(y)$
$\qquad \Rightarrow y \in A)$.

The latter complicated condition on the acceptance set is just the combination of the convex and the union closures.

Let τ be a ground type and σ a ground communication effect. We define the space of dynamic routines D_Routine(τ, σ) that may return results of type τ together with a communication effect bounded by σ as the greatest subset of

$$(\; \mathcal{P}_f(\text{D\_Type}(\tau)) \times$$
$$\text{D\_Input\_Map}(\tau, \sigma) \times$$
$$\text{D\_Output\_Map}(\tau, \sigma) \times$$
$$\text{D\_Acceptance\_Set}(\tau, \sigma)$$
$$)$$
$$\cup$$
$$\{\bot\},$$

which satisfies the following condition:

$$\forall d \in \text{D\_Routine}(\tau, \sigma). \; d \neq \bot \Rightarrow$$
$$dom(\pi_2(d)) \; = \; \bigcup\{\pi_1(z) \mid z \in \pi_4(d)\} \wedge$$
$$dom(\pi_3(d)) \; = \; \bigcup\{\pi_2(z) \mid z \in \pi_4(d)\} \wedge$$
$$\sqrt{} \in \bigcup\{\pi_3(z) \mid z \in \pi_4(d)\} \Leftrightarrow \pi_1(d) \neq \emptyset,$$

where $\pi_i(x)$ stands for the ith ($i = 1, .., 4$) projection of the structure x. The condition above states that whenever a process is not divergent (not $\bot$ but a 4-tuple), then the input events (respectively output events) appearing in its input map (respectively output map) are exactly those appearing in its acceptance set. Furthermore, whenever termination is possible (i.e., there exists some acceptance state containing the symbol $\sqrt{}$), then there must be some values available in the result set among which one will be returned nondeterministically if the termination take place immediately.

Let τ be a ground type and σ a ground communication effect. We define the preorder $\sqsubseteq_{\tau, \sigma}$ on the space "D_Routine(τ, σ)" by

1. $\forall d \in$ D_Routine(τ, σ). $\perp \sqsubseteq_{\tau,\sigma} d$;

2. Let (R, I, O, A) and (R', I', O', A') be elements of D_Routine(τ, σ). We write $(R, I, O, A) \sqsubseteq_{\tau,\sigma} (R', I', O', A')$ if and only if

   (a) $R' \subseteq R \ \wedge \ A' \subseteq A$,
   (b) $dom(I') \subseteq dom(I) \ \wedge \ dom(O') \subseteq dom(O)$,
   (c) $\forall x \in dom(I'). \ \forall v. \ I(x)(v) \sqsubseteq_{\tau,\sigma} I'(x)(v)$,
   (d) $\forall y \in dom(O')$.
       $(dom(O'(y)) \subseteq dom(O(y))) \ \wedge$
       $(\forall v \in dom(O'(y)). \ O(y)(v) \sqsubseteq_{\tau,\sigma} O'(y)(v))$.

The process space is reflexive. Its existence can be easily derived from the proof of the process space presented in [28]. The latter uses the general theory of domains [158] or cpo's. In fact, we have a recursive domain specification of the form $D = F(D)$. In order to show the existence of our process space, we have to show that our constructor "F" can be turned into a continuous functor in the category of cpo's CPO and then define the process space D as the least fixpoint of the functor F (i.e., the initial object in the category of F-algebras).

Proposition 6.5.1. For all ground types τ and ground communication effects σ, (D_Routine$(\tau, \sigma), \sqsubseteq_{\tau,\sigma}$) is a complete partial order (cpo).

Proof. The result is derived from the standard construction of the process space.   □

The intention hereafter is to establish the algebraicity of the process space. For the sake of conciseness and in order to maintain the readability of the presentation, we will drop, without loss of generality, the invariants on input maps, output maps, and acceptance sets. The generalization of the proof to these invariants is straightforward. The following result characterizes the compact elements of the space D_Routine(τ, σ).

Proposition 6.5.2. Let τ be a ground type and σ a ground communication effect. Let $K(\tau, \sigma)$ be the following set:

$K(\tau, \sigma) =$
   $((\ \mathcal{P}_f(\text{D\_Type}(\tau))) \ \times$
      $(\cup \{\text{D\_Type}(chan_\rho(\tau')) \mid chan_\rho(\tau') \in in(\sigma)\}) \ \overrightarrow{m}$
      $(\cup \{\text{D\_Type}(\tau') \xrightarrow{f} K(\tau, \sigma) \mid chan_\rho(\tau') \in in(\sigma)\}) \ \times$
      $(\cup \{\text{D\_Type}(chan_\rho(\tau')) \mid chan_\rho(\tau') \in in(\sigma)\}) \ \overrightarrow{m}$
      $(\cup \{\text{D\_Type}(\tau') \ \overrightarrow{m} \ K(\tau, \sigma) \mid chan_\rho(\tau') \in in(\sigma)\}) \ \times$
      D_Acceptance_Set(τ, σ)
   $)$
   $\cup \{\perp\},$

where $\xrightarrow{f}$ denotes the function constructor that satisfies: $g \in A \xrightarrow{f} B \Leftrightarrow \{x | g(x) \neq \perp\} \in \mathcal{P}_f(A)$. Let $C(\tau, \sigma)$ be the set of all the elements of $K(\tau, \sigma)$ having a finite depth. The space $C(\tau, \sigma)$ is then the set of compact elements of D_Routine(τ, σ).

Proof. First of all, let us point out that $K(\tau, \sigma)$ is reflexive. Its existence could be derived from that of D_Routine(τ, σ) since it is just a nonempty subset of the latter, hence, the existence of $C(\tau, \sigma)$. Now we shall prove that the elements of $C(\tau, \sigma)$ are compact; afterwards we will prove that these are the only compact elements of D_Routine(τ, σ).

Let P be an element of $C(\tau, \sigma)$. We will proceed by induction on the depth of P. If P is of depth 1 then obviously P is $\perp$, which is trivially compact. Now, let $P = (R, I, O, A)$ be a nondivergent process of depth n, where R is the result set, I is the input map, O the output map, and A the acceptance set. Assume that

$$\forall P_i \in \text{D\_Routine}(\tau, \sigma). \; P_0 \sqsubseteq_{\tau,\sigma} P_1 \sqsubseteq_{\tau,\sigma} \cdots$$

Assume that $P \sqsubseteq_{\tau,\sigma} \bigsqcup_{i=0}^{\infty} P_i$. The least upper bound exists since D_Routine(τ, σ) is a cpo. By definition of $\sqsubseteq_{\tau,\sigma}$, we get

$$\bigsqcup_{i=0}^{\infty} P_i = (\bigcap_{i=0}^{\infty} R_i, \bigsqcup_{i=0}^{\infty} I_i, \bigsqcup_{i=0}^{\infty} O_i, \bigcap_{i=0}^{\infty} A_i).$$

Thus, $R \supseteq \bigcap_{i=0}^{\infty} R_i \subseteq \cdots \subseteq R_j \subseteq \cdots \subseteq R_0$. Since R_i is finite for all i, the chain $R_0 \supseteq R_1 \supseteq \cdots$ is obviously terminating. So, $\exists i_0 \in \mathbb{N} \mid R_{i_0} = \bigcap_{i=0}^{\infty} R_i$. Hence $R \supseteq R_{i_0}$.

By using the same argument applied to the A_i, we obtain $\exists j_0 \in \mathbb{N} \mid A \supseteq A_{j_0}$. By taking $k_0 = max(i_0, j_0)$, we get

$$R \supseteq R_{k_0},$$
$$A \supseteq A_{k_0}.$$

We also have $I \sqsubseteq_{\tau,\sigma} \bigsqcup_{i=0}^{\infty} I_i \sqsupseteq_{\tau,\sigma} \cdots \sqsupseteq_{\tau,\sigma} I_1 \sqsupseteq_{\tau,\sigma} I_0$ and $dom(I) \supseteq \bigcap_{i=0}^{\infty} dom(I_i) \subseteq \cdots \subseteq dom(I_0)$. But since $dom(I_i)$ is finite, $\exists l_0 \in \mathbb{N} \mid dom(I) \supseteq dom(I_{l_0})$.

We know that

$$\forall e \in \bigcap_{m=0}^{\infty} dom(I_m). \forall v. I(e)(v) \sqsubseteq_{\tau,\sigma} (\bigsqcup_{m=0}^{\infty} I_m)(e)(v)$$

and

$$I_0(e)(v) \sqsubseteq_{\tau,\sigma} I_1(e)(v) \sqsubseteq_{\tau,\sigma} \cdots \sqsubseteq_{\tau,\sigma} (\bigsqcup_{m=0}^{\infty} I_m)(e)(v).$$

But the terms of the form $I_m(e)(v)$ are processes of depth $n-1$. Hence, by applying the induction hypothesis, we get

$$\exists m_{e,v} \in \mathbb{N} \mid I(e)(v) \sqsubseteq_{\tau,\sigma} I_{m_{e,v}}(e)(v).$$

Now let

$$\eta = max(\{m_{e,v} \mid e \in dom(I_{m_{e,v}}) \;\wedge\; I(e)(v) \neq \bot\}).$$

The maximum exists because the set above is obviously finite since the spaces of the maps I_i are finite and also because $I(e)$ is constructed via the constructor $\xrightarrow{f}$. It should be noted that given a particular input event e, if $I(e)(v)$ is $\bot$ then any positive integer $m_{e,v}$ matches, i.e., $I(e)(v) \sqsubseteq_{\tau,\sigma} I_{m_{e,v}}(e)(v)$.

By applying the same argument to O we will obtain

$$\nu = max(\{n_{e,v} \mid e \in dom(O_{n_{e,v}}), v \in dom(O_{n_{e,v}}(e))\}).$$

Now, by taking $\mu = max(\{\eta, \nu, k_0, l_0\})$ we get $I \sqsubseteq_{\tau,\sigma} I_\mu$ i.e.,

- $R_\mu \subseteq R$,

- $A_\mu \subseteq A$,

- $dom(I_\mu) \subseteq dom(I)$,

- $dom(O_\mu) \subseteq dom(O)$,

- $\forall x \in dom(I_\mu). \; \forall v. \; I(x)(v) \sqsubseteq_{\tau,\sigma} I_\mu(x)(v)$,

- $\forall y \in dom(O_\mu).$
  $(dom(O_\mu(y)) \subseteq dom(O(y))) \;\wedge\; (\forall v \in dom(O_\mu(y)). \; O(y)(v) \sqsubseteq_{\tau,\sigma} O_\mu(y)(v)).$

Hence $C(\tau,\sigma)$ is a set of compact elements in D_Routine(τ,σ).

Now let us prove that $C(\tau,\sigma)$ is the set of *all* compact elements of D_Routine(τ,σ). Consider P a compact element in D_Routine(τ,σ), and we shall prove that it must belong to $C(\tau,\sigma)$. First, notice that this is straightforward when P is $\bot$. Now if P is in D_Routine$(\tau,\sigma)_\infty \backslash \{\bot\}$, it can be written as: $P = (x_0, x_1, ..., x_{i-1}, x_i, x_{i+1}, ...) = \bigsqcup_{i=0}^\infty P_i$ where

$$
\begin{aligned}
P_0 &= (x_0, x_0, ...),\\
P_1 &= (x_0, x_1, x_1, ...),\\
P_2 &= (x_0, x_1, x_2, x_2, ...),\\
&\;\;\vdots\\
P_i &= (x_0, x_1, ..., x_{i-1}, x_i, x_i, ...),\\
&\;\;\vdots
\end{aligned}
$$

Recall that $D\_Routine(\tau, \sigma)_0, D\_Routine(\tau, \sigma)_1, ..., D\_Routine(\tau, \sigma)_i, ...$ is the chain of approximations (projections) of the space $D\_Routine(\tau, \sigma)$ obtained via the inverse limit construction [72, 65]. The construction is standard; we detailed it in [31, 28]. Let us recall also that $D\_Routine(\tau, \sigma)_\infty$ is the least upper bound of these approximations. In fact, $D\_Routine(\tau, \sigma)_\infty$ is the solution of our reflexive domain equation $D\_Routine(\tau, \sigma) = F(D\_Routine(\tau, \sigma))$.

We have $P_0 \sqsubseteq_{\tau, \sigma} P_1 \sqsubseteq_{\tau, \sigma} ... \sqsubseteq_{\tau, \sigma} P_i \sqsubseteq_{\tau, \sigma} ...$, but P is compact in $D\_Routine(\tau, \sigma)$, so $\exists k \in \mathbb{N} \mid P \sqsubseteq_{\tau, \sigma} P_k$. We know also that $P_k \sqsubseteq_{\tau, \sigma} P$. Hence, $P = P_k$, which means that P is of depth k. Thus each compact element in $D\_Routine(\tau, \sigma)$ is of finite depth. For the rest of the proof, we need the following definition: Given a process $Q \in D\_Routine(\tau, \sigma) \backslash \{\bot\}$, let $Sequels(Q)$ be the least set that satisfies

1. $Q \in Sequels(Q)$,

2. $S \in Sequels(Q) \Rightarrow \forall e \in dom(\pi_2(S)). \forall v. (\pi_2(S)(e)(v) \neq \bot \Rightarrow \pi_2(S)(e)(v) \in Sequels(Q))$.

Continuing the proof, we distinguish two cases:

- P satisfies $\forall R \in Sequels(P). \forall e \in dom(\pi_2(R)).\{v \mid \pi_2(R)(e)(v) \neq \bot\}$ is finite. In this case, P is trivially in $C(\tau, \sigma)$.

- Now assume that there exists $R_0 \in Sequels(P)$ such that $\exists e_0 \in dom(\pi_2(R_0)).\{v \mid \pi_2(R_0)(e_0)(v) \neq \bot\}$ is infinite. Let us write the latter set as $\bigcup_{i \in \mathbb{N}} X_i$ such that $X_i \neq \emptyset$ and $X_i \cap X_j = \emptyset$ for $i \neq j$. It should be noted that such a partition exists. In fact, this is quite immediate for our type universe, but the proof is more intricate in the general case. Thus one can define

$$\forall i \in \mathbb{N}. P_i = P[R_0 \leftarrow R_{i0}],$$

which stands for the process P, where the sequel process R_0 is replaced by R_{i0} and

$$R_{i0} = R_0 \quad [\pi_2(R_0) \leftarrow \pi_2(R_0)\dagger \quad [\quad e_0 \mapsto \lambda v. \quad \textbf{if} \quad v \in \cup_{j=0}^{i} X_j$$
$$\vdots \qquad \qquad \vdots \qquad \qquad \textbf{then} \quad \pi_2(R_0)(e_0)(v)$$
$$\vdots \qquad \qquad \vdots \qquad \qquad \textbf{else} \quad \bot$$
$$\vdots \qquad \qquad \quad]$$
$$\vdots$$
$$]$$

Thus it is clear that

$$P_0 \sqsubseteq_{\tau, \sigma} P_1 \sqsubseteq_{\tau, \sigma} ... \sqsubseteq_{\tau, \sigma} P_i \sqsubseteq_{\tau, \sigma} ...$$

and $\bigcup_{i=0}^{\infty} P_i = P$; but

$$\forall i \in \mathbb{N}. P_i \neq P$$

which is a contradiction with the fact that P is compact.

Finally, P compact implies that $P \in C(\tau, \sigma)$. Hence, $C(\tau, \sigma)$ is the set of all compact elements in D_Routine(τ, σ).

$\square$

Proposition 6.5.3. D_Routine(τ, σ) is an algebraic complete partial order.

Proof. D_Routine(τ, σ) is by construction a cpo. Now, given $P \in$ D_Routine(τ, σ), the strategy consists of computing a directed set of compact approximations of P, which will be denoted by $Approx(P)$ and which satisfies $\bigsqcup Approx(P) = P$.

To do so, let $P = (x_0, x_1, ..., x_{i-1}, x_i, x_{i+1}, ...)$. We need to consider the following family of functions:

$$
\begin{aligned}
\Delta_0 &= \lambda\perp.\{\perp\} \\
\Delta_{i+1} &= \lambda x. \ \textbf{case } x \textbf{ of} \\
&\qquad \perp \to \perp \\
&\qquad (R, I, O, A) \to \{(R, I', O, A) \mid I' \in \Omega_i^*(I)\} \\
&\quad \textbf{end}
\end{aligned}
$$

where Ω_i^* is defined as

$$\Omega_i^* = \lambda I.\{m \mid m = [x \mapsto f_y \mid x \mapsto y \in I \ \wedge \ f_y \in \Omega_i(y)]\}$$

and

$$
\begin{aligned}
\Omega_i = \ &\lambda f. \ \textbf{if } \{v \mid f(v) \neq \perp\} \textit{ is finite} \\
&\textbf{then } \{\lambda v.\Delta_i(f(v))\} \\
&\textbf{else} \\
&\qquad \{f_{X_j} \mid (j \in \mathbb{N}) \ \wedge \\
&\qquad\quad \exists X_j.(|X_j| = j) \wedge (v \in X_j \Rightarrow f_{X_j}(v) = \Delta_i(f(v))) \ \wedge \\
&\qquad\quad (v \notin X_j \Rightarrow f_{X_j}(v) = \perp)\}.
\end{aligned}
$$

Let us now write $Approx(P) = \bigcup_{k=0}^{\infty}\{\theta_{k\infty}(x_k') \mid x_k' \in \Delta_k(x_k)\}$ where

$$
\begin{aligned}
\theta_{k\infty} &= \lambda x \in \text{D\_Routine}(\tau, \sigma)_k. \ (\theta_{k0}(x), \theta_{k1}(x), \ldots, \theta_{kj}(x), \ldots), \\
\theta_{\infty k} &= \lambda x \in \text{D\_Routine}(\tau, \sigma)_\infty.\pi_k(x),
\end{aligned}
$$

and the functions θ_{ki} are defined by

$$\begin{aligned}
\textbf{if } k < i \quad &\textbf{then} \quad \theta_{ki} = \phi_{i-1} \circ \phi_{i-2} \circ \ldots \circ \phi_k, \\
\textbf{if } k = i \quad &\textbf{then} \quad \theta_{ki} = Id_{\text{D\_Routine}(\tau,\sigma)_k}, \\
\textbf{if } k > i \quad &\textbf{then} \quad \theta_{ki} = \psi_i \circ \psi_{i-1} \ldots \circ \phi_{k-1},
\end{aligned}$$

where $Id_{\text{D\_Routine}(\tau,\sigma)_k}$ represents the identity function on the kth approximation of D_Routine(τ,σ), written D_Routine$(\tau,\sigma)_k$. Let us recall also the functions ϕ_i and ψ_i, which denote respectively the standard embeddings and projections on the approximations of the form D_Routine$(\tau,\sigma)_i$:

$$\begin{aligned}
\phi_0 &: \text{D\_Routine}(\tau,\sigma)_0 \to \text{D\_Routine}(\tau,\sigma)_1 \\
\phi_i &: \text{D\_Routine}(\tau,\sigma)_i \to \text{D\_Routine}(\tau,\sigma)_{i+1} \\
\psi_0 &: \text{D\_Routine}(\tau,\sigma)_1 \to \text{D\_Routine}(\tau,\sigma)_0 \\
\psi_i &: \text{D\_Routine}(\tau,\sigma)_{i+1} \to \text{D\_Routine}(\tau,\sigma)_i
\end{aligned}$$

It is clear that $Approx(P)$ is directed since for all $Q, R \in Approx(P)$ we have that $Q \sqcup R$ exists. Let $Q = \theta_{m\infty}(x'_m)$ and $R = \theta_{n\infty}(x'_n)$; if $m \neq n$ then $Q \sqcup R = \theta_{max(m,n)\infty}(x'_{max(m,n)})$, otherwise let

$$\begin{aligned}
x'_m &= (R, I, O, A), \\
x'_n &= (R, I', O, A).
\end{aligned}$$

Then obviously $x''_m = (R, I \sqcup I', O, A)$ is a least upper bound for Q and R. Hence, $Approx(P)$ is directed.

One can also see that elements of $Approx(P)$ are compact since they have finite depth and are obtained after the application of Δ_i. Now, to achieve the algebraicity proof we must show that $\bigsqcup Approx(P) = P$, which holds since it is straightforward that for a given $k \in \mathbb{N}$, we have

$$\sqcup \{\theta_{k\infty}(x'_k) \mid x'_k \in \Delta_k(x_k)\} = P_k.$$

This concludes the proof. □

6.5.4 Semantics Presentation

We have presented in the previous sections some semantic domains and we have established some algebraic properties of the dynamic space of processes. Now, the intention is to ascribe a meaning to the syntactic constructions using the previously introduced domains. The semantics description technique that will be used here is borrowed from [51], which generalizes and improves the work done in [32, 29].

First of all, let us introduce the following static domains:

$$
\begin{array}{rcll}
\tau & \in & \text{S\_Type} & \text{Types,} \\
x & \in & \text{Id} & \text{Identifiers,} \\
\forall v_1, ..., v_n.\tau & \in & \text{TypeScheme} & \text{Type schemes,} \\
\mathcal{E} & \in & \text{S\_Env} = \text{Id} \xrightarrow{m} \text{TypeScheme} & \text{Static environments,} \\
\sigma & \in & \text{S\_Ceff} & \text{Communication effects,} \\
\mathcal{E}'{\to}'\tau'{\to}'\sigma & \in & \text{S\_Res} & \text{Static evaluation results.}
\end{array}
$$

In order to lighten the notation and to improve the clarity of the presentation of the semantic equations, we will write triples of the form $\mathcal{E}'{\to}'\tau'{\to}'\sigma$ without the static marks '$\to$', i.e.,

$$(\mathcal{E}, \tau, \sigma) \in \text{S\_Res}.$$

Thus, the static domain "S_Res" is defined by

$$\text{S\_Res} = \text{S\_Env} \times \text{S\_Type} \times \text{S\_Ceff}.$$

As previously explained, the dynamic domain "P_Type(τ)" that corresponds to a not necessarily ground type τ is defined as

$$\text{P\_Type}(\tau) = \prod \theta \in \mathcal{GS}(fv(\tau)). \text{ D\_Type}(\theta\tau),$$

where D_Type is the function used to construct the dynamic type D_Type(τ) from a ground static type τ.

Type schemes are interpreted dynamically as dependent types that take ground substitutions that instantiate all the free variables in the body of a given type scheme, in order to apply afterwards the function that generates the corresponding dynamic types:

$$\text{P\_TypeScheme}(\forall v_1, ..., v_n.\tau) = \prod \theta \in \mathcal{GS}(\{v_1, ..., v_n\}). \text{ D\_Type}(\theta\tau).$$

Dynamic environments are defined as dependent types that take static environments to mappings that associate to identifiers the dynamic domains associated with the corresponding type schemes. In other words,

$$\text{D\_Env}(\mathcal{E}) = \prod x \in dom(\mathcal{E}). \text{ P\_TypeScheme}(\mathcal{E}(x)).$$

Notice that D_Env does not appear in P_TypeScheme($\mathcal{E}(x)$). Accordingly, the definition of D_Env is well-founded.

The function that performs the static evaluation corresponds to the translation of typing sequents. Given an expression e drawn from the syntactic domain "Exp" of expressions, and given a static environment $\mathcal{E}$, the static evaluation function yields a set whose elements are pairs of the form (τ, σ), where τ is a type from "Type" and σ a channel effect from "S_Ceff". Its signature is

$$[\![\, \_ \,]\!]_{\_} : \text{Exp} \to \text{S\_Env} \xrightarrow{\sim} \mathcal{P}(\text{S\_Type} \times \text{S\_Ceff}),$$

where "$\overset{\sim}{\rightarrow}$" stands for the partial function constructor. The presence of such a constructor is due to the side conditions and the formation constraints appearing in the semantic rules.

We adopt the syntactic convention that consists in writing $[\![\, e\,]\!]\mathcal{E} \ni (\tau, \sigma)$ instead of $[\![\, e\,]\!]\mathcal{E} = (\tau, \sigma)$, since the relation between the arguments of the static evaluation and the static result is one-to-many. In other words, an expression may have different types and effects but all are instances of the most general static result (maximal type and minimal effect). Furthermore, we will write $\theta \in \mathcal{GS}(tv)$ to denote a ground substitution whose domain includes the set of all type and effect variables.

Concerning the function that performs the dynamic evaluation, its signature is given by the following:

$$[\![\, \_ \,]\!]_{\_} : \mathrm{Exp} \rightarrow$$
$$\textstyle\prod(\mathcal{E}, \tau, \sigma) \in \mathrm{S\_Res.\ P\_Res}(\mathcal{E}, \tau, \sigma).$$

Given an expression e, the dynamic evaluation yields a dependent type value. This value takes a possible result of the static evaluation of e to an appropriate dynamic result.

At this level, we consider as a result of the static evaluation of a given expression e, a triple of the form $(\mathcal{E}, \tau, \sigma)$. This triple states that the expression e has a type τ and a communication effect σ, under the static environment $\mathcal{E}$. In other words, this means that the sequent $\mathcal{E} \vdash e : \tau, \sigma$ is provable in the type system of Figure 6.2.

The dynamic domain "$\mathrm{P\_Res}(\mathcal{E}, \tau, \sigma)$" is member of the domain family "P_Z". Thus, it takes ground substitutions that instantiate completely $\mathcal{E}$, τ, and σ to an element of "$\mathrm{D\_Res}(\theta\mathcal{E}, \theta\tau, \theta\sigma)$":

$$\mathrm{P\_Res}(\mathcal{E}, \tau, \sigma) \;=\; \textstyle\prod \theta \in \mathcal{GS}(fv(\mathcal{E}) \cup fv(\tau) \cup fv(\sigma)).\ \mathrm{D\_Res}(\theta\mathcal{E}, \theta\tau, \theta\sigma).$$

Analogously, a dynamic result is merely a function that associates dynamic denotations to dynamic environments:

$$\mathrm{D\_Res}(\mathcal{E}, \tau, \sigma) \;=\; \mathrm{D\_Env}(\mathcal{E}) \rightarrow \mathrm{D\_Den}(\tau, \sigma).$$

The dynamic denotations are defined by

$$\mathrm{D\_Den}(\tau, \sigma) \;=\; \mathrm{D\_Routine}(\tau, \sigma).$$

As pointed out before, the description technique used relies on a dependence between the static and the dynamic semantics. Accordingly, the semantic rules hereafter will be structured in three parts. The first part expresses the formation constraints. The second part is devoted to the static evaluation. The third part is devoted to the denotational dynamic evaluation. The semantic rules obey to the following schema:

Context free side conditions
Static applicability conditions
Static evaluation of subexpressions

Static evaluation of the expression

Dynamic evaluation of the expression

The semantic functions together with the semantic rules are given respectively in Appendix 6.A and Appendix 6.B of this chapter.

6.6   Conclusion

We have reported in this chapter a semantic theory for a set of ML higher-order concurrency primitives. The theory consists in a new effect-based type system and a dynamic denotational semantics. The type system computes, in addition to principal types, minimal communication effects. The consistency and the decidability results of the presented static semantics can be derived easily from the proofs we presented previously in [29, 51]. We have also reported a denotational model based on an extension of the acceptance trees model for handling polymorphism, input, output, communication, value-passing, and higher-order objects. The model is constructed in a nonclassical way since it does not refer to domain theory except for the process space. It is made dependent on the static semantics thanks to a new method for constructing dynamic spaces in a denotational setting. The method establishes a dependency between the static and the dynamic semantics. The dynamic domains are typed according to the hierarchy laid down by the static domains.

Appendix 6.A   Semantic Functions

The function "*return*" takes a dynamic value and returns a process. The latter does not communicate; it terminates immediately and returns the argument value as a result:

$$return = \lambda v. \, (\{v\}, [\,], [\,], \{(\emptyset, \emptyset, \{\sqrt{}\})\}).$$

We adopt the convention of identifying $\lambda\theta \in \mathcal{GS}(\emptyset).v$ with the computable value v. Thus, it is possible for us to write $\Gamma \dagger [x \mapsto v]$.

The function "*process_set*" takes a process to the set of its deterministic processes, thus with only one acceptance state such that the application of $\sqcap$ on this set yields the original process:

$$process\_set : \mathrm{D\_Routine}(\tau, \sigma) \to \mathcal{P}_f(\mathrm{D\_Routine}(\tau, \sigma)),$$

$process\_set(\bot) = \emptyset$
$process\_set(R, I, O, A) = \{$
    $(R,$
    $[e \mapsto I(e) \mid e \in dom(I) \cap \pi_1(x)],$
    $[e \mapsto O(e) \mid e \in dom(O) \cap \pi_2(x) \,],$
    $acceptance(x)$
    $) \mid x \in A\},$

where $acceptance(x)$ is the result of applying closures (union, convexity, and "$\sqrt{}$") to the one-element set $\{x\}$.

The function "γ" can be seen as a piping operator. It evaluates its first argument and passes the value that is the result of the evaluation to the second argument. It is like a sequencing operator but on process denotations:

$$\_\gamma\_ : \mathrm{D\_Routine}(\tau, \sigma) \times (\mathrm{D\_Type}(\tau) \to \mathrm{D\_Routine}(\tau', \sigma')) \to$$
$$\mathrm{D\_Routine}(\tau', \sigma \cup \sigma'),$$

$d\gamma g = \mathbf{case} \; d \; \mathbf{of}$
    $\bot \to \bot$
    $(R, I, O, A) \to$
        $\sqcap\{\mathbf{let}$
                $internal\_process\_set = \{g(v) \mid v \in R\},$
                $external\_process = (\emptyset \,, \; I_1\gamma g \,, \; O_1\gamma g \,, \; A_1)$
          $\mathbf{in}$
             $\mathbf{if} \; internal\_process\_set = \emptyset$
             $\mathbf{then} \; external\_process$
             $\mathbf{else}$
                $(external\_process \, [] \, (\sqcap internal\_process\_set)$
                $\sqcap (\sqcap internal\_process\_set))$
          $\mathbf{end}$

$$\textbf{end}$$
$$| \ (R_1, I_1, O_1, A_1) \ \in \ process\_set(R, I, O, A)$$
$$\}$$
$$\textbf{end}$$

$$\_\gamma\_ : \text{D\_Input\_Map}(\tau, \sigma) \ \times \ (\text{D\_Type}(\tau) \rightarrow \text{D\_Routine}(\tau', \sigma')) \rightarrow$$
$$\text{D\_Input\_Map}(\tau', \sigma \ \cup \ \sigma')$$

$$I\gamma g = [e \mapsto (\lambda v. \ (I(v)\gamma g)) \ | \ e \ \in \ dom(I)]$$

$$\_\gamma\_ : \text{D\_Output\_Map}(\tau, \sigma) \ \times \ (\text{D\_Type}(\tau) \rightarrow \text{D\_Routine}(\tau', \sigma')) \rightarrow$$
$$\text{D\_Output\_Map}(\tau', \sigma \ \cup \ \sigma')$$

$$O\gamma g = [e \mapsto [v \mapsto (O(e)(v)\gamma g) \ | \ v \ \in \ dom(O(e))]$$
$$| \ e \ \in \ dom(I)$$
$$].$$

The following semantic functions perform the internal choice of two process denotations:

$$\_\sqcap\_ : \text{D\_Routine}(\tau, \sigma) \ \times \ \text{D\_Routine}(\tau, \sigma'), \rightarrow \text{D\_Routine}(\tau, \sigma \ \cup \ \sigma'),$$

$$d \sqcap d' = \textbf{case } d, d' \ \textbf{of}$$
$$(R_1, I_1, O_1, A_1),$$
$$(R_2, I_2, O_2, A_2) \rightarrow (R_1 \ \cup \ R_2, I_1 \sqcap I_2, O_1 \sqcap O_2, A_1 \sqcap A_2)$$
$$\textbf{else } \bot$$
$$\textbf{end},$$

$$\_\sqcap\_ : \text{D\_Input\_Map}(\tau, \sigma) \ \times \ \text{D\_Input\_Map}(\tau, \sigma') \rightarrow$$
$$\text{D\_Input\_Map}(\tau, \sigma \ \cup \ \sigma'),$$

$$I_1 \sqcap I_2 = [e \mapsto I_1(e) \ | \ e \ \in \ dom(I_1)]\dagger$$
$$[e \mapsto I_2(e) \ | \ e \ \in \ dom(I_2)]\dagger$$
$$[e \mapsto \lambda v. \ I_1(e)(v) \sqcap I_1(e)(v) | e \ \in \ dom(I_1) \ \cap \ dom(I_2)],$$

$$\_\sqcap\_ : \text{D\_Output\_Map}(\tau, \sigma) \ \times \ \text{D\_Output\_Map}(\tau, \sigma') \rightarrow$$
$$\text{D\_Output\_Map}(\tau, \sigma \ \cup \ \sigma'),$$

$$O_1 \sqcap O_2 = [e \mapsto O_1(e) \ | \ e \ \in \ dom(O_1)] \ \dagger$$
$$[e \mapsto O_2(e) \ | \ e \ \in \ dom(O_2)] \ \dagger$$
$$[e \mapsto [v \mapsto O_1(e)(v) \sqcap O_2(e)(v) \ | \ v \ \in \ dom(O_1(e)) \ \cap \ dom(O_2(e))]$$
$$| \ e \ \in \ dom(O_1) \ \cap \ dom(O_2)],$$

$\_\lceil\!\lceil\_ : \text{D\_Acceptance\_Set}(\tau, \sigma) \times \text{D\_Acceptance\_Set}(\tau, \sigma') \rightarrow$
    $\text{D\_Acceptance\_Set}(\tau, \sigma \cup \sigma'),$

$$A_1 \lceil\!\lceil A_2 = \{x \mid x \in \mathcal{P}_f(\mathcal{P}_f(\cup \{\text{D\_Type}(c) \mid c \in in(\sigma)\}) \times$$
$$\mathcal{P}_f(\cup \{\text{D\_Type}(c) \mid c \in out(\sigma)\}) \times$$
$$\mathcal{P}_f(\{\surd\})$$
$$).$$
$$\pi_1(x) \subseteq \cup \{\pi_1(y) \mid y \in A_1 \cup A_2\} \wedge$$
$$\pi_2(x) \subseteq \cup \{\pi_2(y) \mid y \in A_1 \cup A_2\} \wedge$$
$$\pi_3(x) \subseteq \cup \{\pi_3(y) \mid y \in A_1 \cup A_2\} \wedge$$
$$(\exists y \in A_1 \cup A_2.\ \pi_1(x) \supseteq \pi_1(y) \wedge \pi_2(x) \supseteq \pi_2(y) \wedge$$
$$\pi_3(x) \supseteq \pi_3(y))$$
$$\}.$$

The following semantic functions perform the external choice of two process denotations:

$\_\lceil\!\rceil\_ : \text{D\_Routine}(\tau, \sigma) \times \text{D\_Routine}(\tau, \sigma') \rightarrow \text{D\_Routine}(\tau, \sigma \cup \sigma'),$

$d \lceil\!\rceil d' = \textbf{case } d, d' \textbf{ of}$
        $(R_1, I_1, O_1, A_1),$
        $(R_2, I_2, O_2, A_2) \rightarrow (R_1 \cup R_2,\ I_1 \lceil\!\lceil I_2,\ O_1 \lceil\!\lceil O_2,\ A_1 \lceil\!\rceil A_2)$
$\textbf{else } \perp$
$\textbf{end},$

$\_\lceil\!\rceil\_ : \text{D\_Acceptance\_Set}(\tau, \sigma) \times \text{D\_Acceptance\_Set}(\tau, \sigma') \rightarrow$
    $\text{D\_Acceptance\_Set}(\tau, \sigma \cup \sigma'),$

$$A_1 \lceil\!\rceil A_2 = \{x \mid x \in \mathcal{P}_f(\mathcal{P}_f(\cup \{\text{D\_Type}(c) \mid c \in in(\sigma)\}) \times$$
$$\mathcal{P}_f(\cup \{\text{D\_Type}(c) \mid c \in out(\sigma)\}) \times$$
$$\mathcal{P}_f(\{\surd\})$$
$$).$$
$$\pi_1(x) \subseteq \cup \{\pi_1(y) \mid y \in A_1 \cup A_2\} \wedge$$
$$\pi_2(x) \subseteq \cup \{\pi_2(y) \mid y \in A_1 \cup A_2\} \wedge$$
$$\pi_3(x) \subseteq \cup \{\pi_3(y) \mid y \in A_1 \cup A_2\} \wedge$$
$$(\exists (y, z) \in A_1 \times A_2.\pi_1(x) = \pi_1(y) \cup \pi_1(z) \wedge$$
$$\pi_2(x) = \pi_2(y) \cup \pi_2(z) \wedge$$
$$\pi_3(x) = \pi_3(y) \cup \pi_3(z)$$
$$)$$
$$\}.$$

The following semantic functions perform the parallel composition of two process denotations. The semantics of the parallel composition described here is inspired by the work on CCS without τ's [52]. More accurately, our semantics may be viewed as an extension of input, output, communication, value-passing, return of results, and higher-order objects. The behavior of the concurrency combinator described here is similar to the one of CCS up to the accommodations mentioned previously. In fact, it provides both synchronizations and interleavings.

$$\_\|\_ : \mathrm{D\_Routine}(\tau, \sigma) \times \mathrm{D\_Routine}(\tau, \sigma') \to \mathrm{D\_Routine}(\tau, \sigma \cup \sigma'),$$

$$d\|\bot = \bot$$
$$\bot\|d = \bot$$
$$(R, I, O, A)\|s\|(R', I', O', A') =$$
$$\qquad \sqcap\{$$

       let

          $(R_1, I_1, O_1, A_1) = process_1,$
          $(R_2, I_2, O_2, A_2) = process_2,$
          $internal\_process\_set =$
              $(R_1 \gamma process_2) \cup (R_2 \gamma process_1) \cup$
              $(I_1\|O_2) \cup (I_2\|O_1),$
          $external\_process =$
              $(\emptyset , I_1\|process_2 , O_1\|process_2 , A_1)$
              $\square$
              $(\emptyset , I_2\|process_1 , O_2\|process_1, A_2)$

       in

          if $internal\_process\_set = \emptyset$
          then $external\_process$
          else $(external\_process \square (\sqcap internal\_process\_set))$
              $\sqcap (\sqcap internal\_process\_set)$
       end

     end|

     $(process_1, process_2) \in process\_set(R, I, O, A) \times$
     $process\_set(R', I', O', A')\},$

$$\_\|\_ : \mathrm{D\_Input\_Map}(\tau, \sigma) \times \mathrm{D\_Output\_Map}(\tau, \sigma') \to$$
$$\qquad \mathcal{P}_f(\mathrm{D\_Routine}(\tau, \sigma \cup \sigma')),$$

$$I\|O = \bigcup\{I(e)\|O(e) \mid e \in dom(I) \cap dom(O)\},$$

$$\_\|\_ : (\mathrm{D\_Type}(\tau') \to \mathrm{D\_Routine}(\tau, \sigma)) \times (\mathrm{D\_Type}(\tau') \xrightarrow{m} \mathrm{D\_Routine}(\tau, \sigma'))$$
$$\qquad \to \mathrm{D\_Routine}(\tau, \sigma \cup \sigma'),$$

$$I(e)\|O(e) = \{I(e)(v)\|O(e)(v) \mid v \in dom(O(e))\},$$

$$\_\|\_ : \mathrm{D\_Input\_Map}(\tau, \sigma) \times \mathrm{D\_Routine}(\tau, \sigma') \to \mathrm{D\_Input\_Map}(\tau, \sigma \cup \sigma'),$$

$$I'\|(R, I, O, A) =$$

$$[e \mapsto \lambda v. \; I'(e)(v) \| (R, I, O, A) \mid e \in \mathit{dom}(I')],$$

$$\_\|\_ : \text{D\_Output\_Map}(\tau, \sigma) \; \times \; \text{D\_Routine}(\tau, \sigma') \rightarrow$$
$$\text{D\_Output\_Map}(\tau, \sigma \cup \sigma'),$$

$$O' \| (R, I, O, A) = [e \mapsto O'(e) \| (R, I, O, A) \mid e \in \mathit{dom}(O')],$$

$$\_\|\_ : ((\text{D\_Type}(\tau') \rightharpoonup \text{D\_Routine}(\tau, \sigma)) \; \times \; \text{D\_Routine}(\tau, \sigma')) \rightarrow$$
$$\text{D\_Type}(\tau') \rightharpoonup \text{D\_Routine}(\tau, \sigma \cup \sigma'),$$

$$O'(e) \| (R, I, O, A) = [v \mapsto O'(e)(v) \| (R, I, O, A) \mid v \in \mathit{dom}(O'(e))].$$

Appendix 6.B   Semantic Rules

Constants

$$\theta \in \mathcal{GS}(tv)$$

$$[\![\ ()\ ]\!]\mathcal{E} \ni (Unit, \emptyset)$$

$$[\![\ ()\ ]\!](\mathcal{E}, (Unit, \emptyset))(\theta) =$$
$$\lambda \Gamma \in \text{D\_Env}(\theta\mathcal{E}).\ return((\ ))$$

$$\theta \in \mathcal{GS}(tv)$$

$$[\![\ \text{true}\ ]\!]\mathcal{E} \ni (Bool, \emptyset)$$

$$[\![\ \text{true}\ ]\!](\mathcal{E}, Bool, \emptyset)(\theta) =$$
$$\lambda \Gamma \in \text{D\_Env}(\theta\mathcal{E}).\ return(tt)$$

$$\theta \in \mathcal{GS}(tv)$$

$$[\![\ \text{false}\ ]\!]\mathcal{E} \ni (Bool, \emptyset)$$

$$[\![\ \text{false}\ ]\!](\mathcal{E}, Bool, \emptyset)(\theta) =$$
$$\lambda \Gamma \in \text{D\_Env}(\theta\mathcal{E}).\ return(f\!f)$$

$$\theta \in \mathcal{GS}(tv)$$

$$[\![\ \text{skip}\ ]\!]\mathcal{E} \ni (Unit, \emptyset)$$

$$[\![\ \text{skip}\ ]\!](\mathcal{E}, Unit, \emptyset)(\theta) =$$
$$\lambda \Gamma \in \text{D\_Env}(\theta\mathcal{E}).\ return((\ ))$$

Lookup

$$\mathcal{E}(x) = \forall v_1, ..., v_n.\ \tau'$$
$$\theta' \in \mathcal{GS}(\{v_1, ..., v_n\})$$
$$\tau = \theta'\tau'$$
$$\theta \in \mathcal{GS}(tv)$$

$$[\![\, x\,]\!]\mathcal{E}\ \ni\ (\tau, \emptyset)$$

$$[\![\, x\,]\!](\mathcal{E}, \tau, \emptyset)(\theta)\ =$$
$$\quad \lambda\Gamma \in \text{D\_Env}(\theta\mathcal{E}).\ return(\Gamma(x)(\theta \circ \theta'))$$

Abstraction

$$[\![\, e\,]\!](\mathcal{E}_x \dagger [x \mapsto \tau])\ \ni\ (\tau', \sigma)$$
$$\theta \in \mathcal{GS}(tv)$$

$$[\![\, \lambda x.e\,]\!]\mathcal{E}\ \ni\ (\tau \xrightarrow{\sigma} \tau', \emptyset)$$

$$[\![\, \lambda x.e\,]\!](\mathcal{E}, \tau \xrightarrow{\sigma} \tau', \emptyset)(\theta)\ =$$
$$\quad \lambda\Gamma \in \text{D\_Env}(\theta\mathcal{E}).$$
$$\qquad \textbf{let}$$
$$\qquad\quad f = \lambda v \in \text{D\_Type}(\theta\tau).[\![\, e\,]\!](\mathcal{E} \dagger [x \mapsto \tau], \tau', \sigma)(\theta)(\Gamma_x \dagger [x \mapsto v])$$
$$\qquad \textbf{in}$$
$$\qquad\quad return(f)(s)$$
$$\qquad \textbf{end}$$

Application

$$\begin{array}{l} [\![\ e_1\ ]\!]\mathcal{E} \ni (\tau \xrightarrow{\sigma} \tau', \sigma') \\ [\![\ e_2\ ]\!]\mathcal{E} \ni (\tau, \sigma'') \\ \sigma''' = \sigma \cup \sigma' \cup \sigma'' \\ \theta \in \mathcal{GS}(tv) \end{array}$$

$$[\![\ e_1\ e_2\ ]\!]\mathcal{E} \ni (\tau', \sigma''')$$

$$\begin{array}{l} [\![\ e_1\ e_2\ ]\!](\mathcal{E}, \tau', \sigma''')(\theta) = \\ \quad \lambda\Gamma \in \mathrm{D\_Env}(\theta\mathcal{E}). \\ \quad\quad [\![\ e_2\ ]\!](\mathcal{E}, \tau, \sigma'')(\theta)(\Gamma) \\ \quad\quad\quad \gamma\lambda v \in \mathrm{D\_Type}(\theta\tau). [\![\ e_1\ ]\!](\mathcal{E}, \tau \xrightarrow{\sigma} \tau', \sigma')(\theta)(\Gamma) \\ \quad\quad\quad\quad \gamma\lambda f \in \mathrm{D\_Type}(\theta(\tau \xrightarrow{\sigma} \tau')). (f\ v) \end{array}$$

Sequencing

$$\begin{array}{l} [\![\ e_1\ ]\!]\mathcal{E} \ni (\tau, \sigma) \\ [\![\ e_2\ ]\!]\mathcal{E} \ni (\tau', \sigma') \\ \sigma'' = \sigma \cup \sigma' \\ \theta \in \mathcal{GS}(tv) \end{array}$$

$$[\![\ e_1 ; e_2\ ]\!]\mathcal{E} \ni (\tau', \sigma'')$$

$$\begin{array}{l} [\![\ e_1 ; e_2\ ]\!](\mathcal{E}, \tau', \sigma'')(\theta) = \\ \quad \lambda\Gamma \in \mathrm{D\_Env}(\theta\mathcal{E}). \\ \quad\quad [\![\ e_1\ ]\!](\mathcal{E}, \tau, \sigma)(\theta)(\Gamma) \\ \quad\quad\quad \gamma\lambda v \in \mathrm{D\_Type}(\theta\tau). [\![\ e_2\ ]\!](\mathcal{E}, \tau', \sigma')(\theta)(\Gamma) \end{array}$$

Input

$[\![\, e \,]\!]\mathcal{E} \ni (chan_\rho(\tau), \sigma)$
$\sigma' = \sigma \cup in(\rho, \tau)$
$\theta \in \mathcal{GS}(tv)$

$[\![\, \texttt{receive}(e) \,]\!]\mathcal{E} \ni (\tau, \sigma)$

$[\![\, \texttt{receive}(e) \,]\!](\mathcal{E}, \tau, \sigma)(\theta) =$
  $\lambda\Gamma \in \text{D\_Env}(\theta\mathcal{E}).$
    $[\![\, e \,]\!](\mathcal{E}, chan_\rho(\tau), \sigma)(\theta)(\Gamma)$
      $\gamma\lambda c \in \text{D\_Type}(\theta chan_\rho(\tau)).$
        $(\{\},$
          $[c \mapsto \lambda v.\, return(v)],$
          $[\,],$
          $\{(\{c\}, \emptyset, \emptyset)\}$
        $)$

Output

$[\![\, e_1 \,]\!]\mathcal{E} \ni (chan_\rho(\tau), \sigma)$
$[\![\, e_2 \,]\!]\mathcal{E} \ni (\tau, \sigma')$
$\sigma'' = \sigma \cup \sigma' \cup out(\rho, \tau)$
$\theta \in \mathcal{GS}(tv)$

$[\![\, \texttt{send}(e_1, e_2) \,]\!]\mathcal{E} \ni (Unit, \sigma'')$

$[\![\, \texttt{send}(e_1, e_2) \,]\!](\mathcal{E}, Unit, \sigma'')(\theta) =$
  $\lambda\Gamma \in \text{D\_Env}(\theta\mathcal{E}).$
    $[\![\, e_2 \,]\!](\mathcal{E}, \tau, \sigma')(\theta)(\Gamma)$
      $\gamma\lambda v \in \text{D\_Type}(\theta\tau).$
        $[\![\, e_1 \,]\!](\mathcal{E}, chan_\rho(\tau), \sigma)(\theta)(\Gamma)$
          $\gamma\lambda c \in \text{D\_Type}(\theta chan_\rho(\tau)).$
            $\lambda s.\, (\emptyset,$
              $[\,],$
              $[c \mapsto [v \mapsto return(v)]]$
              $\{(\emptyset, \{c\}, \emptyset)\}$
            $)$

Internal Choice

$$\llbracket\ e_1\ \rrbracket\mathcal{E}\ \ni\ (\tau,\sigma)$$
$$\llbracket\ e_2\ \rrbracket\mathcal{E}\ \ni\ (\tau,\sigma')$$
$$\sigma''\ =\ \sigma\ \cup\ \sigma'$$
$$\theta\ \in\ \mathcal{GS}(tv)$$

$$\overline{\qquad\qquad\qquad\qquad\qquad\qquad\qquad}$$

$$\llbracket\ e_1\sqcap e_2\ \rrbracket\mathcal{E}\ \ni\ (\tau,\sigma'')$$

$$\overline{\qquad\qquad\qquad\qquad\qquad\qquad\qquad}$$

$$\llbracket\ e_1\sqcap e_2\ \rrbracket(\mathcal{E},\tau,\sigma'')(\theta)\ =$$
$$\lambda\Gamma\ \in\ \mathrm{D\_Env}(\theta\mathcal{E}).$$
$$(\ \llbracket\ e_1\ \rrbracket(\mathcal{E},\tau,\sigma)(\theta)(\Gamma)$$
$$\sqcap$$
$$\llbracket\ e_2\ \rrbracket(\mathcal{E},\tau,\sigma')(\theta)(\Gamma)$$
$$)$$

External Choice

$$\llbracket\ e_1\ \rrbracket\mathcal{E}\ \ni\ (\tau,\sigma)$$
$$\llbracket\ e_2\ \rrbracket\mathcal{E}\ \ni\ (\tau,\sigma')$$
$$\sigma''\ =\ \sigma\ \cup\ \sigma'$$
$$\theta\ \in\ \mathcal{GS}(tv)$$

$$\overline{\qquad\qquad\qquad\qquad\qquad\qquad\qquad}$$

$$\llbracket\ e_1\Box e_2\ \rrbracket\mathcal{E}\ \ni\ (\tau,\sigma'')$$

$$\overline{\qquad\qquad\qquad\qquad\qquad\qquad\qquad}$$

$$\llbracket\ e_1\Box e_2\ \rrbracket(\mathcal{E},\tau,\sigma'')(\theta)\ =$$
$$\lambda\Gamma\ \in\ \mathrm{D\_Env}(\theta\mathcal{E}).$$
$$(\ \llbracket\ e_1\ \rrbracket(\mathcal{E},\tau,\sigma)(\theta)(\Gamma)$$
$$\Box$$
$$\llbracket\ e_2\ \rrbracket(\mathcal{E},\tau,\sigma')(\theta)(\Gamma)$$
$$)$$

Parallel Composition

$$\llbracket\, e_1 \,\rrbracket\mathcal{E} \ni (\tau, \sigma)$$
$$\llbracket\, e_2 \,\rrbracket\mathcal{E} \ni (\tau, \sigma')$$
$$\sigma'' = \sigma \cup \sigma'$$
$$\theta \in \mathcal{GS}(tv)$$

$$\llbracket\, e_1 \| e_2 \,\rrbracket\mathcal{E} \ni (\tau, \sigma'')$$

$$\llbracket\, e_1 \| e_2 \,\rrbracket(\mathcal{E}, \tau, \sigma'')(\theta) =$$
$$\quad \lambda\Gamma \in \text{D\_Env}(\theta\mathcal{E}).$$
$$\qquad (\llbracket\, e_1 \,\rrbracket(\mathcal{E}, \tau, \sigma)(\theta)$$
$$\qquad \|$$
$$\qquad \llbracket\, e_2 \,\rrbracket(\mathcal{E}, \tau, \sigma')(\theta)$$
$$\qquad)$$

7
Communication Analysis for Concurrent ML

Hanne Riis Nielson and Flemming Nielson

ABSTRACT   Concurrent ML (CML) is an extension of the functional language Standard ML (SML) with primitives for dynamic creation of processes and channels and for communication of values over channels. Because of the powerful abstraction mechanisms, the communication topology of a given program may be very complex and therefore an efficient implementation may be facilitated by knowledge of the topology.

This paper presents a framework for analyzing the communication topology of CML programs. We proceed by extending a polymorphic type system for SML to deduce not only the types of CML programs but also their communication *behaviors* expressed as terms in a process algebra. This involves a syntactic ordering for expressing when one behavior has more communication possibilities than another. We then provide an annotated version of the published operational semantics for CML and we provide an operational semantics for the behaviors similar to the operational semantics of other process algebras. Based on this we define a notion of simulation for behaviors and prove that the syntactic ordering is sound (but not complete). We then prove the *semantic correctness* of the *type and behavior inference system* by an extended subject reduction result: types of CML programs are preserved during evaluation whereas their behaviors may evolve as expressed by the semantics of behaviors. Finally we show that the simulation ordering is undecidable whereas the syntactic ordering (with the exclusion of the axiom for unfolding recursive behaviors) is decidable.

Acknowledgment This work is partially supported by ESPRIT BRA 8130 LOMAPS and by the DART-project funded by the Danish Science Research Council.

7.1   Introduction

In the previous chapters we have seen the design of a number of functional languages that incorporate constructs for achieving concurrency and distribution: CML [150, 151, 152] in Chapter 2, Poly/ML in Chapter 3, LCS [25] in Chapter 4, and FACILE [140] in Chapter 5. Despite the differences between the languages there are a number of similarities: they are all higher-order functional languages, they are all eager (as opposed to lazy) languages, they allow the spawning of new processes and the creation of new channels, and they allow the sending and receiving of values over typed channels.

The design of these languages allows for a high degree of modularization and abstraction in programming but also has the undesirable consequence that the overall communication structure of a given program is not immediately clear from its structure. It is worth pointing out that similar phenomena arise when functional languages are extended with first-class continuations (or imperative languages are extended with goto's). This is somewhat unfortunate, despite the increased expressibility, because knowledge of the communication structure is essential for the implementation as well as for the programmer reasoning about the correctness of programs. To be more specific: as regards implementation, knowledge of the communication structure may facilitate processor allocation so as to match the network configuration; as regards the programmer, it may be important for him to establish that certain communication protocols are adhered to.

In Section 7.2 we therefore present an *analysis of the communication structure* of CML programs by extracting the communication behavior of the program. The development is inspired by the effect systems developed in [95, 160] for polymorphic type inference of functional languages with references. The approach of these papers has been modified to express the communications that take place during execution: in [167] an analysis is defined and in Chapter 6 the effects are used to define the denotational semantics of a concurrent functional language. However, these modifications retain the main characteristics of [95, 160] that effects are *sets* of individual actions. In contrast, the development to be performed here (building upon [122] and [125]) will retain the precise picture of the communication topology by including far more *causality* into the effects. This involves defining a syntactic ordering on behaviors for when one behavior has more communication possibilities than another; this then replaces the simple subset relation of [95, 160].

For the semantics in Section 7.3 we adapt the operational semantics of [151, 152] to include additional annotations that will be useful for our proofs; this technique was also used in [18] and is merely a convenient way of stating results without interfering with the dynamic properties of the semantics. Unlike [167] we then define an operational semantics of behaviors; this is in the spirit of operational semantics of process algebras. Based on this we define a notion of simulation on behaviors and we show that the syntactic ordering on behaviors is a sound (but not complete) axiomatization.

Unlike previous approaches to relating programming languages and process algebras, that tend to regard a programming language as a process algebra with value passing, we establish in Section 7.4 an extended *subject reduction result*; it says that types for CML programs are preserved during evaluation but that the behaviors may evolve as expressed by the operational semantics for behaviors.

We then show in Section 7.5 that the simulation ordering is undecidable by a reduction from language containment for simple grammars. We also show that the syntactic ordering is decidable (except for the inclusion of the axiom for unfolding recursive behaviors). Finally, we discuss the prospects and consequences of achieving decidability.

Our conclusions in Section 7.6 outline a few more specific analyses that can be built on top of the behaviors. Full details of the developments may be found in the appendices.

7.2   Extracting the Communication Topology

We shall follow [18, 152] and study a polymorphic subset of CML with *expressions* $e \in$ **Exp** given by

$$e ::= \quad c \mid x \mid \text{fn } x \Rightarrow e \mid e_1\ e_2$$
$$\mid \quad \text{let } x = e_1 \text{ in } e_2 \mid \text{rec } f\ x \Rightarrow e$$
$$\mid \quad \text{if } e \text{ then } e_1 \text{ else } e_2$$

Here x and f are program identifiers. In addition to function abstraction and function application we have a polymorphic let-construct, recursion, and a conditional. The *constants* $c \in$ **Const** are given by

$$c ::= \quad () \mid \text{true} \mid \text{false} \mid n$$
$$\mid \quad + \mid * \mid = \mid \cdots$$
$$\mid \quad \text{pair} \mid \text{fst} \mid \text{snd}$$
$$\mid \quad \text{nil} \mid \text{cons} \mid \text{hd} \mid \text{tl} \mid \text{isnil}$$
$$\mid \quad \text{send} \mid \text{receive} \mid \text{choose}$$
$$\mid \quad \text{wrap} \mid \text{sync} \mid \text{channel}_l \mid \text{fork}_\pi$$

We have constants corresponding to the base types unit, bool, and int together with operations for constructing and destructing pairs and lists. We may send a value v over a channel ch by sync(send(ch,v)), receive a value over a channel ch by sync(receive(ch)), and choose between a list $[e_1, \cdots, e_n]$ of communications by sync(choose([$e_1, \cdots, e_n$])), where the case $n = 0$ is written sync(noevent) and acts as a blocking statement. Here the primitives send, receive, choose, and noevent do not actually perform the communications but produce *delayed communications* that are then *activated* by the sync operator. The operation wrap(e_1, e_2) then modifies the delayed communication e_1 to another that applies e_2 to the resulting value; so sync(wrap(e_1, e_2)) may be thought of as e_2(sync(e_1)) provided that e_2 performs no communications. Finally, we may fork a process to the pool of processes and we may allocate a new free channel to be used for communication; as is clear from the syntax we shall assume that these primitives are annotated with labels l, π from the set **Lab**.

Example 7.2.1. Consider the following CML program:

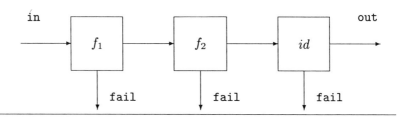

FIGURE 7.1. pipe $[f_1,\ f_2]$ in out

```
let node = fn f => fn in => fn out =>
    forkπ (rec loop d =>
        sync (choose [wrap (receive in,
                        fn x => sync (send (out, f x));
                            loop d),
                    send(fail,())]))
in rec pipe fs => fn in => fn out =>
    if isnil fs
    then node (fn x => x) in out
    else let ch = channel_l ()
        in (node (hd fs) in ch; pipe (tl fs) ch out)
```

For the sake of readability we write $e_1;e_2$ for (fn dummy => e_2) e_1. Given a list of functions and two channels, the program will construct a pipeline of the functions using local channels for interconnecting the functions. Each of the functions may successfully be applied to its argument or cause a failure. This is illustrated in Figure 7.1 for a list with two elements.   □

7.2.1   Types, Behaviors, and Regions

As usual we shall use *types* to classify the values that expressions can evaluate to. When executing a CML program, channels and processes may be created and values may be communicated, and we shall extend the type system with *behaviors* to record this. We do not know the identity of channels but can use the notion of *regions* to track the program points where a given channel could have been allocated.

For *types* $t \in \mathbf{Typ}$ we take

$$
\begin{aligned}
t \quad ::= \quad &\text{unit} \mid \text{bool} \mid \text{int} \mid \alpha \\
\mid \quad &t_1 \to^b t_2 \mid t_1 \times t_2 \mid t\ \text{list} \\
\mid \quad &t\ \text{chan}\ r \mid t\ \text{com}\ b
\end{aligned}
$$

Here α is a metavariable for *type variables*. The function type is written

$t_1 \rightarrow^b t_2$ indicating that the argument type is t_1, the result type is t_2, and the latent behavior is b; thus when a function is supplied with an argument the resulting behavior will be b. The type of a channel is t chan r, indicating that the channel is allocated in region r and that values of type t can be communicated over it. Finally, t com b is the type of a *suspended* communication: when it is eventually enacted using sync, it will result in a value of type t and the resulting behavior will be b.

Formally, *behaviors* $b \in \mathbf{Beh}$ are given by

$$
\begin{aligned}
b \quad ::= \quad & \epsilon \mid r!t \mid r?t \mid t \text{ CHAN } r \mid \beta \\
\mid \quad & \text{FORK}_\pi \ b \mid b_1; b_2 \mid b_1 + b_2 \mid \text{REC } \beta. b
\end{aligned}
$$

Here ϵ stands for the nonobservable behavior; this will be the behavior associated with pure functional programs. We write $r!t$ for sending a value of type t over a channel in region r and similarly $r?t$ for receiving a value of type t over a channel in region r. The allocation of a new channel in region r is written t CHAN r, where t is the type of values to be communicated. The behavior FORK$_\pi$ b expresses that a process with behavior b and label π is spawned. Behaviors may be combined using sequencing and choice and they may be recursive. We write β for a metavariable for *behavior variables*. So for example REC β. (t CHAN r+FORK$_\pi(r?t;\ \beta)$) is the behavior of a program that either will create a channel, and then no more communications take place, or it will spawn a process that inputs on some channel and then the overall process repeats itself.

Finally, *regions* $r \in \mathbf{Reg}$ are given by

$$
r \quad ::= \quad l \mid r_1 + r_2 \mid \rho
$$

Here ρ denotes a metavariable for *region variables*. We shall think of $+$ as *set union*, so a closed region will be a finite set of (channel) labels from **Lab**; formally, we define $r_1 \subseteq r_2$ to mean that all l's and ρ's appearing in r_1 also appear in r_2.

The *type schemes* are obtained from types by quantifying over type variables, behavior variables, and region variables: they have the form $\forall \vec{\alpha}\vec{\beta}\vec{\rho}.t$ where $\vec{\alpha}$, $\vec{\beta}$, and $\vec{\rho}$ are lists of variables.

As usual a type t is a *generic instance* of a type scheme $ts = \forall \vec{\alpha}\vec{\beta}\vec{\rho}.t_0$, written $ts \succ t$, if there exists a substitution θ with $\mathrm{Dom}(\theta) = \{\vec{\alpha}\vec{\beta}\vec{\rho}\}$ such that $\theta\ t_0 = t$. Here a *substitution* θ is a finite mapping from type variables, behavior variables, and region variables to types, behaviors, and regions, respectively, and we write $\mathrm{Dom}(\theta)$ for its (finite) domain. Furthermore, a type scheme ts' is an *instance* of ts, written $ts \succeq ts'$, if whenever $ts' \succ t$, also $ts \succ t$. See [50] for a different formulation that turns out to be equivalent [49].

We shall sometimes use γ for any of α, β, or ρ and similarly use $\vec{\gamma}$ for $\vec{\alpha}\vec{\beta}\vec{\rho}$. Also we shall follow the conventions of the lambda-calculus [17] and freely perform alpha-renaming of bound behavior variables. As an example we have that int $\rightarrow^{\text{REC}\beta_1.\beta_1}$ int equals int $\rightarrow^{\text{REC}\beta_2.\beta_2}$ int.

Example 7.2.2. The desired type of the function `node` of Example 7.2.1 is

$$\forall \alpha_1, \alpha_2, \beta, \rho_1, \rho_2.$$
$$(\alpha_1 \to^\beta \alpha_2) \to^\epsilon (\alpha_1 \text{ chan } \rho_1) \to^\epsilon (\alpha_2 \text{ chan } \rho_2) \to^b \text{ unit}$$

where

$$b = \text{FORK}_\pi \; (\text{REC } \beta'. \; ((\rho_1?\alpha_1; \; \beta; \; \rho_2!\alpha_2; \; \beta') + \rho_0!\text{unit}))$$

Here we have assumed that `fail` has type `unit chan` ρ_0. Turning to the main program, the type is

$$\forall \alpha, \beta, \rho_1, \rho_2.$$
$$(\alpha \to^\beta \alpha) \text{ list} \to^\epsilon (\alpha \text{ chan } (\rho_1 + l)) \to^\epsilon (\alpha \text{ chan } \rho_2) \to^{b'} \text{ unit}$$

where

$$b' = \text{REC } \beta'. \quad (\text{FORK}_\pi \; (\text{REC } \beta''. \; (((\rho_1 + l)?\alpha; \; \rho_2!\alpha; \; \beta'') + \rho_0!\text{unit}))$$
$$+ \quad (\alpha \text{ CHAN } (\rho_1 + l);$$
$$\text{FORK}_\pi (\text{REC } \beta''. \; (((\rho_1 + l)?\alpha; \; \beta; \; \rho_2!\alpha; \; \beta'') + \rho_0!\text{unit}));$$
$$\beta'))$$

□

7.2.2   Ordering on Behaviors

The behaviors record the communications taking place during evaluation. To obtain a flexible type system it is essential to be able to coerce a precise record of the behavior into a less precise record. This is illustrated in the following example:

Example 7.2.3. Consider the program

```
choose [send (ch, 7), wrap (receive ch', fn x => 1)]
```

where for the sake of readability we write $[e_1, \; e_2]$ for cons e_1 (cons e_2 nil) and $(e_1, \; e_2)$ for pair e_1 e_2. The first element of the list has type `int com r!int` (assuming `ch` has type `int chan r`) and the second element has type `int com r'?bool` (assuming `ch'` has type `bool chan r'`). We want the list to have type

```
(int com (r!int + r'?bool)) list
```

to record that either one of the branches may be chosen at run-time. So we need to coerce the types `int com r!int` and `int com r'?bool` into `int com (r!int + r'?bool)`. □

This leads to the introduction of a subsumption (or coercion) rule into the type and behavior inference system, and this presupposes an ordering on behaviors. We define the ordering ⊑ on behaviors by the axioms and rules of Figure 7.2 (to be explained below) and we write ≡ for the associated equivalence defined by

- pre-order laws

    P1. $b \sqsubseteq b$

    P2. if $b_1 \sqsubseteq b_2$ and $b_2 \sqsubseteq b_3$ then $b_1 \sqsubseteq b_3$

- pre-congruence laws

    C1. If $b_1 \sqsubseteq b_2$ and $b_3 \sqsubseteq b_4$ then $b_1; b_3 \sqsubseteq b_2; b_4$

    C2. If $b_1 \sqsubseteq b_2$ and $b_3 \sqsubseteq b_4$ then $b_1 + b_3 \sqsubseteq b_2 + b_4$

    C3. If $b_1 \sqsubseteq b_2$ then $\text{FORK}_\pi \; b_1 \sqsubseteq \text{FORK}_\pi \; b_2$

    C4. If $b_1 \sqsubseteq b_2$ then $\text{REC } \beta. \; b_1 \sqsubseteq \text{REC } \beta. \; b_2$

- laws for sequencing

    S1. $b_1; (b_2; b_3) \equiv (b_1; b_2); b_3$

    S2. $(b_1 + b_2); b_3 \equiv (b_1; b_3) + (b_2; b_3)$

- laws for ϵ

    E1. $b \equiv \epsilon; b$

    E2. $b; \epsilon \equiv b$

- laws for choice (or join)

    J1. $b_1 \sqsubseteq b_1 + b_2$ and $b_2 \sqsubseteq b_1 + b_2$

    J2. $b + b \equiv b$

- laws for recursion

    R1. $\text{REC } \beta. \; b \equiv b[\beta \mapsto \text{REC } \beta. \; b]$

    R2. $\text{REC } \beta. \; b \equiv \text{REC } \beta'. \; b[\beta \mapsto \beta']$ provided $\beta' \notin FV(b)$

FIGURE 7.2. Ordering on behaviors

$b_1 \equiv b_2$ if and only if $b_1 \sqsubseteq b_2$ and $b_2 \sqsubseteq b_1$.

We require $\sqsubseteq$ to be a pre-order and a pre-congruence. Furthermore, sequencing is an associative operation with ϵ as identity, and we have a left-distributive law with respect to choice. A consequence of the laws for choice is that choice is the least upper bound operator and hence associative and commutative. Finally, we have a couple of laws for recursion. It is always possible to fold and unfold a recursion (**R1**) and to rename the bound behavior variable (**R2**). Actually (**R2**) is implicitly true anyway given our syntactical conventions about alpha-renaming for bound behavior variables.

Unlike [122] we shall not extend the ordering $\sqsubseteq$ to types in order to avoid the complex interplay between polymorphism and subtyping.

Remark. The main difference between the typing system presented in this paper and those developed in [160, 167] is that in the present system the dependencies between the individual communications are recorded. If we were to extend Figure 7.2 with

$$b_1; b_2 \equiv b_1 + b_2$$

$$\text{REC } \beta.\ b \equiv b[\beta \mapsto \epsilon]$$

then our system would degrade to those of [29, 160, 167].   □

Syntactic Properties of the Ordering

For later reference we list a couple of properties holding for the ordering.

Fact 7.2.4. We have $b_1 \sqsubseteq b_2$ if and only if there exists b such that $b_1 + b \equiv b_2$.

Proof. A simple consequence of the laws **C2**, **J1**, and **J2**.   □

Fact 7.2.5. If $b_1 \sqsubseteq b_2$ then $FV(b_1) \subseteq FV(b_2)$.

Proof. A simple induction on the structure of the inference $b_1 \sqsubseteq b_2$.   □

Fact 7.2.6. If $b_1 \sqsubseteq b_2$ and θ is a substitution then $\theta\ b_1 \sqsubseteq \theta\ b_2$.

Proof. A simple induction on the structure of the inference $b_1 \sqsubseteq b_2$.   □

7.2.3   The Type and Behavior Inference System

We are now ready to develop the inference system for extracting types and behaviors. The *typing judgments* have the form

$$tenv \vdash e : t \ \& \ b$$

where *tenv* is a *type environment* mapping identifiers to types or type schemes, t is the type of e, and b is its behavior. Since CML has a call-by-value semantics, there is no observable behavior associated with accessing an identifier and therefore the type environment does not contain any behavior component (except embedded within the types or type schemes). The typing rules are given in Figure 7.3 and are fairly close to the standard ones except that we also collect behavior information; these rules will be explained in detail shortly.

$$tenv \vdash c : t \ \& \ b \qquad \text{if TypeOf}(c) \succ t \text{ and } \epsilon \sqsubseteq b$$

$$tenv \vdash x : t \ \& \ b \qquad \text{if } tenv(x) \succ t \text{ and } \epsilon \sqsubseteq b$$

$$\frac{tenv[x \mapsto t] \vdash e : t' \ \& \ b}{tenv \vdash \texttt{fn } x \texttt{ => } e : t \rightarrow^b t' \ \& \ b'} \qquad \text{if } \epsilon \sqsubseteq b'$$

$$\frac{tenv \vdash e_1 : t \rightarrow^b t' \ \& \ b_1 \qquad tenv \vdash e_2 : t \ \& \ b_2}{tenv \vdash e_1 \ e_2 : t' \ \& \ b'} \qquad \text{if } b_1; b_2; b \sqsubseteq b'$$

$$\frac{tenv \vdash e_1 : t_1 \ \& \ b_1 \qquad tenv[x \mapsto ts] \vdash e_2 : t_2 \ \& \ b_2}{tenv \vdash \texttt{let } x \texttt{ = } e_1 \texttt{ in } e_2 : t_2 \ \& \ b'}$$

$$\text{if } ts = \text{gen}(tenv, b_1)t_1 \text{ and } b_1; b_2 \sqsubseteq b'$$

$$\frac{tenv[f \mapsto t \rightarrow^b t'][x \mapsto t] \vdash e : t' \ \& \ b}{tenv \vdash \texttt{rec } f(x) \texttt{=>} e : t \rightarrow^b t' \ \& \ b'} \qquad \text{if } \epsilon \sqsubseteq b'$$

$$\frac{tenv \vdash e : \texttt{bool} \ \& \ b \qquad tenv \vdash e_1 : t \ \& \ b_1 \qquad tenv \vdash e_2 : t \ \& \ b_2}{tenv \vdash \texttt{if } e \texttt{ then } e_1 \texttt{ else } e_2 : t \ \& \ b'}$$

$$\text{if } b; (b_1 + b_2) \sqsubseteq b'$$

FIGURE 7.3. Typing system

A main decision is how to incorporate the desired notion of subsumption that allows a precise record of the communication possibilities to be coerced into a less precise record. Basically, there are two approaches we may adopt:

- *Late subsumption*: coercions can happen at any time inside any type, as when the type system has a general subsumption rule on types. (In [162] this is called subtyping.)

- *Early subsumption*: generic instantiations produce the required specialized types. (In [162] this is called subeffecting.)

In [122] we used the first approach for a monotyped version of the language, thereby obtaining a type system with subtyping. Here we are in a polymorphic setting, and to avoid the complex interplay between polymorphism and subtyping we shall use the second approach (also taken in [125, 160]). This means that the latent behavior of functions and suspended communications always must be prepared to be larger than what seems to be needed.

The types of identifiers are obtained as generic instances of the appropriate type schemes. The actual behavior is ϵ, but we may want to use a larger behavior, and to express this we exploit the ordering $\sqsubseteq$ on behaviors. This turns out to be a general pattern of the axioms and rules: it is always possible to enlarge the actual behavior. In the rule for function abstraction we record the behavior of the body of the function as the latent behavior of the function type. The construction of a function does not in itself have an observable behavior and so is ϵ. In the rule for function application we see that the actual behavior of the composite construct is that of the operator followed by that of the operand and then the behavior initiated by the function application itself; the latter is exactly the latent behavior of the function type. One may note that it is inherent in this rule that CML has a call-by-value semantics.

In the rule for local definitions we generalize over those type variables, behavior variables, and region variables that neither occur free in the type environment nor in the behavior; this is expressed by

$$\mathsf{gen}(tenv, b)t = \mathsf{let}\ \{\vec{\alpha}\vec{\beta}\vec{\rho}\} = FV(t) \setminus (FV(tenv) \cup FV(b))$$
$$\mathsf{in}\ \forall\vec{\alpha}\vec{\beta}\vec{\rho}.t,$$

where $FV(\cdots)$ denotes the set of free type variables, behavior variables, and region variables. The actual behavior of the let-construct simply expresses that the local value is computed before the body. In the rule for recursive functions we make sure that the actual behavior is equal to the latent behavior of the type of the recursive function. The rule for conditional should be straightforward; an alternative and equivalent definition would be to assume that the b_1 and b_2 occurring in the rule are equal (as may have been obtained by subsumption) and then use $b; b_1$ instead of $b; (b_1 + b_2)$.

This leaves us with the type schemes for constants. Each constant has associated a *constrained type scheme* as shown in Figure 7.4. A constrained type scheme $cts = \forall\vec{\alpha}\vec{\beta}\vec{\rho}.t_0[C]$ is a type scheme that additionally incorporates a constraint C; this is a finite set of inequalities of the form $\beta \geq b$ or $\rho \geq r$. A type t is an instance of this constrained type scheme, written $cts \succ t$, if there exists a substitution θ with $\mathrm{Dom}(\theta) = \{\vec{\alpha}\vec{\beta}\vec{\rho}\}$ such that $\theta\, t_0 = t$ and such that the constraints C are solved by θ, written $\theta \models C$. This latter condition amounts to $\theta\beta \sqsupseteq \theta b$ for each $\beta \geq b$ in C and $\theta\rho \sqsupseteq \theta r$ for each $\rho \geq r$ in C. (Here $\geq$ is a formal symbol whereas $\sqsupseteq$ is the ordering defined in Figure 7.2.)

Note that for the primitives also to be found in SML the constraints only involve ϵ, indicating that no communication need take place. Also, most of the primitives of CML are only constrained to have an ϵ-annotation occur on the function arrows, although more interesting behaviors have to appear elsewhere in the type. The only three constants where function arrows are constrained to have non-ϵ behaviors are sync, which extracts the delayed communication of the argument and enacts it; fork which forks a new process; and channel, which allocates a new channel.

Example 7.2.7. Consider the program of Example 7.2.3, and let *tenv* be a type environment with *tenv* ch = int chan r and *tenv* ch' = bool chan r'. By appropriate instantiations of the constrained type schemes of send

c	TypeOf(c)
+	$\forall \beta_1, \beta_2.\ \texttt{int} \to^{\beta_1} \texttt{int} \to^{\beta_2} \texttt{int}\ [\epsilon \le \beta_1, \epsilon \le \beta_2]$
pair	$\forall \alpha_1, \alpha_2, \beta_1, \beta_2.\ \alpha_1 \to^{\beta_1} \alpha_2 \to^{\beta_2} \alpha_1 \times \alpha_2\ [\epsilon \le \beta_1, \epsilon \le \beta_2]$
fst	$\forall \alpha_1, \alpha_2, \beta.\ \alpha_1 \times \alpha_2 \to^{\beta} \alpha_1\ [\epsilon \le \beta]$
snd	$\forall \alpha_1, \alpha_2, \beta.\ \alpha_1 \times \alpha_2 \to^{\beta} \alpha_2\ [\epsilon \le \beta]$
send	$\forall \alpha, \beta_1, \beta_2, \rho.\ (\alpha\,\texttt{chan}\,\rho) \times \alpha \to^{\beta_1} \alpha\,\texttt{com}\,\beta_2\ [\epsilon \le \beta_1, \rho!\alpha \le \beta_2]$
receive	$\forall \alpha, \beta_1, \beta_2, \rho.\ (\alpha\,\texttt{chan}\,\rho) \to^{\beta_1} \alpha\,\texttt{com}\,\beta_2\ [\epsilon \le \beta_1, \rho?\alpha \le \beta_2]$
choose	$\forall \alpha, \beta_1, \beta_2, \beta_3.\ (\alpha\,\texttt{com}\,\beta_1)\,\texttt{list} \to^{\beta_2} \alpha\,\texttt{com}\,\beta_3\ [\epsilon \le \beta_2, \beta_1 \le \beta_3]$
wrap	$\forall \alpha_1, \alpha_2, \beta_1, \beta_2, \beta_3, \beta_4.$ $(\alpha_1\,\texttt{com}\,\beta_1) \times (\alpha_1 \to^{\beta_2} \alpha_2) \to^{\beta_3} \alpha_2\,\texttt{com}\,\beta_4$ $[\epsilon \le \beta_3, \beta_1; \beta_2 \le \beta_4]$
sync	$\forall \alpha, \beta_1, \beta_2.\ (\alpha\,\texttt{com}\,\beta_1) \to^{\beta_2} \alpha\ [\beta_1 \le \beta_2]$
channel$_l$	$\forall \alpha, \beta, \rho.\ \texttt{unit} \to^{\beta} (\alpha\,\texttt{chan}\,\rho)\ [\alpha\,\text{CHAN}\,\rho \le \beta, l \le \rho]$
fork$_\pi$	$\forall \alpha, \beta_1, \beta_2.\ (\texttt{unit} \to^{\beta_1} \alpha) \to^{\beta_2} \texttt{unit}\ [\text{FORK}_\pi\,\beta_1 \le \beta_2]$

FIGURE 7.4. Type schemes for selected constants

and `receive` we get

$$tenv \vdash \texttt{send: int chan r} \times \texttt{int} \to^{\epsilon} \texttt{int com (r!int + r'?bool)}\ \&\ \epsilon$$

$$tenv \vdash \texttt{receive: bool chan r'} \to^{\epsilon} \texttt{bool com (r!int + r'?bool)}\ \&\ \epsilon$$

Using the typing rules of Figure 7.3 we then get

$$tenv \vdash \texttt{send (ch, 7): int com (r!int + r'?bool)}\ \&\ \epsilon$$

$$tenv \vdash \texttt{wrap (receive ch', fn x => 1)}$$
$$\texttt{: int com (r!int + r'?bool)}\ \&\ \epsilon$$

so the two elements of the list get the same type, and therefore the overall typing of the program succeeds.   □

Syntactic Properties of the Typing System

For later reference we list a couple of standard properties holding for the typing system; most are proved in Appendix 7.A.

Lemma 7.2.8. If $tenv[x \mapsto ts] \vdash e : t\ \&\ b$ and $ts' \succeq ts$ then $tenv[x \mapsto ts'] \vdash e : t\ \&\ b$.

Fact 7.2.9. If $tenv \vdash e : t \& b$ and $b \sqsubseteq b'$ then $tenv \vdash e : t \& b'$.

Proof. Inspection of the last step in the proof of $tenv \vdash e : t \& b$.   □

Lemma 7.2.10. If $tenv \vdash e : t \& b$ and θ is a substitution, then $\theta\, tenv \vdash e : \theta\, t \& \theta\, b$.

We now define the set $IV(tenv \vdash e : t \& b)$ of independent variables occurring in the proof of $tenv \vdash e : t \& b$ to be all the variables in the proof tree except those of $FV(tenv)$.

Fact 7.2.11. Given a finite set X of variables and an inference $tenv \vdash e : t \& b$ one may without loss of generality assume that $X \cap IV(tenv \vdash e : t \& b) = \emptyset$.

Proof. Let $\theta : IV(tenv \vdash e : t \& b) \to \overline{X}$ be a bijective renaming of all independent variables into the complement $\overline{X}$ of X; this is possible because $\overline{X}$ is infinite. Using Lemma 7.2.10 we get $(\theta\, tenv) \vdash e : (\theta\, t) \& (\theta\, b)$. By the definition of independent variables this amounts to $tenv \vdash e : (\theta\, t) \& (\theta\, b)$ and here we have no occurrences of variables from $X \setminus FV(tenv)$.   □

Lemma 7.2.12. If $tenv \vdash e : t \& b$, $\mathrm{Dom}(tenv') \cap \mathrm{Dom}(tenv) = \emptyset$, and $FV(tenv') \cap IV(tenv \vdash e : t \& b) = \emptyset$ then $tenv\, tenv' \vdash e : t \& b$.

Corollary 7.2.13. If $tenv \vdash e : t \& b$ and $\mathrm{Dom}(tenv') \cap \mathrm{Dom}(tenv) = \emptyset$ then $tenv\, tenv' \vdash e : t \& b$.

Lemma 7.2.14. Assume $tenv[x \mapsto ts] \vdash e : t \& b$ and $tenv \vdash e_0 : t_0 \& \epsilon$. If $\mathsf{gen}(tenv, \epsilon)t_0 \succeq ts$ then $tenv \vdash e[x \mapsto e_0] : t \& b$.

7.2.4 Subject Expansion Properties

To increase our faith in the typing rules for recursion and polymorphism it is instructive to compare the typing of the constructs with the typing of their unfolded versions.

The unfolded version of a recursively defined function can always be typed in the same way as the recursively defined function itself. To see this assume that

$$tenv \vdash \mathtt{rec}\ f(x) \Rightarrow e : t \to^b t' \& b',$$

because $\epsilon \sqsubseteq b'$ and $tenv[f \mapsto t \to^b t'][x \mapsto t] \vdash e : t' \& b$. But then

$$tenv[f \mapsto t \to^b t'] \vdash \mathtt{fn}\ x \Rightarrow e : t \to^b t' \& b'$$

as well as $tenv \vdash \mathtt{rec}\ f(x) \Rightarrow e : t \to^b t' \& \epsilon$. We now use Lemma 7.2.14 to obtain

$$tenv \vdash (\text{fn } x \Rightarrow e)[f \mapsto \text{rec } f(x) \Rightarrow e] : t \to^b t' \& b',$$

showing that the expansion $(\text{fn } x \Rightarrow e)[f \mapsto \text{rec } f(x) \Rightarrow e]$ has the same type and behavior as $\text{rec } f(x) \Rightarrow e$.

For the let-construct things are more complicated, as shown by the following example:

Example 7.2.15. Consider the following expression e:

```
let x = sync (receive ch)
in sync (send (ch, 2)); x,
```

where we assume that ch has type int chan r. In the inference system we have

$$\cdots \vdash e : \text{int} \& \text{r?int}; \text{r!int}$$

The expansion of e is

```
sync (send (ch, 2)); sync (receive ch)
```

and here the inference system gives

$$\cdots \vdash e : \text{int} \& \text{r!int}; \text{r?int}$$

The two behaviors $\text{r?int}; \text{r!int}$ and $\text{r!int}; \text{r?int}$ are incomparable, showing that the let-construct need not have the same behavior as its expansion.   □

To obtain a positive result we consider the situation where the let-bound expression involves no communication. To be specific, assume that

$$tenv \vdash \text{let } x = e_1 \text{ in } e_2 : t \& b \qquad \text{because} \qquad tenv \vdash e_1 : t_1 \& \epsilon$$

and note that Lemma 7.2.14 then gives

$$tenv \vdash e_2[x \mapsto e_1] : t \& b,$$

so that in this case the expansion $e_2[x \mapsto e_1]$ has the same type and behavior as $\text{let } x = e_1 \text{ in } e_2$.

7.3 Semantics

We shall now present a structural operational semantics for CML. The formulation is close in spirit to [152] and amounts to three inference systems: one for *sequential* evaluation, one for *concurrent* evaluation, and to handle synchronization we also need one for *matching* the communications against one another. This is mimicked in the specification of the semantics of behaviors where we have one inference system for *sequential* evolution and one for *concurrent* evolution. Matching is much simpler for behaviors than for programs, and therefore no matching relation is needed.

7.3.1   Semantics of CML

We begin with the *sequential evaluation* of expressions. This takes care of all primitives of CML except sync, channel$_l$, and fork$_\pi$, which are the constants of Figure 7.4 that have a nontrivial latent behavior. The transition relation for sequential evaluation has the form

$$e \rightarrow e',$$

where e and e' are *closed* expressions, that is, they do not contain free program identifiers. To enforce a left-to-right evaluation we introduce the concept of an *evaluation context* E [55, 182], which specifies where the next step of the computation may take place:

$$E ::= [\,] \mid E\,e \mid w\,E \mid \text{let } x = E \text{ in } e \mid \text{if } E \text{ then } e_1 \text{ else } e_2.$$

Here w denotes a weakly evaluated expression [142] (see below), that is, an expression that cannot be further evaluated. The idea is that $[\,]$ is an empty context (called a hole), and in general E specifies a context with exactly one hole in it. We shall then write $E[e]$ for the expression E with the hole replaced by e. The next step of the computation will take place at the point indicated by the hole. As an example consider function application. The presence of $E\,e$ means that computations in the operator position are possible whereas the presence of $w\,E$ means that computations in the operand position are possible only when the operator is weakly evaluated (for example to a function abstraction). In this way it is ensured that the operator as well as the operand are evaluated before the function application itself takes place (for example by β-reduction).

The *weakly evaluated expressions* $w \in \mathbf{WExp}$ are given by

$$w ::= c' \mid x \mid \text{fn } x \Rightarrow e \mid \langle c'\,w_1 \rangle \mid \ldots \mid \langle c'\,w_1 \ldots w_n \rangle,$$

where $n \geq 1$ and c' ranges over all constants except sync, channel$_l$, and fork$_\pi$. Weakly evaluated expressions of the form $\langle c'\,w_1 \ldots w_i \rangle$ are used to record the evaluation of constants as indicated in Figure 7.5, where we define the relation $\delta \subseteq \mathbf{WExp} \times \mathbf{WExp} \times \mathbf{WExp}$. Note that δ is partial, so for example hd nil is undefined.

The transition relation is specified in Figure 7.6. The clauses should be fairly straightforward. The first rule expresses the one-level unfolding of a recursive definition. Then we have axioms for β-reduction and for let-reduction. The fourth axiom is an abbreviation for two axioms expressing the evaluation of a conditional depending on the outcome of the test. Finally, there is an axiom for δ-reduction which inspects Figure 7.5 to determine the result.

We shall now introduce the transition relation for *concurrent evaluation*. Channels will be associated with *channel identifiers*, $ci \in \mathbf{CIdent}$, and processes with *process identifiers*, $pi \in \mathbf{PIdent}$. We shall assume that the sets $\mathbf{CIdent}$, $\mathbf{PIdent}$, and $\mathbf{Ident}$ (of program identifiers) are mutually

Operator	Operand	Result
pair	w_1	$\langle$pair $w_1\rangle$
$\langle$pair $w_1\rangle$	w_2	$\langle$pair $w_1\,w_2\rangle$
fst	$\langle$pair $w_1\,w_2\rangle$	w_1
snd	$\langle$pair $w_1\,w_2\rangle$	w_2
cons	w_1	$\langle$cons $w_1\rangle$
$\langle$cons $w_1\rangle$	w_2	$\langle$cons $w_1\,w_2\rangle$
hd	$\langle$cons $w_1\,w_2\rangle$	w_1
tl	$\langle$cons $w_1\,w_2\rangle$	w_2
isnil	nil	true
isnil	$\langle$cons $w_1\,w_2\rangle$	false
send	w	$\langle$send $w\rangle$
receive	w	$\langle$receive $w\rangle$
choose	w	$\langle$choose $w\rangle$
wrap	w	$\langle$wrap $w\rangle$
+	n_1	$\langle$+ $n_1\rangle$
$\langle$+ $n_1\rangle$	n_2	n where $n = n_1 + n_2$
$\vdots$	$\vdots$	$\vdots$

FIGURE 7.5. Tabulation of δ

$$E\,[\,\texttt{rec}\ f(x)\ \texttt{=> }e\,]\quad\to\quad E\,[\,(\texttt{fn}\ x\ \texttt{=> }e)\,[f\mapsto(\texttt{rec}\ f(x)\ \texttt{=> }e)]]$$

$$E\,[\,(\texttt{fn}\ x\ \texttt{=> }e)\ w\,]\quad\to\quad E\,[\,e\,[x\mapsto w]\,]$$

$$E\,[\,\texttt{let}\ x = w\ \texttt{in}\ e\,]\quad\to\quad E\,[\,e\,[x\mapsto w]\,]$$

$$E\,[\,\texttt{if}\ w\ \texttt{then}\ e_1\ \texttt{else}\ e_2\,]\quad\to\quad\begin{cases}E\,[e_1] & \text{if } w = \text{true}\\ E\,[e_2] & \text{if } w = \text{false}\end{cases}$$

$$E\,[\,w_1\,w_2\,]\quad\to\quad E\,[w_3]\qquad\text{if }(w_1,w_2,w_3)\in\delta$$

FIGURE 7.6. Sequential evaluation

$$\frac{E[e] \to E[e']}{CI \,\&\, PP[pi \mapsto E[e]] \longrightarrow_{pi}^{\epsilon} CI \,\&\, PP[pi \mapsto E[e']]}$$

$$CI \,\&\, PP[pi \mapsto E[\texttt{channel}_l \ ()]] \longrightarrow_{pi}^{\text{CHAN}_l \ ci} CI \cup \{ci\} \,\&\, PP[pi \mapsto E[ci]]$$

$$\text{if } ci \notin CI$$

$$CI \,\&\, PP[pi_1 \mapsto E[\texttt{fork}_\pi \ w]] \longrightarrow_{pi_1,pi_2}^{\text{FORK}_\pi \ pi_2}$$
$$CI \,\&\, PP[pi_1 \mapsto E[()]][pi_2 \mapsto w\,()]$$

$$\text{if } pi_2 \notin \text{Dom}(PP) \cup \{pi_1\}$$

$$\frac{(w_1, w_2) \overset{(ci!,ci?)}{\rightsquigarrow} (e_1, e_2)}{CI \,\&\, PP[pi_1 \mapsto E_1[\texttt{sync}\, w_1]][pi_2 \mapsto E_2[\texttt{sync}\, w_2]]}$$
$$\longrightarrow_{pi_1,pi_2}^{(ci!,ci?)} CI \,\&\, PP[pi_1 \mapsto E_1[e_1]][pi_2 \mapsto E_2[e_2]]$$

$$\text{if } pi_1 \neq pi_2$$

FIGURE 7.7. Concurrent evaluation

disjoint. The configurations have the form $CI \,\&\, PP$, where CI is the set of channel identifiers that are in use and PP is a (finite) mapping of process identifiers to expressions. The transition relation is written

$$CI \,\&\, PP \longrightarrow_{ps}^{ev} CI' \,\&\, PP',$$

where ev is the event that takes place and ps is a list of the processes that take part in the event—depending on the event there will be either one or two processes involved. An *event* $ev \in \mathbf{Ev}$ has one of the forms

$$ev ::= \epsilon \mid \text{CHAN}_l \ ci \mid \text{FORK}_\pi \ pi \mid (ci!, ci?)$$

and may record the empty event, the creation of a channel with a given channel identifier, the creation of a process with a given process identifier, and the communication over a channel.

The transition relation is specified in Figure 7.7. The first rule embeds sequential evaluation into concurrent evaluation and the name of the process performing the event is recorded. The second rule captures the creation of a new channel. The channel is associated with a new channel identifier and the transition records the name of the process performing the event together with the event itself. The third rule takes care of process creation, and here we record the process performing the event as well as the one being created by the event. Finally, we have a rule expressing the synchronization of communications, and here we use the matching relation (explained below). The transition records the two processes involved in the communication as well as the channel used for it.

$$(\langle \mathtt{send}\langle\ \mathtt{pair}\ ci\ w\rangle\rangle, \langle \mathtt{receive}\ ci\rangle) \overset{(ci!,ci?)}{\rightsquigarrow} (w, w)$$

$$\frac{(w_1, w_3) \overset{(d_1,d_2)}{\rightsquigarrow} (e_1, e_3)}{(\langle \mathtt{choose}\langle \mathtt{cons}\ w_1\ w_2\rangle\rangle, w_3) \overset{(d_1,d_2)}{\rightsquigarrow} (e_1, e_3)}$$

$$\frac{(\langle \mathtt{choose}\ w_2\rangle, w_3) \overset{(d_1,d_2)}{\rightsquigarrow} (e_2, e_3)}{(\langle \mathtt{choose}\langle \mathtt{cons}\ w_1\ w_2\rangle\rangle, w_3) \overset{(d_1,d_2)}{\rightsquigarrow} (e_2, e_3)}$$

$$\frac{(w_1, w_3) \overset{(d_1,d_2)}{\rightsquigarrow} (e_1, e_3)}{(\langle \mathtt{wrap}\langle \mathtt{pair}\ w_1\ w_2\rangle\rangle, w_3) \overset{(d_1,d_2)}{\rightsquigarrow} (w_2\ e_1, e_3)}$$

$$\frac{(w_1, w_2) \overset{(d_1,d_2)}{\rightsquigarrow} (e_1, e_2)}{(w_2, w_1) \overset{(d_2,d_1)}{\rightsquigarrow} (e_2, e_1)}$$

FIGURE 7.8. Matching communications

Finally, the *matching relation* is given two weakly evaluated expressions that are ready to synchronize, and it specifies the outcome of the communication and records the event that takes place. This is expressed by a relation of the form

$$(w_1, w_2) \overset{(ci!,ci?)}{\rightsquigarrow} (e_1, e_2) \text{ and } (w_1, w_2) \overset{(ci?,ci!)}{\rightsquigarrow} (e_1, e_2)\ .$$

The relation is specified in Figure 7.8. The first axiom captures the communication between a send and a receive construct. The second and third axioms take care of the situation where there are several possible communications available in the first component. The fourth axiom shows how the value communicated may be modified using the wrap construct (as was explained already in Section 7.2). Finally, we have a restructuring rule.

7.3.2 Semantics of Behaviors

We begin with the *sequential evolution* of behaviors. Here the configurations of the transition system are either *closed* behaviors, that is, behaviors without free behavior variables, or the special *terminating configuration* $\sqrt{}$. The transition relation takes the form

$$b \Rightarrow^p \flat,$$

where $\flat$ is either a closed behavior or $\sqrt{}$, and where $p \in \mathbf{ABeh}$ is an *atomic behavior* as given by

$$p \quad ::= \quad \epsilon \mid r!t \mid r?t \mid t\ \mathrm{CHAN}\ r \mid \mathrm{FORK}_\pi\ b.$$

$$p \Rightarrow^p \epsilon \qquad\qquad \epsilon \Rightarrow^\epsilon \sqrt{}$$

$$b \Rightarrow^\epsilon b \qquad \text{REC } \beta.\ b \Rightarrow^\epsilon b[\beta \mapsto \text{REC } \beta.\ b]$$

$$\frac{b_1 \Rightarrow^p b_1'}{b_1; b_2 \Rightarrow^p b_1'; b_2} \qquad\qquad \frac{b_1 \Rightarrow^p \sqrt{}}{b_1; b_2 \Rightarrow^p b_2}$$

$$\frac{b_1 \Rightarrow^p b_1'}{b_1 + b_2 \Rightarrow^p b_1'} \qquad\qquad \frac{b_2 \Rightarrow^p b_2'}{b_1 + b_2 \Rightarrow^p b_2'}$$

FIGURE 7.9. Sequential evolution

Here ϵ is supposed to capture the sequential evaluation steps of CML expressions, whereas the remaining atomic behaviors capture the concurrent steps.

The relation is specified in Figure 7.9. The first axiom expresses that any atomic behavior can be performed and in doing so becomes ϵ. The second axiom expresses that ϵ can terminate. The third axiom means that at any time any number of ϵ actions can be performed by any behavior (observe that the terminal configuration is excluded here so that $\sqrt{}$ is a stuck configuration). It corresponds to the fact that in the semantics of CML any number of evaluation steps can be performed in the functional part of CML between those involving the concurrency primitives. The fourth axiom expresses the unfolding of a recursive behavior. Then we have two rules for the evolution of sequential behaviors: only when the evolution of the first component has reached a terminal configuration is it possible to start evolution of the second component. The last two rules express the evolution of a choice between two behaviors; due to the axiom $b \Rightarrow^\epsilon b$ these rules allow *internal choice* between possibilities.

To express the *concurrent evolution* of behaviors we introduce *process identifiers* as in the semantics of CML. The transitions have the form

$$PB \Longrightarrow^a_{ps} PB',$$

where PB and PB' are mappings from process identifiers to closed behaviors and the special symbol $\sqrt{}$. Furthermore, a is the action that takes place and ps is a list of the processes that take part in the action. As in the semantics of CML, ps has one or two elements depending on the action. The *actions* $a \in \textbf{Act}$ are given by

$$a ::= \epsilon \mid t \text{ CHAN } r \mid \text{FORK}_\pi\ b \mid (r!t, r?t).$$

The transition relation is specified in Figure 7.10. The first four rules embed sequential evolution into the concurrent evolution: the first rule captures the termination of a behavior, the second rule captures a silent action, the third rule captures channel creation, and the fourth rule captures process creation. In all cases the action as well as the processes involved are

$$\frac{b \Rightarrow^{\epsilon} \sqrt{}}{PB[pi \mapsto b] \Longrightarrow^{\epsilon}_{pi} PB[pi \mapsto \sqrt{}]}$$

$$\frac{b \Rightarrow^{\epsilon} b'}{PB[pi \mapsto b] \Longrightarrow^{\epsilon}_{pi} PB[pi \mapsto b']}$$

$$\frac{b \Rightarrow^{t \, \text{CHAN} \, r} b'}{PB[pi \mapsto b] \Longrightarrow^{t \, \text{CHAN} \, r}_{pi} PB[pi \mapsto b']}$$

$$\frac{b \Rightarrow^{\text{FORK}_{\pi} \, b_0} b'}{PB[pi_1 \mapsto b] \Longrightarrow^{\text{FORK}_{\pi} \, b_0}_{pi_1,pi_2} PB[pi_1 \mapsto b'][pi_2 \mapsto b_0]}$$
$$\text{if } pi_2 \notin \text{Dom}(PB) \cup \{pi_1\}$$

$$\frac{b_1 \Rightarrow^{r!t} b_1' \qquad b_2 \Rightarrow^{r?t} b_2'}{PB[pi_1 \mapsto b_1][pi_2 \mapsto b_2] \Longrightarrow^{(r!t,r?t)}_{pi_1,pi_2} PB[pi_1 \mapsto b_1'][pi_2 \mapsto b_2']}$$
$$\text{if } pi_1 \neq pi_2$$

FIGURE 7.10. Concurrent evolution

recorded. The final rule captures the communication between processes. Here the matching simply amounts to ensuring that the channels of the two processes are in *equal* regions and that they specify *equal* types of the values communicated.

7.3.3 Simulation Ordering on Behaviors

In order to formulate and prove the subject reduction result in the next section we need to relate the ordering $\sqsubseteq$ on behaviors to the semantics of behaviors. Basically this amounts to the definition of a simulation ordering on behaviors and a proof showing that $\sqsubseteq$ is a simulation ordering. First define

$$b \Rightarrow^{\widehat{p}} \flat$$

to mean that there exists $n \geq 0$ and behaviors $b_1, \cdots, b_n$ such that

$$b \Rightarrow^{\epsilon} b_1 \Rightarrow^{\epsilon} \cdots \Rightarrow^{\epsilon} b_n \Rightarrow^{p} \flat.$$

Recall that $\flat$ ranges over closed behaviors as well as $\sqrt{}$. Thus the atomic behavior p may be prefixed by any number of trivial atomic behaviors.

We shall say that $\mathcal{S}$ is a *ground simulation* on pairs of closed behaviors if

- $\sqrt{} \; \mathcal{S} \; \flat$ if and only if $\flat = \sqrt{}$,

- if $b_1 \Rightarrow^{p_1} \flat_1$ and $b_1 \; \mathcal{S} \; b_2$ then there exists $\flat_2$ and p_2 such that $b_2 \Rightarrow^{\widehat{p_2}} \flat_2$, $p_1 \; \mathcal{S}^{\partial} \; p_2$ and $\flat_1 \; \mathcal{S} \; \flat_2$, where $\mathcal{S}^\partial$ is defined by

- $p\ \mathcal{S}^\partial\ p$ whenever p is a primitive action of the form $\epsilon, r!t, r?t$ or t CHAN r, and

- $(\text{FORK}_\pi\ b_1)\ \mathcal{S}^\partial\ (\text{FORK}_\pi\ b_2)$ if $b_1\ \mathcal{S}\ b_2$.

We shall say that $\mathcal{S}$ is a *simulation* on pairs of behaviors (b_1, b_2) satisfying $FV(b_1) \subseteq FV(b_2)$ if

- $b_1\ \mathcal{S}\ b_2$ implies $(\theta\ b_1)\ \mathcal{S}\ (\theta\ b_2)$

   for all ground substitutions θ defined on $FV(b_1) \cup FV(b_2)$.

We define $\precsim$ to be the *largest* simulation.

Fact 7.3.1. If $FV(b_1) \subseteq FV(b_2)$ then $b_1 \precsim b_2$ is equivalent to $(\theta\ b_1) \precsim (\theta\ b_2)$ for all ground substitutions θ defined on $FV(b_1) \cup FV(b_2)$.

Proof. Define $\precsim'$ by the property claimed for $\precsim$: $b_1 \precsim' b_2$ if and only if $(\theta\ b_1) \precsim (\theta\ b_2)$ for all ground substitutions θ defined on $FV(b_1) \cup FV(b_2)$. Clearly $\precsim'$ is a simulation so $b_1 \precsim' b_2$ implies $b_1 \precsim b_2$ by the choice of $\precsim$. To see that $b_1 \precsim b_2$ implies $b_1 \precsim' b_2$ simply use that $\precsim$ and $\precsim'$ agree on closed behaviors, that $\precsim$ is a simulation, and the definition of $\precsim'$. $\quad\square$

This definition of simulation is inspired by the notions of bisimilarity as developed for the process algebras CCS [108] and CHOCS [164].
   In order to relate $\precsim$ and $\sqsubseteq$ we extend the ordering $\sqsubseteq$ to configurations by taking $\sqrt{} \sqsubseteq \sqrt{}$. Then we have the following results:

Proposition 7.3.2. $\sqsubseteq$ is a simulation.

Proof. See Appendix 7.B $\quad\square$

Corollary 7.3.3. If $b_1 \sqsubseteq b_2$ then $b_1 \precsim b_2$.

Corollary 7.3.3 shows that $\sqsubseteq$ as defined in Figure 7.2 is a *sound axiomatization* of $\precsim$. It is *not* complete because for $FV(b_1) \subseteq FV(b_2)$ we always have $(\text{REC}\beta.\beta); b_1 \precsim b_2$ whereas $(\text{REC}\beta.\beta); b_1 \sqsubseteq b_2$ does not hold in general given the axioms and rules of Figure 7.2. Similarly we have $\text{REC}\beta.(\beta + b) \precsim \text{REC}\beta.b$ whereas we do not have $\text{REC}\beta.(\beta + b) \sqsubseteq \text{REC}\beta.b$.
   Remark. For certain applications it might be worthwhile to introduce laws like

$$t_1\ \text{CHAN}\ r_1;\ t_2\ \text{CHAN}\ r_2 \sqsubseteq t_2\ \text{CHAN}\ r_2;\ t_1\ \text{CHAN}\ r_1,$$

$$\text{FORK}_{\pi_1}\ b_1;\ \text{FORK}_{\pi_2}\ b_2 \sqsubseteq \text{FORK}_{\pi_2}\ b_2;\ \text{FORK}_{\pi_1}\ b_1,$$

reflecting that the order in which channel identifiers and process identifiers are allocated does not matter. However, these axioms are *not* sound with respect to our definition of simulation. Overcoming this is no easy task; the problems are analogous to those arising for imperative languages in trying to ensure that the order of declarations of identifiers is immaterial.   □

7.4   Subject Reduction Property

We shall prove that the typing system of Section 7.2 has the following subject reduction properties:

- Types are preserved during computation.

- Behaviors evolve during computation.

The formalization and proof of this result is in three main stages: *(i)* We prove a subject reduction property for the sequential evaluation of expressions; *(ii)* then we prove a correctness property for matching; *(iii)* and finally we prove the subject reduction property for concurrent evaluation.

Further Syntactic Properties of the Typing System

But first it is convenient to establish a few additional syntactic properties of the inference system that concern the properties of evaluation contexts. Most of these results are proved in Appendix 7.C.

Fact 7.4.1. If $tenv \vdash E[e_0] : t \,\&\, b$ because $tenv_0 \vdash e_0 : t_0 \,\&\, b_0$ then $tenv = tenv_0$ and $FV(b) \supseteq FV(b_0)$; hence $FV(tenv) \cup FV(b) \supseteq FV(tenv_0) \cup FV(b_0)$.

Proof. This is a straightforward induction on E.   □

Lemma 7.4.2. If $tenv \vdash E[e_0] : t \,\&\, b$ because $tenv \vdash e_0 : t_0 \,\&\, b_0$, and if $FV(tenv') \subseteq FV(b_0)$ and $\mathrm{Dom}(tenv')$ is disjoint with all identifiers occurring in $tenv \vdash E[e_0] : t \,\&\, b$, then $tenv\, tenv' \vdash E[e_0] : t \,\&\, b$ because $tenv\, tenv' \vdash e_0 : t_0 \,\&\, b_0$.

Proof. This is proved by induction on E in Appendix 7.C.   □

Fact 7.4.3. Assume that $tenv \vdash E[e_0] : t \,\&\, b$ because $tenv \vdash e_0 : t_0 \,\&\, b_0$; if $tenv \vdash e_0' : t_0 \,\&\, b_0$ then $tenv \vdash E[e_0'] : t \,\&\, b$ because $tenv \vdash e_0' : t_0 \,\&\, b_0$.

Lemma 7.4.4. Assume that

$$tenv \vdash E[e_0] : t \,\&\, b \qquad \text{because} \qquad tenv \vdash e_0 : t_0 \,\&\, b_0$$

If furthermore $tenv \vdash e'_0 : t_0 \,\&\, b'_0$ where $p; b'_0 \sqsubseteq b_0$ for some atomic behavior p then there exists b' such that

$$tenv \vdash E[e'_0] : t \,\&\, b'$$

and $p; b' \sqsubseteq b$.

7.4.1   Sequential Correctness

It is natural to restrict attention to closed expressions because the definition of an evaluation context is such that we never pass inside the scope of any defining occurrence of a program identifier. However, we have to allow expressions to include channel identifiers that have been allocated in previous computation steps. To formalize this we shall write $cenv$ for a mapping from channel identifiers to types (so $cenv\ ci$ will always have the form t chan r). We shall say that e is *closed* if $cenv \vdash e : t \,\&\, b$ for some $cenv$, t and b; this requires the type environments of Figure 7.3 to range over channel identifiers as well as program identifiers. To express the correctness result we shall also need typing rules for weakly evaluated expressions:

$$\frac{tenv \vdash c' : t \to^\epsilon t' \,\&\, \epsilon \qquad tenv \vdash w_1 : t \,\&\, \epsilon}{tenv \vdash \langle c'\ w_1 \rangle : t' \,\&\, b} \qquad \text{if } \epsilon \sqsubseteq b$$

$$\frac{tenv \vdash \langle c'\ w_1 \cdots w_{n-1} \rangle : t \to^\epsilon t' \,\&\, \epsilon \qquad tenv \vdash w_n : t \,\&\, \epsilon}{tenv \vdash \langle c'\ w_1\ \cdots\ w_n \rangle : t' \,\&\, b} \qquad \text{if } \epsilon \sqsubseteq b$$

It is immediate from these rules that we have

Fact 7.4.5. If $tenv \vdash w : t \,\&\, b$ then $\epsilon \sqsubseteq b$ and $tenv \vdash w : t \,\&\, \epsilon$.

We now have the following result showing that sequential evaluation preserves the type and behavior:

Proposition 7.4.6. Assume $e \to e'$ and $cenv \vdash e : t \,\&\, b$. Then $cenv \vdash e' : t \,\&\, b$.

Proof. The proof is by induction on the inference $e \to e'$ and is given in Appendix 7.C.   □

7.4.2   Correctness of Matching

The matching of two weakly evaluated expressions gives rise to a new pair of expressions. To formalize this we shall define $\mathcal{B}\ cenv\ ci! = r!t$ and $\mathcal{B}\ cenv\ ci? = r?t$ whenever $cenv\ ci = t$ chan r. Then we have the following result showing how behaviors evolve into an atomic behavior and the remaining part of the behavior:

Proposition 7.4.7. Assume $(w_1, w_2) \overset{(d_1, d_2)}{\rightsquigarrow} (e_1, e_2)$ and

$$cenv \vdash w_1 : t_1 \text{ com } b_1 \mathbin{\&} \epsilon \text{ and } cenv \vdash w_2 : t_2 \text{ com } b_2 \mathbin{\&} \epsilon.$$

Then there exists b_1' and b_2' such that

$$cenv \vdash e_1 : t_1 \mathbin{\&} b_1' \text{ and } cenv \vdash e_2 : t_2 \mathbin{\&} b_2'$$

and $(\mathcal{B} \ cenv \ d_1); b_1' \sqsubseteq b_1$ and $(\mathcal{B} \ cenv \ d_2); b_2' \sqsubseteq b_2$.

Proof. The proof is by induction on the inference for matching and is given in Appendix 7.C. $\qquad\qquad\qquad\square$

7.4.3 Concurrent Correctness

The concurrent subject reduction property expresses that each step of the concurrent evaluation of the expression can be mimicked by a number of steps in the concurrent evolution of its behavior.

Let us first relate the *configurations* $CI \mathbin{\&} PP$ of the concurrent evaluation of expressions to the configurations PB of the concurrent evolution of behaviors. We shall say that $CI \mathbin{\&} PP$ is *cenv-related to* PB if

$$\mathrm{Dom}(PP) = \mathrm{Dom}(PB) \text{ and } \mathrm{Dom}(cenv) = CI.$$

This ensures that we are dealing with the same process and channel identifiers. Furthermore, we say that $CI \mathbin{\&} PP$ is *cenv-described by* PB if it is *cenv*-related to PB and if for all $pi \in \mathrm{Dom}(PP)$ there exists a type t_{pi} such that

$$cenv \vdash PP \ pi : t_{pi} \mathbin{\&} PB \ pi.$$

We shall also need to relate the *events* ev of the concurrent evaluation of expressions to the *actions* a of the concurrent evolution of behaviors. So assume that $CI \mathbin{\&} PP$ is *cenv*-described by PB. Clearly we would expect $\mathrm{FORK}_\pi \ pi$ to correspond to $\mathrm{FORK}_\pi \ (PB \ pi)$ and $\mathrm{CHAN}_l \ ci$ to correspond to $t \ \mathrm{CHAN} \ r$ when $cenv \ ci = t \text{ chan } r$ and $l \in r$; this is formalized by an auxiliary function denoted $\mathcal{A} \ (cenv, PB)$:

$$\mathcal{A} \ (cenv, PB) \ \epsilon \quad = \quad \epsilon,$$

$$\mathcal{A} \ (cenv, PB) \ (\mathrm{CHAN}_l \ ci) \quad = \quad t \ \mathrm{CHAN} \ r \quad \text{if } cenv \ ci = t \text{ chan } r,$$
$$\text{and } l \in r,$$

$$\mathcal{A} \ (cenv, PB) \ (\mathrm{FORK}_\pi \ pi) \quad = \quad \mathrm{FORK}_\pi \ b \quad \text{if } PB \ pi = b,$$

$$\mathcal{A} \ (cenv, PB) \ (ci!, ci?) \quad = \quad (r!t, r?t) \quad \text{if } cenv \ ci = t \text{ chan } r.$$

The final preparation is to introduce a notation for a sequence of steps in the concurrent evolution of behaviors. For this we write

$$PB \Longrightarrow_{ps}^{\widehat{a}} PB'$$

to mean that there exists $n \geq 0$ and configurations $PB_1, \cdots, PB_n$ such that

$$PB \Longrightarrow_{pi_1}^{\epsilon} \cdots \Longrightarrow_{pi_n}^{\epsilon} PB_n \Longrightarrow_{ps}^{a} PB',$$

where $pi_1, \cdots, pi_n$ are process identifiers from the list ps. Thus, the processes of ps are allowed to perform some trivial actions before they engage in the joint action a. We then have the following result linking concurrent evaluation to concurrent evolution:

Theorem 7.4.8. Assume that

$$CI \ \& \ PP \longrightarrow_{ps}^{ev} CI' \ \& \ PP'$$

and that $CI \ \& \ PP$ is *cenv*-described by PB. Then there exists *cenv'* and PB' such that

$$PB \Longrightarrow_{ps}^{\widehat{a}} PB',$$

where $CI' \ \& \ PP'$ is *cenv'*-described by PB', $\mathcal{A} \ (cenv', PB') \ ev = a$, and we furthermore have $cenv' \lceil CI = cenv$.

Proof. The proof is by induction on the rules for concurrent evaluation and is given in Appendix 7.C. In this proof we exploit the soundness (Corollary 7.3.3) of the ordering $\sqsubseteq$ (Figure 7.2). However, it may be interesting to note that the laws **P1**, **P2**, **C1**, **C2**, **S1**, **E1**, **E2**, and **J1** suffice for carrying out the proof.   □

7.5   Decidability Issues

We have previously established the soundness (Corollary 7.3.3) of the ordering $\sqsubseteq$ with respect to the simulation ordering $\precsim$; we also showed that we do not have completeness. It is a consequence of the results established in this section that *we do not desire completeness*. The reason is that $\precsim$ turns out to be undecidable whereas $\sqsubseteq$ (for proofs not involving **R1**) turns out to be decidable. We also discuss the consequences of incorporating the use of **R1** into our results.

7.5.1   Undecidability of the Simulation Ordering

We now show that the simulation order $\precsim$ is undecidable by a reduction from the language containment problem for simple grammars [56]. This is in the spirit of the undecidability proof for the Basic Process Algebra [64] but due to the differences between our behaviors and the Basic Process Algebra it is simpler to perform a direct reduction.

Let $G = (V, T, P, S)$ be a simple grammar without useless nonterminals. To be specific, V is a finite and nonempty set of nonterminals, T is a finite and nonempty set of terminals, P is a finite set of productions, and $S \in V$ is the start symbol. Each production of P is of the form $A_0 \rightarrow a\, A_1 \ldots A_n$, where $A_i \in V$ and $a \in T$ and for any two productions $A_0 \rightarrow a\, A_1 \ldots A_n$ and $A_0 \rightarrow a\, A'_1 \ldots A'_{n'}$ we have $A_1 \ldots A_n = A'_1 \ldots A'_{n'}$. For each nonterminal A there is a derivation from S to a sentential form involving A and from this to a terminal string. As a consequence every finite derivation starting from S can be extended to one that ends in a terminal string.

As a first step we transform G to $G' = (V', T', P', S')$, which operates over the symbols of our behaviors. Let V' be a finite subset of behavior variables, T' a finite set of behaviors of the form $1!(\text{unit} \rightarrow^\epsilon)^n \text{unit}$, and let Θ be a bijection from V to V' and from T to T'. Then P' contains $\Theta(A \rightarrow a\, A_1 \ldots A_n)$ whenever P contains $A \rightarrow a\, A_1 \ldots A_n$ and $S' = \Theta(S)$. Clearly G' enjoys the same properties as G: it is simple, and all finite derivations from the start symbol to a sentential form may be extended to one that ends in a terminal string. Furthermore the language $\mathcal{L}_{G'}(S')$ generated by G' is isomorphic to the language $\mathcal{L}_G(S)$ generated by G. Indeed, without loss of generality for the arguments that follow, one might assume $G = G'$.

As a second step we construct a behavior system $B = (b, \{\beta_i = b_i \mid i \le k\})$ as follows: b is S', and if $\beta_i \in V'$ and $\beta_i \rightarrow a^1\, A^1_1 \ldots A^1_{n_1}, \cdots, \beta_i \rightarrow a^m\, A^m_1 \ldots A^m_{n_m}$ are all the β_i-productions in P', we set

$$b_i = (a^1; A^1_1; \ldots; A^1_{n_1}) + \cdots + (a^m; A^m_1; \ldots; A^m_{n_m}).$$

By our assumptions we have $m > 0$ and each $n_j \ge 0$. We define the language $\mathcal{L}(B)$ generated by B as

$$\mathcal{L}(b, \{\beta_i = b_i \mid i \le k\}) = \{w \in T^* \mid b \overset{w}{\underset{B}{\Longrightarrow}}{}^* \surd\},$$

where $\overset{}{\underset{B}{\Longrightarrow}}{}^*$ is the reflexive transitive closure of $\underset{B}{\Longrightarrow}$ and $\underset{B}{\Longrightarrow}$ is like $\Longrightarrow$ for behaviors but with the additional axiom $\beta_i \underset{B}{\Longrightarrow} b_i$. Clearly $\mathcal{L}(B') = \mathcal{L}_{G'}(S')$, and every finite derivation starting from b can be extended to one ending in $\surd$. Also, each b_i has all $a^1, \ldots, a^m$ to be distinct.

As a third step we perform a number of ministeps for reducing the number of equations. Each ministep transforms $(b_0, \{\beta_i = b_i \mid 0 < i \le k\})$ to $(b'_0, \{\beta_i = b'_i \mid 0 < i < k\})$, where $b'_i = b_i[\beta \mapsto \text{REC}\beta_k.b_k]$. We thus end up with $B' = (b', \emptyset)$, where b' has no free behavior variables. The system B' enjoys the same properties as B and has $\mathcal{L}(B') = \mathcal{L}(B)$ because these properties are preserved by all the ministeps.

Focusing the attention on b' and the language $\mathcal{L}(b') = \{w \mid b' \overset{w}{\Longrightarrow}{}^* \surd\}$ generated by it we have $\mathcal{L}(b') = \mathcal{L}(B')$. Also, each finite derivation from b' may be extended to one ending in $\surd$; we write $\models_N b'$ for this, and it is a consequence that b' has no free behavior variables. Note that if $b' \overset{w}{\Longrightarrow}{}^* b''$

then $\models_N b'$ implies $\models_N b''$. Furthermore, each sum of behaviors in b' must have distinct first actions; we record this by decreeing $\vdash_D b'$, where $\vdash_D$ is defined inductively by

$$\vdash_D \epsilon \qquad\qquad \vdash_D 1\,!\,t \qquad\qquad\qquad\qquad \vdash_D \beta$$

$$\frac{\vdash_D b_1 \quad \vdash_D b_2}{\vdash_D b_1; b_2} \qquad \frac{\vdash_D b}{\vdash_D \mathrm{REC}\beta.b}$$

$$\frac{\vdash_D b_1 \ldots \vdash_D b_n}{\vdash_D (p_1; b_1) + \ldots + (p_n; b_n)} \quad (p_1, \ldots, p_n) \text{ simple}$$

where $(p_1, \ldots, p_n)$ is "simple" if $n > 0$ and each p_i is a primitive action different from ϵ and all p_i's are distinct. (Note that we did not define $\vdash_D 1\,?\,t, \vdash_D \mathrm{FORK}_\pi(b)$, or $\vdash_D t$ CHAN r because these constructs cannot appear in b'.)

We now need two technical results:

Lemma 7.5.1. *(i)* If $\vdash_D b_1, \models_N b_1$ and $b_1 \Rightarrow^\epsilon b_2$ then $\vdash_D b_2, \models_N b_2$ and $\mathcal{L}(b_2) \subseteq \mathcal{L}(b_1)$; furthermore, if $pw \in \mathcal{L}(b_2)$ for some $p \neq \epsilon$ then $\{pw \mid pw \in \mathcal{L}(b_1)\} = \{pw \mid pw \in \mathcal{L}(b_2)\}$.

(ii) If $\vdash_D b_1, \models_N b_1$ and $b_1 \Rightarrow^{\widehat{p}} b_2$ with $p \neq \epsilon$ then, $\vdash_D b_2, \models_N b_2$ and $\mathcal{L}(b_2) = \{w \mid pw \in \mathcal{L}(b_1)\}$.

Proof. We already have $\models_N b_2$ from a previous observation. The remaining claims are proved by induction on $\vdash_D b_1$. We omit the details. □

Lemma 7.5.2. If $\vdash_D b', \vdash_D b'', \models_N b', \models_N b''$ then $\mathcal{L}(b') \subseteq \mathcal{L}(b'') \Leftrightarrow b' \mathrel{\underset{\sim}{\sqsubseteq}} b''$.

Proof. See Appendix 7.D. □

We can now state our main result:

Proposition 7.5.3. $\underset{\sim}{\sqsubseteq}$ is undecidable.

Proof. Language containment for simple grammars with no useless nonterminals is undecidable due to [56]. The above procedures transform simple grammars G_1 and G_2 with no useless nonterminals into behaviors b_1' and b_2' such that $\mathcal{L}_{G_1}(S_1) \subseteq \mathcal{L}_{G_2}(S_2)$ amounts to $\mathcal{L}(b_1') \subseteq \mathcal{L}(b_2')$ and where $\vdash_D b_1', \vdash_D b_2', \models_N b_1'$ and $\models_N b_2'$. By Lemma 7.5.2 $\mathcal{L}_{G_1}(S_1) \subseteq \mathcal{L}_{G_2}(S_2)$ is then equivalent to $b_1 \mathrel{\underset{\sim}{\sqsubseteq}} b_2$. If the latter were to be decidable we would have a contradiction. □

7.5.2 Decidability of the Syntactic Ordering

Although $\underset{\sim}{\sqsubseteq}$ is undecidable we can show that the subset of the ordering $\sqsubseteq$ defined by excluding the axiom **R1** from the laws of Figure 7.2 is indeed

$[\![\epsilon]\!]$	$=$	ϵ
$[\![r!t]\!]$	$=$	$r!\lceil t \rceil$
$[\![r?t]\!]$	$=$	$r?\lceil t \rceil$
$[\![t \text{ CHAN } r]\!]$	$=$	$\lceil t \rceil \text{ CHAN } r$
$[\![\beta]\!]$	$=$	β
$[\![\text{FORK}_\pi\, b]\!]$	$=$	$\text{FORK}_\pi\, [\![b]\!]$
$[\![b_1 ; b_2]\!]$	$=$	$\mathsf{seq}([\![b_1]\!], [\![b_2]\!])$
$[\![b_1 + b_2]\!]$	$=$	$[\![b_1]\!] + [\![b_2]\!]$
$[\![\text{REC}\beta.\, b]\!]$	$=$	$\text{REC}\beta.[\![b]\!]$

$$
\mathsf{seq}(bs, bn_0) = \begin{cases} bs & \text{if } bn_0 = \epsilon \\ bn_0 & \text{if } bs = \epsilon \,\wedge\, bn_0 \neq \epsilon \\ bp; bn_0 & \text{if } bs = bp \,\wedge\, bn_0 \neq \epsilon \\ bp; \mathsf{seq}(bn, bn_0) & \text{if } bs = bp; bn \,\wedge\, bn_0 \neq \epsilon \end{cases}
$$

$$
\mathsf{seq}(bn + bn', bn_0) = \mathsf{seq}(bn, bn_0) + \mathsf{seq}(bn', bn_0)
$$

FIGURE 7.11. Transformation to canonical form

decidable. More precisely, we shall give an algorithm that given two behaviors b_1 and b_2 will decide whether $b_1 \sqsubseteq b_2$ without using **R1** and we shall show that it is sound and complete.

The algorithm proceeds in two stages. First it transforms the behaviors into canonical forms and then it checks the ordering between the canonical forms. A behavior is in *canonical form* if it is constructed according to the nonterminal bn of the following grammar:

$$
bn ::= bs \mid bn + bn
$$

$$
bs ::= \epsilon \mid bp \mid bp; bn
$$

$$
bp ::= r!t \mid r?t \mid t \text{ CHAN } r \mid \beta \mid \text{FORK}_\pi\, bn \mid \text{REC}\beta.bn
$$

This means that a canonical behavior is a sum of behaviors. A summand is either ϵ or it begins with a primitive behavior and is possibly followed by a canonical behavior. A primitive behavior is one of $r!t$, $r?t$, t CHAN r, β, $\text{FORK}_\pi\, bn$ and $\text{REC}\beta.bn$, where the last two have bodies in canonical form.

Each behavior b can be transformed into an equivalent canonical behavior $[\![b]\!]$. The translation is specified in Figure 7.11 and proceeds according to the structure of the behavior. It uses the auxiliary operation $\lceil \cdots \rceil$ that will transform a type into a form where bound behavior variables are α-renamed in the manner of deBruin indices. So for example $\text{int} \to^{\text{REC}\beta_1.\beta_1}$

$$\frac{bs \; \mathrm{ord}_s \; bs_0}{bs \; \mathrm{ord} \; bs_0} \qquad \frac{bs \; \mathrm{ord} \; bn_0}{bs \; \mathrm{ord} \; bn_0 + bn_0'}$$

$$\frac{bs \; \mathrm{ord} \; bn_0'}{bs \; \mathrm{ord} \; bn_0 + bn_0'} \qquad \frac{bn \; \mathrm{ord} \; bn_0, \; bn' \; \mathrm{ord} \; bn_0}{bn + bn' \; \mathrm{ord} \; bn_0}$$

$$\epsilon \; \mathrm{ord}_s \; \epsilon \qquad \frac{bp \; \mathrm{ord}_p \; bp_0}{bp \; \mathrm{ord}_s \; bp_0}$$

$$\frac{bp \; \mathrm{ord} \; bp_0 \quad bn \; \mathrm{ord} \; bn_0}{bp; bn \; \mathrm{ord}_s \; bp_0; bn_0}$$

$$r!t \; \mathrm{ord}_p \; r!t \qquad r?t \; \mathrm{ord}_p \; r?t$$

$$t \; \mathrm{CHAN} \; r \; \mathrm{ord}_p \; t \; \mathrm{CHAN} \; r \qquad \beta \; \mathrm{ord}_p \; \beta$$

$$\frac{bn \; \mathrm{ord} \; bn_0}{\mathrm{FORK}_\pi \; bn \; \mathrm{ord}_p \; \mathrm{FORK}_\pi \; bn_0}$$

$$\frac{bn[\beta \mapsto \beta'] \; \mathrm{ord} \; bn_0[\beta_0 \mapsto \beta']}{\mathrm{REC}\beta. \; bn \; \mathrm{ord}_p \; \mathrm{REC}\beta_0. \; bn_0}$$
$$\text{if } \beta' \notin FV(\mathrm{REC}\beta. \; bn) \cup FV(\mathrm{REC}\beta_0. \; bn_0)$$

FIGURE 7.12. Checking the ordering for behaviors in canonical form

int and int $\to^{\mathrm{REC}\beta_2.\beta_2}$ int will be transformed into the same type int $\to^{\mathrm{REC}\beta'.\beta'}$ int for some unique β'. Furthermore, $[\![\cdots]\!]$ uses the auxiliary function seq that takes two behaviors bn_1 and bn_2 in canonical form and constructs a behavior equivalent to $bn_1; bn_2$ but in canonical form. Basically, the translation applies the laws **S1**, **S2**, **E1**, and **E2** to ensure that behaviors are written in a certain form. The translation could easily be extended to remove duplicate summands.

Lemma 7.5.4. For all b: $[\![b]\!]$ is in canonical form and $[\![b]\!] \equiv b$.

Proof. It is easy to verify that $[\![b]\!]$ is in canonical form. The equivalence of b and $[\![b]\!]$ is proved by a straightforward structural induction on b and uses

$$\mathrm{seq}(bn, bn_0) \equiv bn; bn_0,$$

which can easily be proved by structural induction on bn. □

Given two behaviors bn_1 and bn_2 in canonical form, we can now present a method for deciding whether $bn_1 \sqsubseteq bn_2$ holds. It is presented in Figure 7.12 in the form of an inference system that axiomatizes the three relations ord, ord_s, and ord_p. We shall see that bn_1 ord bn_2 amounts to $bn_1 \sqsubseteq bn_2$, that

bs_1 ord$_s$ bs_2 amounts to $bs_1 \sqsubseteq bs_2$, and that bp_1 ord$_p$ bp_2 amounts to $bp_1 \sqsubseteq bp_2$.

Intuitively it should be clear that the inference system may be converted into the definition of three terminating functions ord, ord$_s$, and ord$_p$ defined by pattern matching upon their arguments and with a catch-all case giving *false*. The only case that is slightly nontrivial is

$$\text{ord}(bs, bn_0 + bn_0') \;=\; \text{ord}(bs, bn_0) \;\vee\; \text{ord}(bs, bn_0') \;\vee\; \textit{false},$$

since it is the only case where more than one rule may be appropriate.

Formally, we verify our claim that Figure 7.12 defines an algorithm by

Lemma 7.5.5. The relations ord, ord$_s$, and ord$_p$ are decidable.

Proof. Define $size(b)$ to be the size (say length of presentation) of the behavior b. Define the measure μ by

$$\mu(bn_1 \text{ ord } bn_2) = 2 + 3(size(bn_1) + size(bn_2)),$$
$$\mu(bs_1 \text{ ord}_s bs_2) = 1 + 3(size(bs_1) + size(bs_2)),$$
$$\mu(bp_1 \text{ ord}_p bp_2) = 0 + 3(size(bp_1) + size(bp_2)),$$

and note that μ always produces a nonnegative integer. Next inspect all rules of Figure 7.12 and note that the measure μ of the conclusion is always strictly larger than the maximum of the measure μ of the premises. This shows that an inference tree for a statement has height at most the measure μ of that statement. Since there are finitely many binary trees of a given height it would suffice to search each one in turn.   □

Soundness of the method is expressed by

Theorem 7.5.6. If $\llbracket b \rrbracket$ ord $\llbracket b_0 \rrbracket$ then $b \sqsubseteq b_0$; furthermore, the inference of $b \sqsubseteq b_0$ need not use **R1**.

Proof. Using Lemma 7.5.4 it suffices to prove the (stronger) result

$$\text{if } bn \text{ ord } bn_0 \text{ then } bn \sqsubseteq bn_0, \tag{1}$$
$$\text{if } bs \text{ ord}_s bs_0 \text{ then } bs \sqsubseteq bs_0, \tag{2}$$
$$\text{if } bp \text{ ord}_p bp_0 \text{ then } bp \sqsubseteq bp_0. \tag{3}$$

The proof is by a straightforward induction on the inference tree.   □

To prove completeness of the algorithm we shall first give an alternative formulation of when bn ord bn_0. First we define $\Sigma(bn)$ as the *set of summands* of bn:

$$\Sigma(bs) \quad\;\; = \quad \{bs\},$$
$$\Sigma(bn + bn') \;\; = \quad \Sigma(bn) \cup \Sigma(bn').$$

Then we have (reminiscent of the Egli-Milner ordering)

Lemma 7.5.7. bn_1 ord bn_2 if and only if for all $bs_1 \in \Sigma(bn_1)$ there exists $bs_2 \in \Sigma(bn_2)$ such that bs_1 ord$_s$ bs_2.

Proof. The proof of "only if" is by a straightforward induction on the inference tree of bn_1 ord bn_2 (tracing the lower part involving ord only). The proof of "if" amounts to a straightforward construction of an inference tree.   □

Theorem 7.5.8. If one can infer $b \sqsubseteq b_0$ without using **R1**, then $[\![b]\!]$ ord $[\![b_0]\!]$.

Proof. We prove that $[\![\cdots]\!]$ ord $[\![\cdots]\!]$ is a model for $\cdots \sqsubseteq \cdots$. Consult Appendix 7.D for the details.   □

To see that we do *not* have a counterpart of the law **R1** consider the canonical behavior $\text{REC}\beta.(r!\texttt{int}; \beta + \epsilon)$. Here

$$\Sigma(\text{REC}\beta.(r!\texttt{int}; \beta + \epsilon)) = \{\text{REC}\beta.(r!\texttt{int}; \beta + \epsilon)\},$$

$$\Sigma(r!\texttt{int}; \text{REC}\beta.(r!\texttt{int}; \beta + \epsilon) + \epsilon) = \{r!\texttt{int}; \text{REC}\beta.(r!\texttt{int}; \beta + \epsilon), \epsilon\},$$

and it is easy to see that neither

$$\text{REC}\beta.(r!\texttt{int}; \beta + \epsilon) \text{ ord}_s \ r!\texttt{int}; \text{REC}\beta.(r!\texttt{int}; \beta + \epsilon),$$

nor

$$\text{REC}\beta.(r!\texttt{int}; \beta + \epsilon) \text{ ord}_s \ \epsilon.$$

Towards a Larger and Still Decidable Ordering

There are two approaches that may be pursued in order to extend our algorithm for deciding $\sqsubseteq$ to allow also the use of **R1**. One is to concentrate on **R1** and to build further knowledge into the algorithm. The caveat of this approach is that one risks non-termination due to the unbounded number of times that **R1** might be used. To overcome this one might try to apply automata-based techniques to discover when we repeat the same "pattern of recursion." This leads (we believe) to the second approach, where we must extend Figure 7.2 with new axioms and rules in order to ensure the soundness of the automata-based techniques: in particular, rules that allow some kind of induction to be performed. An example (perhaps derived) rule might allow one to deduce $\text{REC}\beta.b_0 \sqsubseteq b$ from $b_0[\beta \mapsto b] \sqsubseteq b$ (under suitable side conditions).

This then raises an important question. If we decide to extend Figure 7.2, does this invalidate the other results we have established? Let us define *an admissible ordering* to be an inductively defined ordering between behaviors such that *(i)* it is a simulation, *(ii)* all axioms and rules maintain the statements of Facts 7.2.5 and 7.2.6, and *(iii)* it contains all axioms and rules of Figure 7.2 (possibly omitting **C4** and **R1**). We believe that all results (except of course decidability of the ordering) would continue to hold if $\sqsubseteq$ of Figure 7.2 were replaced by another ordering provided it is *admissible*.

At present it is unclear which is the better route to pursue in order to obtain a decidable ordering that is still sound with respect to the simulation ordering

7.6   Conclusion

The starting point of this work has been an existing programming language, namely CML. We have developed a type and behavior inference system for a subset of this language: as usual the *types* talk about the sets of *values* upon which a program operates whereas the *behaviors* talk about the *communications* (or more generally the computations) that take place when the program executes. This is formally expressed by the subject reduction property that states that the execution of the CML program is mimicked by the evolution of its behavior viewed as a term in a process algebra.

Previous work [151, 152] shows how Standard ML's type system can be extended to take care of the concurrency constructs of CML; however, the polymorphic let-construct is handled in a rather restricted way by distinguishing between expansive and nonexpansive let-constructs. This is overcome by our type and behavior system: the behaviors contain information that allows us to handle polymorphism properly much as in the type and effect systems developed for type inference of Standard ML with references [160].

The structure of behaviors is much more refined than the sets of [160], as they also express the *causality* of the various communications that take place during computation. Because of this the behaviors can be used as a basis for a number of interesting program analyses of the communication structure of programs. Let us illustrate this with a few examples.

Analysis for finite communication topology

A CML program may create unboundedly many processes and channels. Since hardware is finite, an implementation may have to map many processes and channels to a "smaller" finite architecture. This task becomes easier if the number of processes and channels created in the program do not exceed the resources (processors and links) that are available at the hardware level. Furthermore, a much smaller version of the run-time system will be needed: there is no need for multitasking and multiplexing. In [125] we develop an analysis of behaviors that detects whether a CML program has a finite topology. As an example consider the behavior

$$\text{FORK}_\pi \ (\text{REC} \ \beta'. \ ((\rho_1?\alpha_1; \ b; \ \rho_2!\alpha_2; \ \beta') + \rho_0!\texttt{unit}))$$

associated with the node function in Example 7.2.2. Here the analysis will determine that if b does not create any processes and channels then the node function will at most create one process and no channels; thus it has a finite topology. On the other hand, the pipe function has behavior

$$
\begin{aligned}
\text{REC} \ \beta'. \ &(\text{FORK}_\pi \ (\text{REC} \ \beta''. \ (((\rho_1 + l)?\alpha; \ \rho_2!\alpha; \ \beta'') + \rho_0!\texttt{unit})) \\
+ \ &(\alpha \ \text{CHAN} \ (\rho_1 + l); \\
&\text{FORK}_\pi \ (\text{REC} \ \beta''. \ (((\rho_1 + l)?\alpha; \ b; \ \rho_2!\alpha; \ \beta'') + \rho_0!\texttt{unit})); \\
&\beta')).
\end{aligned}
$$

The analysis of [125] will deduce that any number of processes and any number of channels may be created so the pipe function does not have a finite topology.

Processor allocation

Often it will be the case that the number of processors of the hardware is less than the number of processes created by the CML program. Thus one has to resort to multitasking and decide how to allocate the various processes on the available processors. Basically there are two approaches: in *static processor allocation* it is decided at compile-time where all instances of a given process should reside at run-time, whereas in *dynamic processor allocation* it is decided at run-time. In both cases it is useful to have information about the requirements of the processes; for example, we might like to know which channels are needed for communication and how many times. In [126] we present an analysis showing how such information can be obtained from the behaviors. We illustrate this for the pipe function.

In the case of static processor allocation we will decide that all processes corresponding to the occurrence of $\texttt{fork}_\pi$ in the CML program will reside on the same processor. Thus the requirements of that processor are obtained by *accumulating* the requirements of *all* the processes with label π. So for the pipe function we see that there will be many inputs over channels in $\rho_1 + l$, many outputs over channels in ρ_2, and *many* outputs over channels in ρ_0. The latter result may be surprising because each of the processes labeled π will communicate at most once over ρ_0. However, there may be many processes labeled π, and since they all will reside on the same processor this processor must be prepared to do many communications over ρ_0. The situation is different for dynamic processor allocation. Here we do not accumulate the requirements of each process with a specific label; instead we estimate the *maximal* requirements of all instances of the process, and for the pipe function we get that each process labeled π will communicate over ρ_0 at most once; the results for $\rho_1 + l$ and ρ_2 are as for static processor allocation.

Acknowledgment

Discussions with Torben Amtoft, Fritz Henglein, Pierre Jouvelot, Jean-Pierre Talpin, Bent Thomsen, and Mads Tofte have been most stimulating.

Appendix 7.A Syntactic Properties of the Typing System

Proof of Lemma 7.2.8. We need a somewhat stronger induction hypothesis. Define $tenv' \succeq tenv$ to mean that $\mathrm{Dom}(tenv') = \mathrm{Dom}(tenv)$ and that $tenv'\, x \succeq tenv\, x$ for all $x \in \mathrm{Dom}(tenv)$. We then claim that

$$\text{if } tenv \vdash e : t \,\&\, b \text{ and } tenv' \succeq tenv \text{ then } tenv' \vdash e : t \,\&\, b.$$

The proof is by induction on the structure of the inference of $tenv \vdash e : t \,\&\, b$. In the case of let-polymorphism the key observation is that $ts' \succeq ts$ implies $FV(ts') \subseteq FV(ts)$. To see that this is indeed the case let $ts \succ t$ be chosen such that $FV(ts) = FV(t)$, for example by mapping all quantified variables of ts to ground terms; since $ts' \succ t$ we immediately have $FV(ts') \subseteq FV(t)$ and this establishes the result. Using this observation it is then immediate that $\mathsf{gen}(tenv',b)t \succeq \mathsf{gen}(tenv,b)t$. □

Proof of Lemma 7.2.10. This is a structural induction on e using Fact 7.2.6. Only the case of let-polymorphism is non-trivial. In this case assume

$$tenv \vdash \texttt{let } x = e_1 \texttt{ in } e_2 : t \,\&\, b.$$

Then $b_1; b_2 \sqsubseteq b$ and

$$tenv \vdash e_1 : t_1 \,\&\, b_1,$$
$$tenv[x \mapsto ts] \vdash e_2 : t \,\&\, b_2,$$

where $ts = \mathsf{gen}(tenv, b_1)\, t_1$. Let $\{\vec{\alpha}\vec{\beta}\vec{\rho}\} = FV(t_1)\backslash(FV(tenv) \cup FV(b_1))$ and let μ be a renaming of $\vec{\alpha}\vec{\beta}\vec{\rho}$ to fresh and distinct variables $\vec{\alpha_0}\,\vec{\beta_0}\,\vec{\rho_0}$. Then the induction hypothesis gives

$$\theta\,(\mu\, tenv) \vdash e_1 : \theta\,(\mu\, t_1) \,\&\, \theta\,(\mu\, b_1),$$
$$(\theta\, tenv)[x \mapsto \theta\, ts] \vdash e_2 : \theta\, t \,\&\, \theta\, b_2,$$

and the former can be rewritten as

$$\theta\, tenv \vdash e_1 : \theta\,(\mu\, t_1) \,\&\, \theta\, b_1.$$

Let $ts' = \mathsf{gen}(\theta\, tenv, \theta\, b_1)(\theta\,(\mu\, t_1))$. One can prove that $ts' \succeq \theta\, ts$, and Lemma 7.2.8 gives

$$(\theta\, tenv)[x \mapsto ts'] \vdash e_2 : \theta\, t \,\&\, \theta\, b_2.$$

From Fact 7.2.6 we get $\theta b_1; \theta b_2 \sqsubseteq \theta b$, and so using the rule for let-polymorphism we get the required

$$\theta\, tenv \vdash \texttt{let } x = e_1 \texttt{ in } e_2 : \theta\, t\ \&\ \theta\, b.$$

This completes the proof. $\square$

Proof of Lemma 7.2.12. We proceed by induction on the structure of the inference $tenv \vdash e : t\ \&\ b$. Due to the assumption that $tenv'$ redefines no identifier of $tenv$ all cases except let-polymorphism are straightforward; in particular the cases for variables and abstraction. For the case of let-polymorphism it suffices by Lemma 7.2.8 to show

$$\mathsf{gen}(tenv\, tenv', b_1)t_1 \succeq \mathsf{gen}(tenv, b_1)t_1,$$

for which it suffices to show

$$FV(t_1)\backslash(FV(b_1)\cup FV(tenv)\cup FV(tenv')) \supseteq FV(t_1)\backslash(FV(b_1)\cup FV(tenv)).$$

For this to be false we must have $\gamma \in FV(t_1)$, $\gamma \in FV(tenv')$, $\gamma \notin FV(b_1)$, and $\gamma \notin FV(tenv)$; but then $\gamma \notin IV(tenv \vdash e : t\ \&\ b)$ and so $\gamma \notin FV(t_1)$, and we have the desired contradiction. $\square$

Proof of Corollary 7.2.13. Let $X = FV(tenv') \setminus FV(tenv)$. Define the substitution θ such that $\mathrm{Dom}(\theta) = X$, such that $\{\gamma_1, \gamma_2\} \subseteq X \wedge \theta\gamma_1 = \theta\gamma_2 \Rightarrow \gamma_1 = \gamma_2$, and such that $\{\theta\gamma \mid \gamma \in X\}$ is disjoint with all variables occurring in the proof of $tenv \vdash e : t\ \&\ b$. Then $FV(\theta(tenv')) \cap IV(tenv \vdash e : t\ \&\ b) = \emptyset$. It follows from Lemma 7.2.12 that $tenv\,(\theta(tenv')) \vdash e : t\ \&\ b$. Next define the substitution θ' such that $\mathrm{Dom}(\theta') = \{\theta\gamma \mid \gamma \in X\}$ and $\theta'(\theta\gamma) = \gamma$ for all $\gamma \in X$. It follows from Lemma 7.2.10 that $\theta'(tenv)\,\theta'(\theta(tenv')) \vdash e : \theta'(t)\ \&\ \theta'(b)$. Clearly $\theta'(tenv) = tenv$, $\theta'(t) = t$ and $\theta'(b) = b$ by the assumptions on $\{\theta\gamma \mid \gamma \in X\}$; furthermore $\theta'(\theta(tenv')) = tenv'$. This proves the result. $\square$

Proof of Lemma 7.2.14. From the assumption and Lemma 7.2.8 we have

$$tenv[x \mapsto \mathsf{gen}(tenv, \epsilon)t_0] \vdash e : t\ \&\ b \tag{1}$$

We shall now assume that the variables of (1) not occurring in $\mathsf{gen}(tenv, \epsilon)t_0$ are disjoint with all variables of

$$tenv \vdash e_0 : t_0\ \&\ \epsilon \tag{2}$$

except those in $FV(tenv)$; this is merely an application of Fact 7.2.11. Furthermore we assume that all defined identifiers of e have been alpha-renamed so as not to occur in $tenv$; this ensures that no alpha-renaming is needed when performing the substitution $e[e_0/x]$.

We now want to modify (1) by replacing each node

$$tenv[x \mapsto \mathsf{gen}(tenv, \epsilon)t_0]tenv' \vdash e' : t' \& b'$$

by

$$tenv\,tenv' \vdash e' : t' \& b' \qquad \text{if } e' \neq x \text{ or } x \in \mathrm{Dom}(tenv'),$$
$$tenv\,tenv' \vdash e_0 : t' \& b' \qquad \text{if } e' = x \text{ and } x \notin \mathrm{Dom}(tenv').$$

The first part of this transformation is immediate, whereas the second part needs to be obtained from (2). First note that

$$\mathsf{gen}(tenv, \epsilon)t_0 \succ t' \quad \text{and} \quad \epsilon \sqsubseteq b'$$

and that $\theta\,t_0 = t'$ for some substitution θ defined on $FV(t_0) \setminus FV(tenv)$. Using Lemma 7.2.12 we get

$$tenv\,tenv' \vdash e_0 : t_0 \& \epsilon,$$

where $\mathrm{Dom}(tenv') \cap \mathrm{Dom}(tenv) = \emptyset$ follows from the alpha-renaming on e, and $FV(tenv') \cap IV(tenv \vdash e_0 : t_0 \& \epsilon) = \emptyset$ follows from the assumption that all variables of (1) not occurring in $\mathsf{gen}(tenv, \epsilon)t_0$ are disjoint with those of (2) except for those in $FV(tenv)$. We now use Lemma 7.2.10 and Fact 7.2.9 to get

$$tenv\,tenv' \vdash e_0 : t' \& b'.$$

This shows the well-definedness of the transformation.

The final step is to prove by structural induction that the constructed structure is indeed a proof of

$$tenv \vdash e[e_0/x] : t \& b.$$

This is a straightforward induction on the proof tree for (1). In the case of `let`-polymorphism note that

$$FV(tenv) = FV(tenv[x \mapsto \mathsf{gen}(tenv, \epsilon)t_0])$$

because $FV(\mathsf{gen}(tenv, \epsilon)t_0) = FV(t_0) \cap FV(tenv)$.   □

Appendix 7.B Semantic Properties of the Ordering

Proof of Proposition 7.3.2. We show that the laws of Figure 7.2 fulfill the requirements, that is, whenever b_1 and b_2 are closed, $b_1 \sqsubseteq b_2$ and

$$b_1 \Rightarrow^{p_1} b_1,$$

then there exists p_2 and b_2 such that

$$b_2 \Rightarrow^{\widehat{p_2}} b_2, \quad p_1 \sqsubseteq^{\partial} p_2 \text{ and } b_1 \sqsubseteq b_2.$$

For open behaviors the result follows from Fact 7.2.6.

The case P1 is immediate.

The case P2. Then $b_1 \sqsubseteq b_3$ because $b_1 \sqsubseteq b_2$ and $b_2 \sqsubseteq b_3$. From $b_1 \Rightarrow^{p_1} b_1$ and the induction hypothesis (IH) we get

$$b_2 \Rightarrow^{\widehat{p_2}} b_2, \tag{1}$$
$$p_1 \sqsubseteq^{\partial} p_2 \text{ and } b_1 \sqsubseteq b_2,$$

for some p_2 and b_2. By induction on the length of the derivation sequence of (1) we will show the required

$$b_3 \Rightarrow^{\widehat{p_3}} b_3, \tag{2}$$
$$p_1 \sqsubseteq^{\partial} p_3 \text{ and } b_1 \sqsubseteq b_3.$$

If the length of (1) is 1 then the induction hypothesis gives

$$b_3 \Rightarrow^{\widehat{p_3}} b_3,$$
$$p_2 \sqsubseteq^{\partial} p_3 \text{ and } b_2 \sqsubseteq b_3,$$

and (2) follows using **P2**. For the induction step assume the length of (1) is $n + 1$. Then

$$b_2 \Rightarrow^{\epsilon} b_2' \Rightarrow^{\widehat{p_2}} b_2,$$

and IH applied to the first step gives

$$b_3 \Rightarrow^{\widehat{p_3'}} b_3',$$
$$\epsilon \sqsubseteq^{\partial} p_3' \text{ and } b_2' \sqsubseteq b_3'.$$

Now $p_3' = \epsilon$ is the only possibility and also $b_3' \neq \sqrt{}$ must be the the case. Next, IH applied to $b_2' \Rightarrow^{\widehat{p_2}} b_2$ with $b_2' \sqsubseteq b_3'$ gives

$$b_3' \Rightarrow^{\widehat{p_3}} b_3,$$
$$p_1 \sqsubseteq^{\partial} p_3 \text{ and } b_1 \sqsubseteq b_3.$$

Thus we have $b_3 \Rightarrow^{\widehat{p_3}} b_3$ and the result follows.

The case C1. Assume $b_1; b_3 \sqsubseteq b_2; b_4$ because $b_1 \sqsubseteq b_2$ and $b_3 \sqsubseteq b_4$. Furthermore assume

$$b_1; b_2 \Rightarrow^{p_1} b_1.$$

There are two interesting subcases:

$$(i) \quad b_1 \Rightarrow^{p_1} b_1' \quad \text{and} \quad b_1 = b_1'; b_2,$$
$$(ii) \quad b_1 \Rightarrow^{p_1} \sqrt{} \quad \text{and} \quad b_1 = b_2.$$

In subcase *(i)* IH gives $b_2 \Rightarrow^{\widehat{p_2}} b_2'$, $p_1 \sqsubseteq^{\partial} p_2$, and $b_1' \sqsubseteq b_2'$. Since $b_1' \neq \sqrt{}$ we have $b_2' \neq \sqrt{}$; so

$$b_2; b_4 \Rightarrow^{\widehat{p_2}} b_2'; b_4.$$

Using **P1**, **P2**, and **C1** we get $b_1 \sqsubseteq b'_2; b_4$ as required. In subcase *(ii)* IH gives $b_2 \Rightarrow^{\widehat{p_2}} b'_2$, $p_1 \sqsubseteq^{\partial} p_2$, and $\sqrt{} \sqsubseteq b'_2$. Thus $b'_2 = \sqrt{}$ must be the case and

$$b_2; \, b_4 \Rightarrow^{\widehat{p_2}} b_4.$$

The result then follows.

   The case C2. Assume $b_1 + b_3 \sqsubseteq b_2 + b_4$ because $b_1 \sqsubseteq b_2$ and $b_3 \sqsubseteq b_4$. Furthermore assume that

$$b_1 + b_3 \Rightarrow^{p_1} b_1.$$

The only interesting case is when $b_i \Rightarrow^{p_1} b_1$ for $i = 1$ or $i = 3$. Then IH gives $b_{i+1} \Rightarrow^{\widehat{p_2}} b_2$ for $p_1 \sqsubseteq^{\partial} p_2$ and $b_1 \sqsubseteq b_2$. So we get the required

$$b_2 + b_4 \Rightarrow^{\widehat{p_2}} b_2.$$

   The case C3. Assume $\text{FORK}_\pi \, b_1 \sqsubseteq \text{FORK}_\pi \, b_2$ because $b_1 \sqsubseteq b_2$. Furthermore, assume

$$\text{FORK}_\pi \, b_1 \Rightarrow^{p_1} b_1.$$

The only interesting case is when $p_1 = \text{FORK}_\pi \, b_1$ and $b_1 = \epsilon$. Clearly $\text{FORK}_\pi \, b_2 \Rightarrow^{\widehat{p_2}} \epsilon$ for $p_2 = \text{FORK}_\pi \, b_2$, and since $\text{FORK}_\pi \, b_1 \sqsubseteq^{\partial} \text{FORK}_\pi \, b_2$ and $\epsilon \sqsubseteq \epsilon$ the result follows.

   The case C4. Assume $\text{REC}\beta.b_1 \sqsubseteq \text{REC}\beta.b_2$ because $b_1 \sqsubseteq b_2$. Furthermore, assume

$$\text{REC}\beta.b_1 \Rightarrow^{p_1} b_1.$$

The only interesting case is when $p_1 = \epsilon$ and $b_1 = b_1[\beta \mapsto \text{REC}\beta.b_1]$. Clearly

$$\text{REC}\beta.b_2 \Rightarrow^{\widehat{\epsilon}} b_2[\beta \mapsto \text{REC}\beta.b_2].$$

We have

$$\begin{aligned}
b_1[\beta \mapsto \text{REC}\beta.b_1] \quad &\sqsubseteq \text{REC}\beta.b_1 \\
&\sqsubseteq \text{REC}\beta.b_2 \\
&\sqsubseteq b_2[\beta \mapsto \text{REC}\beta.b_2]
\end{aligned}$$

using **P2**, **R1**, and the assumption. Thus the result follows.

   The case S1. First we study $b_1; (b_2; b_3) \sqsubseteq (b_1; b_2); b_3$. So assume

$$b_1; (b_2; b_3) \Rightarrow^{p} b.$$

There are two interesting cases:

$$\begin{aligned}
&(i) \quad b_1 \Rightarrow^p b'_1 \quad && \text{and} \quad b = b'_1; (b_2; b_3), \\
&(ii) \quad b_1 \Rightarrow^p \sqrt{} \quad && \text{and} \quad b = b_2; b_3.
\end{aligned}$$

In subcase *(i)* we get $b_1; b_2 \Rightarrow^p b'_1; b_2$ and then $(b_1; b_2); b_3 \Rightarrow^p (b'_1; b_2); b_3$. Since $p \sqsubseteq^{\partial} p$ and $b'_1; (b_2; b_3) \sqsubseteq (b'_1; b_2); b_3$ (follows from **S1**) we get the required result. In subcase *(ii)* we have $b_1; b_2 \Rightarrow^p b_2$ and then $(b_1; b_2); b_3 \Rightarrow^p b_2; b_3$. The result follows using **P1**.

Next we study $(b_1; b_2); b_3 \sqsubseteq b_1; (b_2; b_3)$. So assume

$$(b_1; b_2); b_3 \Rightarrow^p \flat.$$

It cannot be the case that $b_1; b_2 \Rightarrow^p \sqrt{}$; so the only interesting case is when

$$b_1; b_2 \Rightarrow^p b \text{ and } \flat = b; b_3.$$

We have the two subcases

$$
\begin{array}{llll}
(i) & b_1 \Rightarrow^p b_1' & \text{and} & b = b_1'; b_2, \\
(ii) & b_1 \Rightarrow^p \sqrt{} & \text{and} & b = b_2.
\end{array}
$$

In subcase *(i)* we get $b_1; (b_2; b_3) \Rightarrow^p b_1'; (b_2; b_3)$, and since $p \sqsubseteq^\partial p$ and $(b_1'; b_2); b_3 \sqsubseteq b_1'; (b_2; b_3)$ (follows from **S1**) we get the required result. In subcase *(ii)* we have $b_1; (b_2; b_3) \Rightarrow^p b_2; b_3$, and since $\flat = b_2; b_3$ the result follows.

The case S2. First we study $(b_1 + b_2); b_3 \sqsubseteq b_1; b_3 + b_2; b_3$. So assume

$$(b_1 + b_2); b_3 \Rightarrow^p \flat.$$

There are two interesting subcases:

$$
\begin{array}{llll}
(i) & b_1 + b_2 \Rightarrow^p b' & \text{and} & \flat = b'; b_3, \\
(ii) & b_1 + b_2 \Rightarrow^p \sqrt{} & \text{and} & \flat = b_3.
\end{array}
$$

In subcase *(i)* the only interesting case is when $b_i \Rightarrow^p b'$ for $i = 1$ or $i = 2$. Then $b_i; b_3 \Rightarrow^p b'; b_3$, and hence $b_1; b_3 + b_2; b_3 \Rightarrow^p b'; b_3$. The result follows using **P1**. In subcase *(ii)* it must be the case that $b_i \Rightarrow^p \sqrt{}$ for $i = 1$ or $i = 2$. Then $b_i; b_3 \Rightarrow^p b_3$, and hence $b_1; b_3 + b_2; b_3 \Rightarrow^p b_3$, and the result follows.

Next we study $b_1; b_3 + b_2; b_3 \sqsubseteq (b_1 + b_2); b_3$. So assume

$$b_1; b_3 + b_2; b_3 \Rightarrow^p \flat.$$

The only interesting case is when $b_i; b_3 \Rightarrow^p \flat$ for $i = 1$ or $i = 2$. Now there are two interesting subcases:

$$
\begin{array}{llll}
(i) & b_i \Rightarrow^p b_i' & \text{and} & \flat = b_i'; b_3, \\
(ii) & b_i \Rightarrow^p \sqrt{} & \text{and} & \flat = b_3.
\end{array}
$$

In subcase *(i)* we get $b_1 + b_2 \Rightarrow^p b_i'$ and hence $(b_1 + b_2); b_3 \Rightarrow^p b_i'; b_3$. The result follows using **P1**. In subcase *(ii)* we get $b_1 + b_2 \Rightarrow^p \sqrt{}$ and hence $(b_1 + b_2); b_3 \Rightarrow^p b_2$. Again the result follows from **P1**.

The case E1. First we study $b \sqsubseteq \epsilon; b$. So assume $b \Rightarrow^p \flat$. Clearly $\epsilon; b \Rightarrow^\epsilon b \Rightarrow^p \flat$ and the result follows using **P1**.

Next we study $\epsilon; b \sqsubseteq b$. So assume $\epsilon; b \Rightarrow^p b$. There are two interesting subcases:

$$(i) \quad \epsilon \Rightarrow^\epsilon \epsilon \quad \text{and} \quad b = \epsilon; b \quad (\text{and } p = \epsilon),$$
$$(ii) \quad \epsilon \Rightarrow^\epsilon \sqrt{} \quad \text{and} \quad b = b \quad (\text{and } p = \epsilon).$$

Clearly $b \Rightarrow^\epsilon b$. In subcase (i) the result follows from using the assumption (**E1**) that $\epsilon; b \sqsubseteq b$ and in subcase (ii) it follows using **P1**.

The case E2. First we study $b; \epsilon \sqsubseteq b$. So assume $b; \epsilon \Rightarrow^p b$. There are two interesting subcases:

$$(i) \quad b \Rightarrow^p b' \quad \text{and} \quad b = b'; \epsilon,$$
$$(ii) \quad b \Rightarrow^p \sqrt{} \quad \text{and} \quad b = \epsilon.$$

In subcase (i) the result follows using $b'; \epsilon \sqsubseteq b'$ (**E2**). In subcase (ii) it must be the case that $b = \epsilon$ and $p = \epsilon$. Clearly $\epsilon \Rightarrow^\epsilon \epsilon$ and the result follows because $\epsilon \sqsubseteq \epsilon$.

Next we study $b \sqsubseteq b; \epsilon$. So assume $b \Rightarrow^p b$. If $b \neq \sqrt{}$ then $b; \epsilon \Rightarrow^p b; \epsilon$, and the result follows because $b \sqsubseteq b; \epsilon$ (**E2**). If $b = \sqrt{}$ then $p = \epsilon$ must be the case. So we have $b; \epsilon \Rightarrow^\epsilon \epsilon \Rightarrow^\epsilon \sqrt{}$, and since $\sqrt{} \sqsubseteq \sqrt{}$ the result follows.

The case J1. We shall study $b_i \sqsubseteq b_1 + b_2$ for $i = 1$ and $i = 2$. So assume $b_i \Rightarrow^p b$. But then $b_1 + b_2 \Rightarrow^p b$ and the result follows using **P1**.

The case J2. We shall study $b + b \sqsubseteq b$ since $b \sqsubseteq b + b$ follows from **J1**. So assume $b + b \Rightarrow^p b$. The only interesting case is when $b \Rightarrow^p b$ and the result follows immediately.

The case R1. First we study $\text{REC}\beta.b \sqsubseteq b[\beta \mapsto \text{REC}\beta.b]$. So assume

$$\text{REC}\beta.b \Rightarrow^p b.$$

The only interesting case is when $p = \epsilon$ and $b = b[\beta \mapsto \text{REC}\beta.b]$. Since $b[\beta \mapsto \text{REC}\beta.b] \Rightarrow^\epsilon b[\beta \mapsto \text{REC}\beta.b]$ the result follows using **P1**.

Next we study $b[\beta \mapsto \text{REC}\beta.b] \sqsubseteq \text{REC}\beta.b$. So assume

$$b[\beta \mapsto \text{REC}\beta.b] \Rightarrow^p b.$$

We have $\text{REC}\beta.b \Rightarrow^\epsilon b[\beta \mapsto \text{REC}\beta.b] \Rightarrow^p b$ and the result follows using **P1**.

The case R2. We first consider $\text{REC}\beta.b \sqsubseteq \text{REC}\beta'.b[\beta \mapsto \beta']$ for $\beta' \notin FV(b)$. So assume

$$\text{REC}\beta.b \Rightarrow^p b.$$

The only interesting case is when $p = \epsilon$ and $b = b[\beta \mapsto \text{REC}\beta.b]$. Then

$$\text{REC}\beta'.b[\beta \mapsto \beta'] \Rightarrow^p b[\beta \mapsto \text{REC}\beta'.b[\beta \mapsto \beta']].$$

That $b[\beta \mapsto \text{REC}\beta.b] \sqsubseteq b[\beta \mapsto \text{REC}\beta'.b[\beta \mapsto \beta']]$ then follows from **R1**, and $p \sqsubseteq^\partial p$ is immediate. The other direction is similar. $\qquad \square$

Appendix 7.C   Semantic Properties of the Typing System

Proof of Lemma 7.4.2. We proceed by structural induction on E. The interesting case is when $E = \mathtt{let}\ x = E_1\ \mathtt{in}\ e_2$. Then we have

$$tenv \vdash E[e_0] : t\ \&\ b \quad (\text{because } tenv \vdash e_0 : t_0\ \&\ b_0)$$

because

$$tenv \vdash E_1[e_0] : t_1\ \&\ b_1 \quad (\text{because } tenv \vdash e_0 : t_0\ \&\ b_0),$$
$$tenv[x \mapsto ts_1] \vdash e_2 : t\ \&\ b_2,$$
$$b_1 ; b_2 \sqsubseteq b,$$
$$ts_1 = \mathrm{gen}(tenv, b_1)t_1.$$

By the induction hypothesis we get

$$tenv\ tenv' \vdash E_1[e_0] : t_1\ \&\ b_1 \quad (\text{because } tenv\ tenv' \vdash e_0 : t_0\ \&\ b_0),$$

and by Corollary 7.2.13 we get

$$tenv\ tenv'\ [x \mapsto ts_1] \vdash e_2 : t\ \&\ b_2,$$

and clearly

$$b_1 ; b_2 \sqsubseteq b,$$

and finally

$$ts_1 = \mathrm{gen}(tenv\ tenv', b_1)t_1$$

because $FV(tenv') \subseteq FV(b_0)$ by assumption and $FV(b_0) \subseteq FV(b_1)$ by Fact 7.4.1. This completes the proof. □

Proof of Lemma 7.4.4. We proceed by structural induction on E. The more interesting cases are

The case of $E\ e$. Assume $tenv \vdash E[e_0]\ e : t\ \&\ b$. Then $b_1 ; b_2 ; b_0 \sqsubseteq b$ and the premises are $tenv \vdash E[e_0] : t' \to^{b_0} t\ \&\ b_1$ and $tenv \vdash e : t'\ \&\ b_2$. The induction hypothesis gives $tenv \vdash E[e_0'] : t' \to^{b_0} t\ \&\ b_1'$ where $p; b_1' \sqsubseteq b_1$. The rule for application gives $tenv \vdash E[e_0']\ e : t\ \&\ b_1' ; b_2 ; b_0$. Using the laws **P2**, **C1**, and **S1** we get $p; b_1' ; b_2 ; b_0 \sqsubseteq b$ as required.

The case of $w\ E$. Assume $tenv \vdash w\ E[e_0] : t\ \&\ b$. Then $b_1 ; b_2 ; b_0 \sqsubseteq b$ and the premises are $tenv \vdash w : t' \to^{b_0} t\ \&\ b_1$ and $tenv \vdash E[e_0] : t'\ \&\ b_2$. The induction hypothesis gives $tenv \vdash E[e_0'] : t'\ \&\ b_2'$ where $p; b_2' \sqsubseteq b_2$. From Fact 7.4.5 we have $\epsilon \sqsubseteq b_1$ and $tenv \vdash w : t' \to^{b_0} t\ \&\ \epsilon$ so the rule for application gives $tenv \vdash w\ E[e_0'] : t\ \&\ \epsilon; b_2'; b_0$. Using the laws **P1**, **P2**, **C1**, **S1**, **E1**, and **E2** we get $p; \epsilon; b_2'; b_0 \sqsubseteq b$ as required.

The case of $\mathtt{let}\ x = E\ \mathtt{in}\ e$. Assume $tenv \vdash \mathtt{let}\ x = E[e_0]\ \mathtt{in}\ e : t\ \&\ b$. Then $b_1 ; b_2 \sqsubseteq b$ and the premises are $tenv \vdash E[e_0] : t_1\ \&\ b_1$ and $tenv[x \mapsto$

$ts] \vdash e : t \mathbin{\&} b_2$ where $ts = \mathrm{gen}(tenv,\ b_1)\ t_1$. The induction hypothesis gives $tenv \vdash E[e'_0] : t_1 \mathbin{\&} b'_1$ where $p; b'_1 \sqsubseteq b_1$. Clearly $FV(b'_1) \subseteq FV(b_1)$ follows from Fact 7.2.5; so $FV(t_1) \backslash (FV(tenv) \cup FV(b_1)) \subseteq FV(t_1) \backslash (FV(tenv) \cup FV(b'_1))$, and thereby $ts' \succeq ts$, where $ts' = \mathrm{gen}(tenv, b'_1)\ t_1$. Using Fact 7.2.8 we get $tenv[x \mapsto ts'] \vdash e : t \mathbin{\&} b_2$ and then the rule for let-polymorphism gives $tenv \vdash \mathtt{let}\ x = E[e'_0]\ \mathtt{in}\ e : t \mathbin{\&} b'_1; b_2$. Using the laws **P1**, **P2**, **C1**, and **S1**, it follows that $p; b'_1; b_2 \sqsubseteq b$.   □

Proof of Proposition 7.4.6. We proceed by induction on the inference for $e \to e'$. Most cases are similar, and so we only consider the case of let-polymorphism. For this assume that $E[\mathtt{let}\ x = w\ \mathtt{in}\ e] \to E[e[x \mapsto w]]$ and

$$cenv \vdash E[\mathtt{let}\ x = w\ \mathtt{in}\ e] : t \mathbin{\&} b. \tag{1}$$

In this inference we can identify the node corresponding to the hole of E:

$$cenv \vdash \mathtt{let}\ x = w\ \mathtt{in}\ e : t_2 \mathbin{\&} b_1. \tag{2}$$

Its premises are $cenv \vdash w : t_1 \mathbin{\&} b_2$ and

$$cenv[x \mapsto ts] \vdash e : t_2 \mathbin{\&} b_3, \tag{3}$$

where $ts = \mathrm{gen}(cenv, b_2)t_1$ and $b_2; b_3 \sqsubseteq b_1$. From Fact 7.4.5 we have $\epsilon \sqsubseteq b_2$ and

$$cenv \vdash w : t_1 \mathbin{\&} \epsilon. \tag{4}$$

We shall now apply Lemma 7.2.14 to (3) and (4) and get $cenv \vdash e[x \mapsto w] : t_2 \mathbin{\&} b_3$. The laws **P1**, **P2**, **C1**, and **E1** give $b_3 \sqsubseteq b_1$ so using Fact 7.2.9 we get

$$cenv \vdash e[x \mapsto w] : t_2 \mathbin{\&} b_1. \tag{5}$$

Using Fact 7.4.3 with (1), (2), and (5) we get the required

$$cenv \vdash E[e[x \mapsto w]] : t \mathbin{\&} b.$$

This completes the proof.   □

Proof of Proposition 7.4.7. We proceed by induction on the inference for matching.

The cases of send/receive. Assume

$$(\langle \mathtt{send}\ \langle \mathtt{pair}\ ci\ w \rangle \rangle, \langle \mathtt{receive}\ ci \rangle) \overset{(ci!,ci?)}{\rightsquigarrow} (w, w)$$

and

$$cenv \vdash \langle \mathtt{send}\ \langle \mathtt{pair}\ ci\ w \rangle \rangle : t_1\ \mathtt{com}\ b_1 \mathbin{\&} \epsilon,$$
$$cenv \vdash \langle \mathtt{receive}\ ci \rangle : t_2\ \mathtt{com}\ b_2 \mathbin{\&} \epsilon.$$

Furthermore, assume $cenv\ ci\ = t$ chan r. Then the typing rule for weakly evaluated expressions gives $t_1 = t_2 = t$ and $cenv \vdash w : t$ & b_0, and furthermore $b_1 \sqsupseteq r!t$ and $b_2 \sqsupseteq r?t$. Now, $\mathcal{B}\ cenv\ ci! = r!t$ and $\mathcal{B}\ cenv\ ci? = r?t$, and so we only have to show $r!t; \epsilon \sqsubseteq b_1$ and $r?t; \epsilon \sqsubseteq b_2$, but this is immediate.

The case of heads. Assume $(\langle \texttt{choose}\ \langle \texttt{cons}\ w_1\ w_2 \rangle \rangle, w_3) \overset{(d_1,d_3)}{\rightsquigarrow} (e_1, e_3)$ because $(w_1, w_3) \overset{(d_1,d_3)}{\rightsquigarrow} (e_1, e_3)$ and

$$cenv \vdash \langle \texttt{choose}\ \langle \texttt{cons}\ w_1\ w_2 \rangle \rangle : t_1\ \texttt{com}\ b_1\ \&\ \epsilon,$$

$$cenv \vdash w_3 : t_3\ \texttt{com}\ b_3\ \&\ \epsilon.$$

From the typing rule for weakly evaluated expressions we get $cenv \vdash w_1 : t_1\ \texttt{com}\ b_0\ \&\ b$ for some $b \sqsupseteq \epsilon$ and where $b_1 \sqsupseteq b_0$. Using Fact 7.4.5 we have $cenv \vdash w_1 : t_1\ \texttt{com}\ b_0\ \&\ \epsilon$, and the induction hypothesis gives

$$cenv \vdash e_1 : t_1\ \&\ b_0'\ \text{ and } cenv \vdash e_3 : t_3\ \&\ b_3',$$

where $(\mathcal{B}\ cenv\ d_1); b_0' \sqsubseteq b_0$ and $(\mathcal{B}\ cenv\ d_3); b_3' \sqsubseteq b_3$. Using the laws **P2** and **J1** we get $(\mathcal{B}\ cenv\ d_1); b_0' \sqsubseteq b_1$ and the result follows.

The case of tails. This is along the lines of the previous case and we omit the details.

The case of $\texttt{wrap}$. Assume $(\langle \texttt{wrap}\ \langle \texttt{pair}\ w_1\ w_2 \rangle \rangle, w_3) \overset{(d_1,d_3)}{\rightsquigarrow} (w_2\ e_1, e_3)$ because $(w_1, w_3) \overset{(d_1,d_3)}{\rightsquigarrow} (e_1, e_3)$ and assume

$$cenv \vdash \langle \texttt{wrap}\ \langle \texttt{pair}\ w_1\ w_2 \rangle \rangle : t_2\ \texttt{com}\ b_2\ \&\ \epsilon,$$

$$cenv \vdash w_3 : t_3\ \texttt{com}\ b_3\ \&\ \epsilon.$$

From the typing rule for weakly evaluated expressions we get

$$cenv \vdash w_1 : t_1\ \texttt{com}\ b_1\ \&\ b\ \text{ and } cenv \vdash w_2 : t_1 \rightarrow^{b_0} t_2\ \&\ b'$$

and $b_2 \sqsupseteq b_1; b_0$. Using Fact 7.4.5 we get

$$cenv \vdash w_1 : t_1\ \texttt{com}\ b_1\ \&\ \epsilon\ \text{ and } cenv \vdash w_2 : t_1 \rightarrow^{b_0} t_2\ \&\ \epsilon\ .$$

Then the induction hypothesis gives

$$cenv \vdash e_1 : t_1\ \&\ b_1'\ \text{ and } cenv \vdash e_3 : t_3\ \&\ b_3',$$

where $(\mathcal{B}\ cenv\ d_1); b_1' \sqsubseteq b_1$ and $(\mathcal{B}\ cenv\ d_3); b_3' \sqsubseteq b_3$. The rule for function application then gives

$$cenv \vdash w_2\ e_1 : t_2\ \&\ \epsilon; b_1'; b_0,$$

and we have to show $(\mathcal{B}\ cenv\ d_1); \epsilon; b_1'; b_0 \sqsubseteq b_2$. But this is immediate.

The case of swop. This case is straightforward and we omit the details. This completes the proof.   □

Proof of Theorem 7.4.8. We proceed by induction on the inference for concurrent evaluation.

The case of sequential evaluation. Assume that

$$CI \ \& \ PP[pi \mapsto E[e]] \longrightarrow_{pi}^{\epsilon} CI \ \& \ PP[pi \mapsto E[e']]$$

because $E[e] \to E[e']$. Furthermore, assume that $CI\&PP[pi \mapsto E[e]]$ is *cenv*-described by $PB[pi \mapsto b]$. In particular this means that

$$cenv \vdash E[e] : t \ \& \ b$$

for some t. From Proposition 7.4.6 we get

$$cenv \vdash E[e'] : t \ \& \ b.$$

Clearly $b \Rightarrow^\epsilon b$, and thereby

$$PB[pi \mapsto b] \Longrightarrow_{pi}^{\widehat{\epsilon}} PB[pi \mapsto b].$$

We have $\mathcal{A} \ (cenv, PB[pi \mapsto b]) \ \epsilon = \epsilon$. Taking $PB' = PB[pi \mapsto b]$ we get that $CI\&PP[pi \mapsto E[e']]$ is *cenv*-described by PB' as required.

The case of channel allocation. Assume that

$$CI \ \& \ PP[pi \mapsto E[\mathtt{channel}_l \ ()]] \longrightarrow_{pi}^{\mathrm{CHAN}_l \ ci}$$

$$CI \ \cup \ \{ci\} \ \& \ PP[pi \mapsto E[ci]],$$

where $ci \notin CI$. Furthermore, assume that $CI\&PP[pi \mapsto E[\mathtt{channel}_l \ ()]]$ is *cenv*-described by $PB[pi \mapsto b]$. In particular this means that

$$cenv \vdash E[\mathtt{channel}_l \ ()] : t \ \& \ b \tag{1}$$

for some t. In this inference we can identify the node corresponding to the hole of E and it will be of the form

$$cenv \vdash \mathtt{channel}_l \ () : t' \ \mathtt{chan} \ r \ \& \ b_0, \tag{2}$$

where $l \in r$ and $b_1; b_2; t'$ CHAN $r \sqsubseteq b_0$, where $\epsilon \sqsubseteq b_1$ and $\epsilon \sqsubseteq b_2$ (follows from Fact 7.4.5). Now define $cenv' = cenv[ci \mapsto t' \ \mathtt{chan} \ r]$. Then we can replace $cenv$ in (2) and (1) by $cenv'$ and thus obtain (2') and (1'); by Lemma 7.4.2 we still have (1') because (2'). From (2') we then get

$$cenv' \vdash ci : t' \ \mathtt{chan} \ r \ \& \ \epsilon.$$

Also, t' CHAN r; $\epsilon \sqsubseteq b_0$ follows from the laws **P1**, **P2**, **C1**, **E1**, **E2**, and **J1**; so we can apply Lemma 7.4.4 and get

$$cenv' \vdash E[ci] : t \ \& \ b', \tag{3}$$

where t' CHAN r; $b' \sqsubseteq b$. Clearly t' CHAN $r; b' \Rightarrow^{t' \ \mathrm{CHAN} \ r} b'$, and using that $\sqsubseteq$ is a simulation (Proposition 7.3.2) we get $b \Rightarrow^{\widehat{p}} \tilde{b}$ for some p and $\tilde{b}$ satisfying t' CHAN $r \sqsubseteq^\partial p$ and $b' \sqsubseteq \tilde{b}$. Now $p = t'$ CHAN r must be the case; so

$$PB[pi \mapsto b] \Longrightarrow_{pi}^{t' \; \widehat{\text{CHAN}} \; r} \; PB[pi \mapsto \tilde{b}].$$

Clearly $\mathcal{A}\,(cenv', PB[pi \mapsto \tilde{b}])$ CHAN $ci = t'$ CHAN r as required. Taking $PB' = PB[pi \mapsto \tilde{b}]$ we get from (3) and Fact 7.2.9 (and $b' \sqsubseteq \tilde{b}$) that $CI \cup \{ci\}\&PP[pi \mapsto E[ci]]$ is $cenv'$-described by PB'.

The case of process creation. Assume that

$$CI \; \& \; PP[pi_1 \mapsto E[\texttt{fork}_\pi \; w]] \longrightarrow_{pi_1,pi_2}^{\text{FORK}_\pi \; pi_2},$$

$$CI \; \& \; PP[pi_1 \mapsto E[()]][pi_2 \mapsto w()],$$

where $pi_2 \notin \text{Dom}(PP) \cup \{pi_1\}$. Furthermore, assume that $CI\&PP[pi_1 \mapsto E[\texttt{fork}_\pi \; w]]$ is $cenv$-described by $PB[pi_1 \mapsto b_1]$. In particular this means that

$$cenv \vdash E[\texttt{fork}_\pi \; w] : t_1 \; \& \; b_1$$

for some t_1. In this inference we can identify the node corresponding to the hole of E. It has the form

$$cenv \vdash \texttt{fork}_\pi \; w : \texttt{unit} \; \& \; b_0, \tag{1}$$

where $b_1; b_2; \text{FORK}_\pi \; b \sqsubseteq b_0$ for some b and where $\epsilon \sqsubseteq b_1$ and $\epsilon \sqsubseteq b_2$ follows from Fact 7.4.5. We also have

$$cenv \vdash () : \texttt{unit} \; \& \; \epsilon,$$

and $(\text{FORK}_\pi \; b); \epsilon \sqsubseteq b_0$ follows from the laws **P1**, **P2**, **C1**, **E1**, **E2**, and **J1**. We can then apply Lemma 7.4.4 and get

$$cenv \vdash E[()] : t_1 \; \& \; b_1', \tag{2}$$

where $(\text{FORK}_\pi \; b); b_1' \sqsubseteq b_1$. Clearly $(\text{FORK}_\pi \; b); b_1' \Rightarrow^{\text{FORK}_\pi \; b} b_1'$, and using that $\sqsubseteq$ is a simulation (Proposition 7.3.2) we get $b_1 \Rightarrow^{\tilde{p}} \tilde{b}_1$ for some p and $\tilde{b}_1$ with $\text{FORK}_\pi \; b \sqsubseteq^{\partial} p$ and $b_1' \sqsubseteq \tilde{b}_1$. Now it follows that $p = \text{FORK}_\pi \; b'$ for some b' where $b \sqsubseteq b'$. Also we have

$$PB[pi_1 \mapsto b_1] \Longrightarrow_{pi_1,pi_2}^{\widehat{\text{FORK}_\pi} \; b'} \; PB[pi_1 \mapsto \tilde{b}_1][pi_2 \mapsto b'].$$

We have $\mathcal{A}\,(cenv, PB[pi_1 \mapsto \tilde{b}_1][pi_2 \mapsto b'])$ FORK$_\pi$ $pi_2 = $ FORK$_\pi$ b' as required. We shall now take $PB' = PB[pi_1 \mapsto \tilde{b}_1][pi_2 \mapsto b']$. From (1) and Fact 7.4.5 we get

$$cenv \vdash w : \texttt{unit} \; \rightarrow^b t \; \& \; \epsilon$$

for some type t, and thereby

$$cenv \vdash w \; () : t \; \& \; b.$$

Using this and (2) together with Fact 7.2.9 (and $b'_1 \sqsubseteq \tilde{b}_1$ and $b \sqsubseteq b'$) we get that $CI\&PP[pi_1 \mapsto E[()][pi_2 \mapsto w()]$ is *cenv*-described by PB'.

The case of matching. Assume that

$$CI \ \& \ PP[pi_1 \mapsto E_1[\text{sync } w_1]][pi_2 \mapsto E_2[\text{sync } w_2]] \longrightarrow^{(ci!,ci?)}_{pi_1,pi_2},$$

$$CI \ \& \ PP[pi_1 \mapsto E_1[e_1]][pi_2 \mapsto E_2[e_2]],$$

because $(w_1, w_2) \overset{(ci!,ci?)}{\rightsquigarrow} (e_1, e_2)$. Furthermore, assume that $CI\&PP[pi_1 \mapsto E_1[\text{sync } w_1]] [pi_2 \mapsto E_2[\text{sync } w_2]]$ is *cenv*-described by $PB[pi_1 \mapsto b_1][pi_2 \mapsto b_2]$. In particular this means that

$$cenv \vdash E_1[\text{sync } w_1] : t_1 \ \& \ b_1 \text{ and } cenv \vdash E_2[\text{sync } w_2] : t_2 \ \& \ b_2$$

for some t_1 and t_2. In these inferences we can identify the node corresponding to the hole of E_1 and E_2, respectively, and they have the forms

$$cenv \vdash \text{sync } w_1 : t'_1 \ \& \ \overline{b_1} \text{ and } cenv \vdash \text{sync } w_2 : t'_2 \ \& \ \overline{b_2},$$

where $b_{11}; b_{12}; b_{01} \sqsubseteq \overline{b_1}$ and $b_{21}; b_{22}; b_{02} \sqsubseteq \overline{b_2}$ for some b_{01} and b_{02}. The premises include

$$cenv \vdash w_1 : t'_1 \text{ com } b_{01} \ \& \ b_{12} \text{ and } cenv \vdash w_2 : t'_2 \text{ com } b_{02} \ \& \ b_{22},$$

and from Fact 7.4.5 we get $\epsilon \sqsubseteq b_{11}, \epsilon \sqsubseteq b_{12}, \epsilon \sqsubseteq b_{21}, \epsilon \sqsubseteq b_{22}$, and

$$cenv \vdash w_1 : t'_1 \text{ com } b_{01} \ \& \ \epsilon \text{ and } cenv \vdash w_2 : t'_2 \text{ com } b_{02} \ \& \ \epsilon.$$

Using Proposition 7.4.7 we get

$$cenv \vdash e_1 : t'_1 \ \& \ b'_{01} \text{ and } cenv \vdash e_2 : t'_2 \ \& \ b'_{02},$$

where $(\mathcal{B} \ cenv \ ci!); b'_{01} \sqsubseteq b_{01}$ and $(\mathcal{B} \ cenv \ ci?); b'_{02} \sqsubseteq b_{02}$. Using the laws **P1**, **P2**, **C1**, **E1**, and **J1** we get $(\mathcal{B} \ cenv \ ci!); b'_{01} \sqsubseteq \overline{b_1}$ and $(\mathcal{B} \ cenv \ ci?); b'_{02} \sqsubseteq \overline{b_2}$. We can now apply Lemma 7.4.4 and get

$$cenv \vdash E_1[e_1] : t_1 \ \& \ b'_1 \text{ and } cenv \vdash E_2[e_2] : t_2 \ \& \ b'_2, \tag{1}$$

where $(\mathcal{B} \ cenv \ ci!); b'_1 \sqsubseteq b_1$ and $(\mathcal{B} \ cenv \ ci?); b'_2 \sqsubseteq b_2$. Clearly $(\mathcal{B} \ cenv \ ci!); b'_1 \Rightarrow^{(\mathcal{B} \ cenv \ ci!)} b'_1$ and $(\mathcal{B} \ cenv \ ci?); b'_2 \Rightarrow^{(\mathcal{B} \ cenv \ ci?)} b'_2$. Using that $\sqsubseteq$ is a simulation (Proposition 7.3.2), we get $b_1 \Rightarrow^{\widehat{p_1}} \tilde{b}_1$ and $b_2 \Rightarrow^{\widehat{p_2}} \tilde{b}_2$, where $(\mathcal{B} \ cenv \ ci!) \sqsubseteq^{\partial} p_1, (\mathcal{B} \ cenv \ ci?) \sqsubseteq^{\partial} p_2, b'_1 \sqsubseteq \tilde{b}_1$, and $b'_2 \sqsubseteq \tilde{b}_2$. It must be the case that $(p_1, p_2) = ((\mathcal{B} \ cenv \ ci!), (\mathcal{B} \ cenv \ ci?)) = (r!t, r?t)$ for some r and t; so we get

$$PB[pi_1 \mapsto b_1][pi_2 \mapsto b_2] \Longrightarrow^{\widehat{(r!t,r?t)}}_{pi_1,pi_2} PB[pi_1 \mapsto \tilde{b}_1][pi_2 \mapsto \tilde{b}_2].$$

Now $\mathcal{A} \ (cenv, PB[pi_1 \mapsto \tilde{b}_1][pi_2 \mapsto \tilde{b}_2]) \ (ci!, ci?) = (r!t, r?t)$ as required. Taking $PB' = PB[pi_1 \mapsto \tilde{b}_1][pi_2 \mapsto \tilde{b}_2]$ we get that

$$CI\&PP[pi_1 \mapsto E_1[e_1]][pi_2 \mapsto E_2[e_2]] \text{ is } cenv\text{-described by } PB',$$

using (1) together with Fact 7.2.9 (and $b'_1 \sqsubseteq \tilde{b}_1$ and $b'_2 \sqsubseteq \tilde{b}_2$). $\qquad \square$

Appendix 7.D   Decidability Issues Concerning the Orderings

Proof of Lemma 7.5.2. We prove the two implications separately. Proving "$\Leftarrow$": Let $b' \subseteq_{\approx} b''$ and let $w \in \mathcal{L}(b')$. Then there exists

$$b' \Rightarrow^{p'_1} b'_1 \ldots \Rightarrow^{p'_n} b'_n \text{ with } b'_n = \sqrt{}$$

such that $w = p'_1 \ldots p'_n$ (and where some p'_i may be ϵ and hence disappear). By $b' \subseteq_{\approx} b''$ we get

$$b'' \Rightarrow^{\widehat{p''_1}} b''_1 \ldots \Rightarrow^{\widehat{p''_n}} b''_n,$$

with $b'_i \subseteq_{\approx} b''_i$ and $p'_i \subseteq^{\partial} p''_i$ for all i. As each p'_i is either ϵ or of the form $1 \mathbin{!} t$ it follows that $p''_i = p'_i$ for all i. Also, b''_n equals $\sqrt{}$. It follows that $w \in \mathcal{L}(b'')$.

Proving "$\Rightarrow$": We define

$$S = \{(b_1, b_2) \mid \mathcal{L}(b_1) \subseteq \mathcal{L}(b_2), \vdash_D b_1, \vdash_D b_2, \models_N b_1, \models_N b_2\} \cup \{(\sqrt{}, \sqrt{})\}$$

and show that S is a simulation on closed behaviors; since $b' S b''$ the desired $b' \subseteq_{\approx} b''$ follows. First we note that $\sqrt{} S b$ if and only if $b = \sqrt{}$. Next let $(b_1, b_2) \in S \setminus \{(\sqrt{}, \sqrt{})\}$ and suppose $b_1 \Rightarrow^{p_1} b_{11}$; if $b_{11} \neq \sqrt{}$ we have (using Lemma 7.5.1) that $\vdash_D p_1, \vdash_D b_{11}, \models_N p_1, \models_N b_{11}$. We now perform a case analysis.

(i) If $p_1 = \epsilon$ and $b_{11} \neq \sqrt{}$ we have $b_2 \Rightarrow^{\widehat{\epsilon}} b_2$ with $(b_{11}, b_2) \in S$ and $(\epsilon, \epsilon) \in S^{\partial}$, where we have used Lemma 7.5.1.

(ii) If $p_1 = \epsilon$ and $b_{11} = \sqrt{}$ we have $\epsilon \in \mathcal{L}(b_1)$, and hence $\epsilon \in \mathcal{L}(b_2)$, so that $b_2 \Rightarrow^{\widehat{\epsilon}} \sqrt{}$ with $(\sqrt{}, \sqrt{}) \in S$ and $(\epsilon, \epsilon) \in S^{\partial}$.

(iii) If $p_1 = 1 \mathbin{!} t$ (for some 1 and t) we have $b_{11} \overset{w}{\Longrightarrow}^* \sqrt{}$, so that $p_1 w \in \mathcal{L}(b_1)$ and $p_1 w \in \mathcal{L}(b_2)$. Hence $b_2 \Rightarrow^{\widehat{p_1}} b_{21} \overset{w}{\Longrightarrow}^* \sqrt{}$. From Lemma 7.5.1 we have

$$\mathcal{L}(b_{11}) = \{w \mid p_1 w \in \mathcal{L}(b_1)\},$$
$$\mathcal{L}(b_{21}) = \{w \mid p_1 w \in \mathcal{L}(b_2)\},$$

and since $\mathcal{L}(b_1) \subseteq \mathcal{L}(b_2)$ we get $\mathcal{L}(b_{11}) \subseteq \mathcal{L}(b_{21})$. Using Lemma 7.5.1 we have $(b_{11}, b_{21}) \in S$ and $(p_1, p_1) \in S^{\partial}$.   □

Proof of Lemma 7.5.8. We inspect each of the laws:

The case P1: We shall prove the (stronger) result

$$bn \text{ ord } bn, \tag{1}$$

$$bs \text{ ord}_s bs, \tag{2}$$

$$bp \text{ ord}_p bp. \tag{3}$$

We proceed by induction on the *size* of the behaviors bn, bs, bp proving (3), (2), and (1) in order.

First we prove (3). If bp is one of $r!t$, $r?t$, t CHAN r, and β, then the result is immediate from the definition of ord_p. If $bp = \mathrm{FORK}_\pi \ bn$, then the induction hypothesis gives bn ord bn and the result follows from the definition of ord_p. The case where $bp = \mathrm{REC}\beta.bn$ is similar.

Then we prove (2). If $bs = \epsilon$ the result is immediate from the definition of ord_s. If $bs = bp$ then the result follows from (3) and the definition of ord_s. So assume $bs = bp; bn$. Then the induction hypothesis gives bp ord bp and bn ord bn and the result follows from the definition of ord_s.

Finally we prove (1). If $bn = bs$ the result follows from (2) and the definition of ord. So assume $bn = bn' + bn''$. Then the induction hypothesis gives bn' ord bn' and bn'' ord bn''. We then get bn' ord $bn' + bn''$ and bn'' ord $bn' + bn''$. From the definition of ord it now follows that $bn' + bn''$ ord $bn' + bn''$.

The case P2. We shall prove the (stronger) result

$$bn_1 \text{ ord } bn_2 \text{ and } bn_2 \text{ ord } bn_3 \text{ imply } bn_1 \text{ ord } bn_3 \tag{1}$$

$$bs_1 \text{ ord}_s \ bs_2 \text{ and } bs_2 \text{ ord}_s \ bs_3 \text{ imply } bs_1 \text{ ord}_s \ bs_3 \tag{2}$$

$$bp_1 \text{ ord}_p \ bp_2 \text{ and } bp_2 \text{ ord}_p \ bp_3 \text{ imply } bp_1 \text{ ord}_p \ bp_3 \tag{3}$$

We proceed by induction on the *size* of the behaviors bn_1, bs_1, bp_1, proving (3), (2), and (1) in order.

First we prove (3). If bp_1 is one of $r!t$, $r?t$, t CHAN r, and β, then $bp_2 = bp_1$ must be the case because of the definition of ord_p, and similarly $bp_3 = bp_2$ also must be the case. The result now follows from the definition of ord_p. If $bp_1 = \mathrm{FORK}_\pi \ bn_1$ then $bp_2 = \mathrm{FORK}_\pi \ bn_2$ must be the case because of the definition of ord_p, and furthermore bn_1 ord bn_2 holds. Similarly, $bp_3 = \mathrm{FORK}_\pi \ bn_3$ must be the case and bn_2 ord bn_3 holds. The induction hypothesis gives bn_1 ord bn_3, and the result follows using the definition of ord_p. The case where $bp_1 = \mathrm{REC}\beta.bn_1$ is similar.

Then we prove (2). If $bs_1 = \epsilon$ then the definition of ord_s gives that $bs_2 = \epsilon$ must be the case, and similarly $bs_3 = \epsilon$ must be the case. Then the result follows trivially from the definition of ord_s. If $bs_1 = bp_1$ then $bs_2 = bp_2$ must be the case because of the definition of ord_s, and similarly $bs_3 = bp_3$ must be the case. Then the result follows from (3) and the definition of ord_s. So assume $bs_1 = bp_1; bn_1$. Then $bs_2 = bp_2; bn_2$ must be the case because of the definition of ord_s, and furthermore bp_1 ord bp_2 and bn_1 ord bn_2. Similarly, $bs_3 = bp_3; bn_3$ must be the case, and bp_2 ord bp_3 and bn_2 ord bn_3. The induction hypothesis gives bp_1 ord bp_3 and bn_1 ord bn_3 and the result follows using the definition of ord_s.

Finally we prove (1). If $bn_1 = bs_1$ then Lemma 7.5.7 gives that there exists $bs_2 \in \Sigma(bn_2)$ such that $bs_1 \text{ ord}_s \ bs_2$. But then there exists $bs_3 \in \Sigma(bn_3)$ such that $bs_2 \text{ ord}_s \ bs_3$. From (2) we get $bs_1 \text{ ord}_s \ bs_3$ and we have

bs_1 ord bn_3 using Lemma 7.5.7. Next assume $bn_1 = bn_1' + bn_1''$. From $bn_1' + bn_1''$ ord bn_2 we get bn_1' ord bn_2 and bn_1'' ord bn_2 and the induction hypothesis gives bn_1' ord bn_3 and bn_1'' ord bn_3. But then the result follows using the definition of ord.

The case C1. Using Lemma 7.5.7 it suffices to prove the (stronger) result

$$\text{if } bn_1 \text{ ord } bn_2 \text{ and } bn_3 \text{ ord } bn_4 \text{ then } \mathsf{seq}(bn_1, bn_3) \text{ ord } \mathsf{seq}(bn_2, bn_4) \quad (1)$$

$$\text{if } bs_1 \text{ ord}_s bs_2 \text{ and } bn_3 \text{ ord } bn_4 \text{ then } \mathsf{seq}(bs_1, bn_3) \text{ ord } \mathsf{seq}(bs_2, bn_4) \quad (2)$$

To do this we need

$$\Sigma(\mathsf{seq}(bn, bn_0)) = \bigcup\{\Sigma(\mathsf{seq}(bs, bn_0)) \mid bs \in \Sigma(bn)\}, \qquad (*)$$

which can be proved by a straightforward structural induction on bn. The proofs of (1) and (2) proceed by induction on the *size* of the behaviors bn_1, bs_1, proving (2) and (1) in order.

First we prove (2). To prove $\mathsf{seq}(bs_1, bn_3)$ ord $\mathsf{seq}(bs_2, bn_4)$ it is sufficient to prove that whenever $bs \in \Sigma(\mathsf{seq}(bs_1, bn_3))$ then there exists $bs' \in \Sigma(\mathsf{seq}(bs_2, bn_4))$ such that bs ord$_s$ bs', and the result follows from Lemma 7.5.7. So assume $bs \in \Sigma(\mathsf{seq}(bs_1, bn_3))$. If $bs_1 = \epsilon$ then $bs_2 = \epsilon$ must be the case because of the definition of ord$_s$, and furthermore $bs \in \Sigma(bn_3)$ must be the case. From bn_3 ord bn_4 and Lemma 7.5.7 we get that there exists $bs' \in \Sigma(bn_4)$ such that bs ord$_s$ bs'. Since $bs' \in \Sigma(\mathsf{seq}(\epsilon, bn_4))$ the result follows. Next assume $bs_1 = bp_1$. Then $bs_2 = bp_2$ must be the case because of the definition of ord$_s$, and furthermore $bs = bp_1; bn_3$ must be the case. Using the definition of ord$_s$ we get $bp_1; bn_3$ ord$_s$ $bp_2; bn_4$ and the result follows since $bp_2; bn_4 \in \Sigma(\mathsf{seq}(bp_2, bn_4))$. Finally, assume $bs_1 = bp_1; bn_1$. Then $bs_2 = bp_2; bn_2$ must be the case because of the definition of ord$_s$, and furthermore bp_1 ord bp_2 and bn_1 ord bn_2. From $bs \in \Sigma(\mathsf{seq}(bp_1; bn_1, bn_3))$ we see that $bs = bp_1; \mathsf{seq}(bn_1, bn_3)$. The induction hypothesis gives $\mathsf{seq}(bn_1, bn_3)$ ord $\mathsf{seq}(bn_2, bn_4)$. Thus we have $bp_1; \mathsf{seq}(bn_1, bn_3)$ ord$_s$ $bp_2; \mathsf{seq}(bn_2, bn_4)$ using the definition of ord$_s$ and since $bp_2; \mathsf{seq}(bn_2, bn_4) \in \Sigma(\mathsf{seq}(bp_2; bn_2, bn_4))$, this is the required result.

Then we prove (1). To prove $\mathsf{seq}(bn_1, bn_3)$ ord $\mathsf{seq}(bn_2, bn_4)$ it suffices to prove that whenever $bs \in \Sigma(\mathsf{seq}(bn_1, bn_3))$ then there exists $bs' \in \Sigma(\mathsf{seq}(bn_2, bn_4))$ such that bs ord$_s$ bs', and the result follows from Lemma 7.5.7. So assume $bs \in \Sigma(\mathsf{seq}(bn_1, bn_3))$. Using $(*)$ this means that $bs \in \Sigma(\mathsf{seq}(bs_1, bn_3))$ for some $bs_1 \in \Sigma(bn_1)$. From bn_1 ord bn_2 and Lemma 7.5.7 we get that bs_1 ord$_s$ bs_2 for some $bs_2 \in \Sigma(bn_2)$. Then (2) and Lemma 7.5.7 gives that there is $bs' \in \Sigma(\mathsf{seq}(bs_2, bn_4))$ such that bs ord$_s$ bs'. But $bs' \in \Sigma(\mathsf{seq}(bn_2, bn_4))$ due to $(*)$, and the result follows.

The case C2. We shall prove

$$\text{if } bn_1 \text{ ord } bn_2 \text{ and } bn_3 \text{ ord } bn_4 \text{ then } bn_1 + bn_3 \text{ ord } bn_2 + bn_4.$$

Using Lemma 7.5.7 it is sufficient to prove that whenever $bs \in \Sigma(bn_1 + bn_3)$

then there exists $bs' \in \Sigma(bn_2 + bn_4)$ such that bs ord_s bs'. It is immediate that

$$\Sigma(bn_i + bn_{i+2}) = \Sigma(bn_i) \cup \Sigma(bn_{i+2})$$

for $i = 1, 2$. So given $bs \in \Sigma(bn_1 + bn_3)$ we have $bs \in \Sigma(bn_i)$, and Lemma 7.5.7 together with bn_i ord bn_{i+1} gives that there exists $bs' \in \Sigma(bn_{i+1})$ such that bs ord_s bs'. Since $bs' \in \Sigma(bn_2 + bn_4)$ the result follows.

The case C3. We shall prove

if bn_1 ord bn_2 then FORK_π bn_1 ord FORK_π bn_2.

But this follows from the definitions of ord, ord_s, and ord_p.

The case C4. We shall prove

if bn_1 ord bn_2 then $\mathrm{REC}\beta$. bn_1 ord $\mathrm{REC}\beta$. bn_2.

But this follows from the definitions of ord, ord_s, and ord_p.

The case S1. We shall prove

$$\mathsf{seq}(bn_1, \mathsf{seq}(bn_2, bn_3)) \text{ ord } \mathsf{seq}(\mathsf{seq}(bn_1, bn_2), bn_3),$$

$$\mathsf{seq}(\mathsf{seq}(bn_1, bn_2), bn_3) \text{ ord } \mathsf{seq}(bn_1, \mathsf{seq}(bn_2, bn_3)).$$

Below we show that

$$\mathsf{seq}(bn_1, \mathsf{seq}(bn_2, bn_3)) = \mathsf{seq}(\mathsf{seq}(bn_1, bn_2), bn_3). \qquad (*)$$

Since ord fulfills the law **P1** we have bn ord bn for all bn, and the result follows.

Turning to the proof of $(*)$, note that the result is immediate if $bn_3 = \epsilon$, so henceforth assume that $bn_3 \neq \epsilon$. In a similar way note that the result is immediate if $bn_2 = \epsilon$; so henceforth assume that also $bn_2 \neq \epsilon$. We now proceed by structural induction on bn_1.

First assume that $bn_1 = bs_1$. If $bs_1 = \epsilon$ then the result holds trivially since

$$\begin{aligned} \mathsf{seq}(\epsilon, \mathsf{seq}(bn_2, bn_3)) &= \mathsf{seq}(bn_2, bn_3) \\ &= \mathsf{seq}(\mathsf{seq}(\epsilon, bn_2), bn_3). \end{aligned}$$

If $bs_1 = bp_1$ then the result follows from

$$\begin{aligned} \mathsf{seq}(bp_1, \mathsf{seq}(bn_2, bn_3)) &= bp_1; \mathsf{seq}(bn_2, bn_3) \\ &= \mathsf{seq}(\mathsf{seq}(bp_1, bn_2), bn_3). \end{aligned}$$

Finally, if $bs_1 = bp_1; bn_1'$ then the result follows from

$$\begin{aligned} \mathsf{seq}(bp_1; bn_1', \mathsf{seq}(bn_2, bn_3)) &= bp_1; \mathsf{seq}(bn_1', \mathsf{seq}(bn_2, bn_3)) \\ &= bp_1; \mathsf{seq}(\mathsf{seq}(bn_1', bn_2), bn_3) \\ &= \mathsf{seq}(bp_1; \mathsf{seq}(bn_1', bn_2), bn_3) \\ &= \mathsf{seq}(\mathsf{seq}(bp_1; bn_1', bn_2), bn_3), \end{aligned}$$

where we have used the induction hypothesis to obtain the second equality. Next assume $bn_1 = bn'_1 + bn''_1$. Then

$$
\begin{aligned}
&\mathsf{seq}(bn'_1 + bn''_1, \mathsf{seq}(bn_2, bn_3)) \\
&= \mathsf{seq}(bn'_1, \mathsf{seq}(bn_2, bn_3)) + \mathsf{seq}(bn''_1, \mathsf{seq}(bn_2, bn_3)) \\
&= \mathsf{seq}(\mathsf{seq}(bn'_1, bn_2), bn_3) + \mathsf{seq}(\mathsf{seq}(bn''_1, bn_2), bn_3) \\
&= \mathsf{seq}(\mathsf{seq}(bn'_1, bn_2) + \mathsf{seq}(bn''_1, bn_2), bn_3) \\
&= \mathsf{seq}(\mathsf{seq}(bn'_1 + bn''_1, bn_2), bn_3),
\end{aligned}
$$

where we have used the induction hypothesis to obtain the second equality.

The case S2. We shall prove

$$\mathsf{seq}(bn_1 + bn_2, bn_3) \text{ ord } \mathsf{seq}(bn_1, bn_3) + \mathsf{seq}(bn_2, bn_3),$$

$$\mathsf{seq}(bn_1, bn_3) + \mathsf{seq}(bn_2, bn_3) \text{ ord } \mathsf{seq}(bn_1 + bn_2, bn_3).$$

Clearly we have

$$\mathsf{seq}(bn_1 + bn_2, bn_3) = \mathsf{seq}(bn_1, bn_3) + \mathsf{seq}(bn_2, bn_3).$$

Since ord fulfills the law **P1** we have bn ord bn for all bn and the result follows.

The case E1. We shall prove

$$\mathsf{seq}(\epsilon, bn) \text{ ord } bn \text{ and } bn \text{ ord } \mathsf{seq}(\epsilon, bn).$$

We have $\mathsf{seq}(\epsilon, bn) = bn$ and the result follows from the law **P1**.

The case E2. We shall prove

$$\mathsf{seq}(bn, \epsilon) \text{ ord } bn \text{ and } bn \text{ ord } \mathsf{seq}(bn, \epsilon).$$

We have $\mathsf{seq}(bn, \epsilon) = bn$ and the result follows from the law **P1**.

The case J1. We shall prove

$$bn_i \text{ ord } bn_1 + bn_2$$

for $i = 1, 2$. We have $\Sigma(bn_i) \subseteq \Sigma(bn_1 + bn_2)$ and the result follows from the law **P1** (for ord_s) and Lemma 7.5.7.

The case J2. We shall prove

$$bn \text{ ord } bn + bn \text{ and } bn + bn \text{ ord } bn.$$

We have $\Sigma(bn) = \Sigma(bn + bn)$ and the result follows from the law **P1** (for ord_s) and Lemma 7.5.7.

The case R2. We shall prove

$$\text{REC}\beta.bn \text{ ord } \text{REC}\beta'.bn[\beta \mapsto \beta'], \tag{1}$$

$$\text{REC}\beta'.bn[\beta \mapsto \beta'] \text{ ord } \text{REC}\beta.bn, \tag{2}$$

for $\beta' \notin FV(bn)$. Clearly $bn[\beta \mapsto \beta''] = (bn[\beta \mapsto \beta'])[\beta' \mapsto \beta'']$. Since ord fulfills the law **P1** we have bn' ord bn' for all bn'; so in particular,

$$bn[\beta \mapsto \beta''] \text{ ord } (bn[\beta \mapsto \beta'])[\beta' \mapsto \beta''].$$

From the definition of ord_p we then get

$$\text{REC}\beta.bn \text{ ord}_p \text{ REC}\beta'.bn[\beta \mapsto \beta'],$$

and (1) follows from the definition of ord and ord_s. The proof of (2) is similar. □

References

[1] S. Abramsky. Observation equivalence as a testing equivalence. *Theoretical Computer Science* 53, pages 225–241, 1987.

[2] L. Aceto. A Static View of Localities. *Formal Aspects of Computing* 6(2):201-222, 1994.

[3] M.J. Acetta, R.V. Baron, W. Bolosky, D.B. Golub, R.F. Rashid, A. Jr. Tevanian, and M.W. Young. Mach: A New Kernel Foundation for UNIX Development. In *Proceedings of the Summer 1986 USENIX Conference*, pages 93–113, 1986.

[4] G. Agha. *Actors, A Model of Concurrent Computation in Distributed Systems.* MIT Press, 1987.

[5] K. Ahlers, D.E. Breen, C. Crampton, E. Rose, M. Tucheryan, R. Whitaker, and D. Greer. An augmented vision system for industrial applications. In *SPIE Photonics for Industrial Applications Conference Proceedings*, October 1994.

[6] K.H. Ahlers, A. Kramer, D.E. Breen, P.-Y. Chevalier, C. Crampton, E. Rose, M. Tucheryan, R.T. Whitaker, and D. Greer. Distributed Augmented Reality for Collaborative Design Applications. Technical Report ECRC-95-03, European Computer-Industry Research Centre, 1995.

[7] R. Amadio, L. Leth, and B. Thomsen. From a Concurrent λ-calculus to the π-calculus. In *Proceedings of Fundamentals of Computation Theory*, 10th International Conference, FCT'95, Dresden Germany, August 1995, LNCS 965, Springer Verlag 1995, pp. 106–115. Full version in technical report ECRC-95-18.

[8] ANSA: An Engineer's Introduction to the Architecture. ANSA Number TR.03.02, Architecture Projects Management Limited, November 1989.

[9] M.V. Aponte and P. Cregut. Making functors and signatures true module-class objects, manuscript 1993.

[10] A.W. Appel. *Compiling with Continuations.* Cambridge University Press, 1992.

[11] J.L. Armstrong and R. Virding. Erlang—An Experimental Telephony Programming Language. In *Proceedings of the International Switching Symposium, Stockholm*, vol 3, pages 43–48, 1990.

[12] D.K. Arvind, B. Kraft, and J. Schneiders. Functional Programming, MultiSpace and Distributed Simulation. In preparation, 1995.

[13] E. Astesiano and E. Zucca. Parametric channels via label expressions in CCS*. *Theoretical Computer Science* 33, 1984.

[14] P. Bailey and M. Newey. Implementing ML on Distributed Memory Multiprocessors. In *Proceedings of Boulder Workshop on Languages for Distributed Memory Multiprocessors*, Boulder, USA, 1992.

[15] H.E. Bal, J.G. Steiner, and A.S. Tanenbaum. Programming Languages for Distributed Computing Systems. In *ACM Computing Surveys* 21, no. 3, pages 261–322, 1989.

[16] J.-P. Banâtre and D. Le Métayer. The Gamma model and its discipline of programming. *Science of Computer Programming* 15, pages 55–77, 1990.

[17] H.P. Barendregt. *The Lambda Calculus: Its Syntax and Semantics*. North-Holland, 1984.

[18] D. Berry, R. Milner, and D. N. Turner. A Semantics for ML Concurrency Primitives. In *Proceedings of ACM Symposium on Principles of Programming Languages*, pages 89–104, 1992.

[19] G. Berry and G. Boudol. The Chemical Abstract Machine. In *Proceedings of 1990 POPL Conference*, pages 81–94, 1990.

[20] G. Berry and G. Boudol. The chemical abstract machine. *Theoretical Computer Science* 96, pages 217–248, 1992.

[21] B. Berthomieu. LCS: une implantation de CCS. In A. Arnold, editor, *Troisième colloque C-cube*, Angoulème, France, December 1988.

[22] B. Berthomieu. Process calculi at work—an account of the LCS project. In *Workshop on Parallel Symbolic Languages and Systems*, Beaune, France, 1995, Springer Lecture Notes in Computer Science 1068, 1996.

[23] B. Berthomieu, D. Giralt, and J.P. Gouyon. *LCS users manual*. Technical Report 91226, CNRS-LAAS, September 1991.

[24] B. Berthomieu and C. le Moniès de Sagazan. A calculus of tagged types, with applications to process languages. In *TAPSOFT Workshop on Types for Program Analysis*, Aarhus, Denmark, 1995. (DAIMI report PB-493, University of Aarhus.)

[25] B. Berthomieu and T. Le Sergent. Programming with behaviors in an ML framework: the syntax and semantics of LCS. In *Proceedings of Programming Languages and Systems, ESOP '94*, Springer Lecture Notes in Computer Science 788, 1994.

[26] K. Birman. The Process Group Approach to Reliable Distributed Computing. *Communication of the ACM*, December 1993.

[27] K. Birman, T. Joseph, and F. Schmuck. *ISIS – A Distributed Programming Environment, Version 2.1 – User's Guide and Reference Manual*, 1987.

[28] D. Bolignano and M. Debbabi. Higher order communicating processes with value-passing, assignment and return of results. In *Proceedings of the ISAAC'92 Conference*, Springer Lecture Notes in Computer Science 650, 1992.

[29] D. Bolignano and M. Debbabi. A Coherent Type System for a Concurrent, Functional and Imperative Programming Language. In *Proceedings of AMAST '93*, Springer Lecture Notes in Computer Science, 1993.

[30] D. Bolignano and M. Debbabi. A semantics theory for CML. In *Proceedings of TACS'94 Conference*, 1994.

[31] D. Bolignano and M. Debbabi. On the foundations of the RAISE specification language. Technical report, Bull-ORDA, May 1992.

[32] D. Bolignano and M. Debbabi. A denotational model for the integration of concurrent functional and imperative programming. In *Proceedings of the ICCI'93 Conference*. IEEE, 1993.

[33] D. Bolignano and M. Debbabi. A semantic theory for ML higher order concurrency primitives. In *Proceedings of the NAPAW'93 Workshop*. Cornell University, August 1993.

[34] G. Boudol. Some Chemical Abstract Machines. *A Decade of Concurrency—Reflections and Perspectives*, Proceedings of the REX School/Symposium, Noordwijkerout, The Netherlands, J.W. de Bakker, W.-P. de Roever, G. Rozenberg (eds.), Springer Lecture Notes in Computer Science 803, 1994.

[35] G. Boudol, I. Castellani, M. Hennessy, and A. Kiehn. Observing localities. Technical Report No. 4/91, University of Sussex, Computer Science, 1991.

[36] S.D. Brooks. On the relationship of CCS and CSP. Technical report, Carnegie-Mellon University, 1985.

[37] S.D. Brooks, C.A.R. Hoare, and A.W. Roscoe. A theory of communicating sequential processes. Journal of the ACM 31(3):560–599. ACM Press, 1984.

[38] S.D. Brooks and A.W. Roscoe. An improved failure set model for communicating processes. In *Seminar on Concurrency*, pages 281–305. Springer-Verlag, 1985.

[39] G. Buckley and A. Silberschatz. An Effective Implementation of the Generalized Input/Output Construct of CSP. *ACM Toplas* 5 no. 2, 1983.

[40] W.H. Burge. *Recursive Programming Techniques*. The Systems Programming. Addison-Wesley, 1975.

[41] A. Burns, A.M. Lister, and A.J. Wellings. *A Review of Ada Tasking*. Lecture Notes in Computer Science. Springer-Verlag, 1987.

[42] V. Cahill, R. Balter, X. Rousset de Pina, and N. Harris, editors. *The Comandos Distributed Application Platform*. ESPRIT Research Reports Series. Springer-Verlag, Berlin Heidelberg, 1993.

[43] L. Cardelli. Amber. In *Combinators and Functional Programming Languages*, Springer Lecture Notes in Computer Science 242. Springer-Verlag, 1986.

[44] K. Mani Chandy and J. Misra. *Parallel Program Design: A Foundation*. Addison-Wesley, Reading, Mass., 1988.

[45] D. Clément, J. Despeyroux, T. Despeyroux, and G. Kahn. A simple applicative language: Mini-ML. In *Conference record of the 1986 ACM Conference on Lisp and Functional Programming*, pages 13–27, 1986.

[46] E.C. Cooper and J.G. Morrisett. Adding Threads to Standard ML. Technical Report CMU/CS/90-186, Carnegie Mellon University, School of Computer Science, December 1990.

[47] P. Cregut. Safe Dynamic Connection of Distributed Applications. In *ACM SIGPLAN Workshop on ML and its Applications*, 1994.

[48] P. Cregut and D. MacQueen. An implementation of higher-order functors. In *ACM SIGPLAN Workshop on ML and its Applications*, 1994.

[49] L. Damas. *Type Assignment in Programming Languages*. Ph.D. thesis, Department of Computer Science, University of Edinburgh, 1985. Report CST-33-85.

[50] L. Damas and R. Milner. Principal type-schemes for functional programs. In *Proceedings of POPL'82*. ACM Press, 1982.

[51] M. Debbabi. *Intégration des paradigmes de programmation parallèle, fonctionnelle et impérative : fondements sémantiques*. Ph.D. thesis, Université Paris Sud, Centre d'Orsay, 1994.

[52] R. DeNicola and M. Hennessy. CCS without τs. In *Proceedings of TAPSOFT'87*, Springer Lecture Notes in Computer Science 250. Springer-Verlag, 1987.

[53] J.R. Ellis, K. Li, and A.W. Appel. Real-time Concurrent Collection on Stock Multiprocessors. Technical Report 25, DEC Systems Research Center, 1988.

[54] U. Engberg and M. Nielsen. A Calculus of Communicating Systems with Label Passing. Technical Report DAIMI PB-208, Aarhus University Computer Science Department, 1986.

[55] M. Felleisen and D.P. Friedman. Control Operators, the SECD-Machine, and the λ-Calculus. In M. Wirsing, editor, *Formal Descriptions of Programming Concepts III*, pages 193–219. North-Holland, 1986.

[56] E.P. Friedman. The Inclusion Problem for Simple Languages. *Theoretical Computer Science*, 1:297–316, 1976.

[57] E.R. Gansner and J.H. Reppy. *A Multi-threaded Higher-order User Interface Toolkit*, volume 1 of *Software Trends*, pages 61–80. John Wiley & Sons, 1993.

[58] A. Giacalone, P. Mishra, and S. Prasad. Facile: A Symmetric Integration of Concurrent and Functional Programming. In *Proceedings of 1989 TAPSOFT Conference*, Springer Lecture Notes in Computer Science 352. Springer-Verlag, 1989.

[59] A. Giacalone, P. Mishra, and S. Prasad. Facile: A Symmetric Integration of Concurrent and Functional Programming. *International Journal of Parallel Programming, Vol. 18, No. 2*, pages 121–160, 1989.

[60] D.K. Gifford, P. Jouvelot, J.M. Lucassen, and M.A. Sheldon. Fx-87 reference manual. Technical Report MIT/LCS/TR-407, MIT Laboratory for Computer Science, September 1987.

[61] R. Goldman and R.P. Gabriel. Qlisp: Experience and new directions. *ACM SIGPLAN Notices*, 23(9):111–123, 1988.

[62] M. Gordon, R. Milner, and C. Wadsworth. *Edinburgh LCS*. Springer Lecture Notes in Computer Science 78, 1979.

[63] J. Greiner. Standard ML weak polymorphism can be sound. Technical Report CMU-CS-93-160, Department of Computer Science, Carnegie-Mellon University, May 1993.

[64] J.F. Groote and H. Hüttel. Undecidable Equivalences for Basic Process Algebra. *Information and Computation* 112:2, pages 354–371, 1994.

[65] C.A. Gunter and D.S. Scott. Semantic domains. In J. van Leeuwen, editor, *Handbook of Theoretical Computer Science*, pages 633–674. Elsevier Science Publishers B.V., Amsterdam, the Netherlands, 1990.

[66] R.H. Halstead. Implementation of multilisp: Lisp on a multiprocessor. In *Conference Record of the 1984 ACM Symposium on LISP and Functional Programming*, Austin, TX, pages 9–17, New York, ACM Press, 1984.

[67] R.W. Harper. Introduction to Standard ML. Technical Report ECS-LFCS-86-14, Laboratory for Foundation of Computer Science, Computer Science Department, Edinburgh University, 1986.

[68] M. Hennessy. Acceptance trees. *ACM* 32:896–928, 1985.

[69] M. Hennessy. *Algebraic Theory of Process*. MIT Press, 1988.

[70] M. Hennessy and A. Ingólfsdóttir. A theory of communicating processes with value passing. In *Proc. 17th ICALP*, Springer Lecture Notes in Computer Science. Springer Verlag, 1990.

[71] M. Hennessy and A. Ingólfsdóttir. Communicating processes with value-passing and assignments. Technical report, University of Sussex, June 1991.

[72] J.R. Hindley and J.P. Seldin. *Introduction to Combinators and λ-Calculus*. Cambridge University Press, Cambridge, 1986. London Mathematical Society Student Texts 1.

[73] M. Hoang, J. Mitchell, and R. Viswanathan. Standard ML weak polymorphism and imperative constructs. Draft, Department of Computer Science, Stanford University, 1992.

[74] C.A.R. Hoare. *Communicating Sequential Processes*. International Series in Computer Science Prentice-Hall, 1985.

[75] C.A.R. Hoare. Communicating sequential processes. *Communications of the ACM* 21(8):666–677, 1978.

[76] S. Holmström. PFL: A Functional Language for Parallel Programming, and its Implementation. Technical report, Programming Methodologies Group 7, University of Göteborg and Chalmers Institute of Technology, September 1983.

[77] S. Holmström. PFL: A functional language for parallel programming languages. In *Declarative Programming Workshop, Chalmers Univ. of Technology, Univ. of Göteborg, Sweden*, 1983.

[78] ISO. ISO-LOTOS behaviour, 1989. Int. Standard ISO 8807, ISO.

[79] A. Jeffrey. A fully-abstract semantics for a concurrent functional language with monadic types. In *Proceedings of the Tenth Annual IEEE Symposium on Logic in Computer Science*, pages 255–264, 1995.

[80] A. Jeffrey. Remarks on CML. Private communication, 1995.

[81] B.C. Johnson. A Distributed Computing Environment Framework: An OSF perspective. Technical Report DEV-DCE-TP6-1, Open Software Foundation, Inc., Cambridge, MA, 1991.

[82] P. Jouvelot and D.K. Gifford. Algebraic reconstruction of types and effects. In *Proceedings of 18th Annual Symposium on Principles of Programming Languages*, pages 303–310, 1991.

[83] F. Knabe. A Distributed Protocol for Channel-Based Communication with Choice. In *Proceedings of PARLE '92*, 1992. Poster in Springer Lecture Notes in Computer Science 605, Springer-Verlag, 1992. Full version in tech. Report ECRC–92–16, European Computer-Industry Research Centre, 1992.

[84] F. Knabe. *Language and Compiler Support for Mobile Agents*. Ph.D. thesis, Carnegie-Mellon University, 1995.

[85] F. Knabe, P.-Y. Chevalier, A. Kramer, T.-M. Kuo, L. Leth, S. Prasad, J.-P. Talpin, and B. Thomsen. Mobile Service Agents. Technical Report Internal report ECRC-94-2i, European Computer-Industry Research Centre, 1994.

[86] C. le Moniès de Sagazan. Un système de types étiquetés polymorphes pour typer les calculs de processus à liaisons noms-canaux dynamiques. Thèse de doctorat de l'Université Paul Sabatier, Toulouse, l'Université Paul Sabatier, Toulouse, Report LAAS 95077, November 1995.

[87] T. Le Sergent. Méthodes d'exécution, et machines virtuelles parallèles pour l'implantation distribuée du langage de programmation parallèle LCS. Thèse de doctorat de l'Université Paul Sabatier, Toulouse, February 1993.

[88] T. Le Sergent and B. Berthomieu. Incremental multi-threaded garbage collection on virtually shared memory architectures. In *Memory Management—International Workshop IWMM'92, St. Malo, france*, Springer Lecture Notes in Computer Science 637, 1992.

[89] T. Le Sergent and B. Berthomieu. Balancing load under large and fast load changes in distributed systems—a case study. In *CONPAR 94 International Conference on Parallel Processing, Linz, Austria,* Springer Lecture Notes in Computer Science 854, 1994.

[90] X. Leroy. *Typage polymorphe d'un langage algorithmique.* Ph.D. thesis, Université de Paris VII, June 1992.

[91] X. Leroy and P. Weis. Polymorphic type inference and assignment. In *Proceedings of the 18th ACM Symposium on Principles of Programming Languages,* pages 291–302, 1991.

[92] L. Leth. *Functional Programs as Reconfigurable Networks of Communicating Processes.* Ph.D. thesis, Imperial College, Department of Computing, 1991.

[93] L. Leth and B. Thomsen. Some Facile Chemistry. *Formal Aspects of Computing* 7, no. 3, pages 314–328, 1995.

[94] K. Li and P. Hudak. Memory coherence in shared virtual memory systems. *ACM Transactions on Computer Systems* 7(4):321–359, 1989.

[95] J.M. Lucassen and D.K. Gifford. Polymorphic Effect Systems. In *Proceedings of POPL'88,* pages 47–57. ACM Press, 1988.

[96] J.M. Lucassen. *Type and Effects: Towards an Integration of Functional and Imperative Programming.* Ph.D. thesis, Laboratory of Computer Science, MIT, 1987.

[97] D.B. MacQueen. Modules for standard ML. Polymorphism, 2(2), 1985. An earlier version appeared in *Proceedings of 1984 ACM Symposium on Lisp and Functional Programming.*

[98] D.C.J. Matthews. An Overview of the Poly Programming Language. In P. Atkinson, M. Buneman and R. Morrison, editors, *Data Types and Persistence.* Springer-Verlag, 1988.

[99] D.C.J. Matthews. Papers on Poly/ML. Technical report, Computer Laboratory, University of Cambridge, 1989.

[100] D.C.J. Matthews. A distributed concurrent implementation of Standard ML. In *EurOpen Autumn 1991 Conference,* Budapest, Hungary, 1991.

[101] D.C.J. Matthews and T. Le Sergent. LEMMA: A Distributed Shared Memory with Global and Local Garbage Collection. In Henry G. Baker, editor, *Memory Management—International Workshop IWMM'95,* Kinross, Scotland, Springer Lecture Notes in Computer Science 986, pages 297–311. Springer-Verlag, 1995.

[102] D.C.J. Matthews and T. Le Sergent. LEMMA Interface Definition. Technical Report LFCS Report ECS-LFCS-95-316, Department of Computer Science, University of Edinburgh, 1995.

[103] R.E. Milne. Concurrency models and axioms. Technical Report RAISE/CRI/DOC/4/V1, CRI, 1988.

[104] R.E. Milne. Semantic foundations of RSL. Technical Report RAISE/CRI/DOC/4/V1, CRI, 1990.

[105] R.E. Milne. The formal basis for the RAISE specification language. In D.J. Andrews, J.F. Groote, and C.A. Middelburg, editors, *Proceedings of the 1st Conference on Semantics of Specification Languages, SoSL'93*, Workshops in computing series. Springer-Verlag, 1993.

[106] R. Milner. A theory of type polymorphism in programming. *Computer and systems sciences*, 17:348–375, 1978.

[107] R. Milner. A calculus of communicating systems. In *Lecture Notes in Computer Science 92*. Springer-Verlag, 1980.

[108] R. Milner. *Communication and Concurrency*. Prentice Hall, 1989.

[109] R. Milner, J. Parrow, and D. Walker. A calculus of mobile processes. Technical Report ECS-LFCS–89–85 and –86, Laboratory for Foundations of Computer Science, Edinburgh University, 1989.

[110] R. Milner, J. Parrow, and D. Walker. A calculus of mobile processes *I* and *II*. *Information and Computation*, 100:1–77, 1992.

[111] R. Milner and M. Tofte. *Commentary on Standard ML*. MIT Press, 1991.

[112] R. Milner, M. Tofte, and R. Harper. *The Definition of Standard ML*. MIT Press, 1990.

[113] E. Moggi. Notions of computation and monads. *Information and Computation*, 93:55–92, 1991.

[114] J.G. Morrisett and A. Tolmach. A Portable Multiprocessor Interface for Standard ML of New Jersey. Technical Report CMU-CS-92-155, Carnegie Mellon, and Princeton Technical Report 376-92, 1992.

[115] T.J. Mowbray and T. Brando. Interoperability and CORBA-based Open Systems. *Object Magazine*, pages 50–54, September–October, 1993.

[116] S. Mudambi, R. Whitaker, and B. Thomsen. Report of the Mobility Working Group. Technical Report Internal report ECRC-94-5i, European Computer-Industry Research Centre, 1994.

[117] G. Nelson, editor. *Systems Programming with Modula-3*. Prentice-Hall, 1991.

[118] Standard ML of New Jersey – Base Environment (version 0.93). AT& T Bell Laboratories, February 15 1993.

[119] Standard ML of New Jersey – System Modules (version 0.93). AT& T Bell Laboratories, February 15 1993.

[120] X. Nicollin and J. Sifakis. An overview and synthesis on timed process algebras. Presented at CAV'91, Aalborg, Denmark, 1991.

[121] F. Nielson. The Typed Lambda-Calculus with First-Class Processes. In *Proceedings of PARLE'89*, Springer Lecture Notes in Computer Science 366, 1989.

[122] F. Nielson and H.R. Nielson. From CML to Process Algebras. In *Proceedings of CONCUR'93*, Springer Lecture Notes in Computer Science 715, 1993.

[123] F. Nielson and H.R. Nielson. Constraints for Polymorphic Behaviours of Concurrent ML. In *Proceedings of CCL'94*, Springer Lecture Notes in Computer Science 845, pages 73–88, 1994.

[124] F. Nielson and H.R. Nielson. From CML to its process algebras. *Theoretical Computer Science* 155, pages 179–219, 1996.

[125] H.R. Nielson and F. Nielson. Higher-Order Concurrent Programs with Finite Communication Topology. In *Proceedings of POPL'94*, pages 84–97. ACM Press, 1994.

[126] H.R. Nielson and F. Nielson. Static and Dynamic Processor Allocation for Higher-Order Concurrent Languages. In *Proceedings of TAP-SOFT'95*, Springer Lecture Notes in Computer Science 915, pages 590–604, 1995.

[127] Object Management Group: Common Object Request Broker: Architecture and Specification. Document 92.12.1, OMG Inc., Framingham, Mass., December, 1992.

[128] Object Management Group: Object Management Architecture Guide. Document 92.11.1, OMG Inc., Framingham, Mass., November, 1992.

[129] *occam Programming Manual*. Prentice-Hall, 1984. See also the *occam2 Reference Manual*, Prentice-Hall, 1988.

[130] P. Panangaden and V. Shanbhogue. The expressive power of indeterminate dataflow primitives. *Information and Computation*, 98(1):99–131, 1992.

[131] P. Panangaden and K.E. Taylor. Concurrent common knowledge. *Distributed Computing* 6:73–93, 1992.

[132] D. Park. Concurrency and Automata on Infinite Sequences. Springer Lecture Notes in Computer Science 104. Springer-Verlag, 1981.

[133] L.C. Paulson. *ML for the working programmer*. Cambridge University Press, 1991.

[134] N. Perry. Hope$^+$C, A Continuation extension for Hope$^+$. Technical Report IC/FPR/LANG/2.5.1/7, Issue 5, Department of Computing, Imperial College, 1988.

[135] S. Peyton Jones, A. Gordon, and S. Finne. Concurrent Haskell. In *Conference Record of The 23rd ACM SIGPLAN-SIGACT Symposium on Principles of Programming Languages*, pages 295–308, 1996.

[136] B.C. Pierce, D. Rémy, and D.N. Turner. A typed higher-order programming language based on the pi-calculus. Technical report, Edinburgh University, 1993.

[137] B.C. Pierce and D.N. Turner. Concurrent objects in a process calculus. In Takayasu Ito and Akinori Yonezawa, editors, *Theory and Practice of Parallel Programming (TPPP), Sendai, Japan (Nov. 1994)*, Springer Lecture Notes in Computer Science 907, pages 187–215. Springer-Verlag, 1995.

[138] G. Plotkin. A Structural Approach to Operational Semantics. Technical Report DAIMI FN-19, Computer Science Department, Aarhus University, 1981.

[139] S. Prasad. *Towards A Symmetric Integration of Concurrent and Functional Programming*. Ph.D. thesis, State University of New York at Stony Brook, 1991.

[140] S. Prasad, A. Giacalone, and P. Mishra. Operational and Algebraic Semantics for Facile: A Symmetric Integration of Concurrent and Functional Programming. In *Proceedings of ICALP 90*, Springer Lecture Notes in Computer Science 443, pages 765–780. Springer-Verlag, 1990.

[141] C. Queinnec. A concurrent and distributed extension to scheme. In D. Etiemble and J.-C. Syre, editors, *PARLE '92, Parallel Architectures and Languages Europe*, Springer Lecture Notes in Computer Science 605, pages 431–448. Springer-Verlag, Berlin, 1992.

[142] C. Reade. *Elements of Functional Programming*. Addison-Wesley, 1989.

[143] D. Rémy. Typechecking records and variants in a natural extension of ML. In *Proceedings of the 16th ACM Symposium on Principles of Programming Languages*, 1989.

[144] D. Rémy. Syntactic theories and the algebra of record terms. Technical Report 1869, INRIA-Rocquencourt, March 1993.

[145] J.H. Reppy. First-class synchronous operations in Standard ML. Technical Report TR89-1068, Dept. of Computer Science, Cornell University, 1989.

[146] J.H. Reppy. Concurrent programming with events—the Concurrent ML manual. Technical report, Department of Computer Science, Cornell University, November 1990.

[147] J.H. Reppy. An operational semantics of first-class synchronous operations. Technical Report TR 91-1232, Department of Computer Science, Cornell University, August 1991.

[148] J.H. Reppy. *Concurrent Programming in ML*. Cambridge University Press. To appear.

[149] J.H. Reppy. Synchronous Operations as First-Class Values. In *Proceedings of the SIGPLAN Conference on Programming Language Design and Implementation*, pages 250–259, 1988.

[150] J.H. Reppy. CML: A Higher-Order Concurrent Language. In *Proceedings of PLDI'91*, pages 293–305. ACM Press, 1991.

[151] J.H. Reppy. *Higher-Order Concurrency*. Ph.D. thesis, Department of Computer Science, Cornell University, 1992. Report 92-1285.

[152] J.H. Reppy. Concurrent ML: Design, Application and Semantics. In *Proceedings of Functional Programming, Concurrency, Simulation and Automated Reasoning*, Springer Lecture Notes in Computer Science 693, pages 165–198, 1993.

[153] J.C. Reynolds. The essence of Algol. In J.W. de Bakker and J.C. van Vliet, editors, *Algorithmic Languages*, pages 345–372. North-Holland, Amsterdam, 1981.

[154] A.W. Roscoe Denotational semantics for occam. In *Proc. Seminar on Concurrency*, Springer Lecture Notes in Computer Science 197, pages 306–329. Springer Verlag, 1985.

[155] D.E. Rydeheard and R.M. Burstall. *Computational Category Theory*. Prentice Hall, 1988.

[156] D. Sangiorgi. π-calculus, internal mobility and agent-passing calculi. Technical Report 2539, INRIA Sophia-Antipolis, April 1995.

[157] D. Sannella and A. Tarlecki. Program specification and development in Standard ML. In *Proc. 12th ACM Symposium on Principles of Programming Languages*, 1985.

[158] M.B. Smyth and G.D. Plotkin. The category-theoretic solution of recursive domain equations. *SIAM Journal of Computing*, 11(4):761–783, 1982.

[159] J.-P. Talpin. The Calumet Experiment in Facile—A Model for Group Communication and Interaction Control in Cooperative Applications. Technical Report ECRC-94-26, European Computer-Industry Research Centre, 1994.

[160] J.-P. Talpin and P. Jouvelot. The type and effect discipline. In *Proceedings of LICS'92*, pages 162–173, 1992.

[161] J.-P. Talpin, P. Marchal, and K. Ahlers. Calumet—A Reference Manual. Technical Report ECRC-94-30, European Computer-Industry Research Centre, 1994.

[162] Y.M. Tang. *Control Flow Analysis by Effect Systems and Abstract Interpretation*. Ph.D. thesis, Ecoles des Mines de Paris, 1994. Report A/258/CRI.

[163] C.P. Thacker, L.C. Stewart, and E.H. Satterthwaite Jr. Firefly: A Multiprocessor Workstation. Technical Report 23, DEC Systems Research Center, 1987.

[164] B. Thomsen. A Calculus of Higher Order Communicating Systems. In *Proceedings of POPL'89*. ACM Press, 1989.

[165] B. Thomsen. *Calculi for Higher Order Communicating Systems*. Ph.D. thesis, Imperial College, London University, 1990.

[166] B. Thomsen. Facile vs. CML. Magic Note Nr. 56, European Computer-Industry Research Centre, 1993.

[167] B. Thomsen. Polymorphic sorts and types for concurrent functional programs. Technical Report ECRC-93-10, European Computer-Industry Research Centre, 1993.

[168] B. Thomsen. A Second Generation Calculus for Higher Order Processes. *Acta Informatica* 30, pages 1–59, 1993. Preliminary version in Technical Report 89/04, Imperial College 1989.

[169] B. Thomsen. Polymorphic Sorts and Types for Concurrent Functional Programs. In J. Glauert, editor, *Proceedings of the 6th International Workshop on the Implementation of Functional Languages, UEA Norwich, UK*, 1994. Preliminary version in Technical report ECRC-93-10, 1993.

[170] B. Thomsen. A Theory of Higher Order Communicating Systems. *Information and Computation* 116, no. 1, pages 38–57, 1995.

[171] B. Thomsen, F. Knabe, L. Leth, and P.-Y. Chevalier. Mobile agents set to work. *Communications International*, July 1995.

[172] B. Thomsen, L. Leth, and A. Giacalone. Some Issues in the Semantics of Facile Distributed Programming. In *Proceedings of the 1992 REX Workshop on "Semantics: Foundations and Applications,"* Springer Lecture Notes in Computer Science 666. Springer-Verlag, 1992.

[173] B. Thomsen, L. Leth., F. Knabe, and P.-Y. Chevalier. Mobile agents. Technical Report ECRC-95-21, European Computer-Industry Research Centre, 1995.

[174] B. Thomsen, L. Leth, S. Prasad, T.-M. Kuo, A. Kramer, F. Knabe, and A. Giacalone. Facile Antigua Release Programming Guide. Technical Report ECRC-93-20, European Computer-Industry Research Centre, 1993.

[175] M. Tofte. *Operational Semantics and Polymorphic Type Inference.* Ph.D. thesis, Department of Computer Science, University of Edinburgh, 1988.

[176] M. Tofte and D. MacQueen. A Semantics for Higher-Order Functors. In *Proceedings of the 5th European Symposium on Programming (ESOP)*, Springer Lecture Notes in Computer Science 788, pages 409–423. Springer-Verlag 1994.

[177] M. Tofte. Type inference for polymorphic references. *Information and Computation* 89:1–34, 1990.

[178] J.D. Ullman. *Elements of ML Programming.* Prentice-Hall International, Inc., 1994.

[179] M. Wand. Complete type inference for simple objects. In *Symposium on Logic in Computer Science*, Ithaca, New York, 1987.

[180] M. Wand. Type Inference for Objects with Instance Variables and Inheritance. In C. Gunter and J. C. Mitchell, editors, *Theoretical Aspects of Object-Oriented Programming*, MIT Press, 1994.

[181] Å. Wikström. *Functional Programming using Standard ML.* Prentice Hall, 1987.

[182] A. Wright and M. Felleisen. A Syntactic Approach to Type Soundness. Technical Report TR 91-160, Dept. of Computer Science, Rice University, 1991.

[183] A.K. Wright. Typing references by effect inference. In *Proceedings of European Symposium on Programming*, Springer Lecture Notes in Computer Science 582. Springer-Verlag, 1992.

[184] A.K. Wright. Simple imperative polymorphism. *Lisp and Symbolic Computation* 8(4):343–356, 1995.

Index